National Pastime

National Pastime

How Americans Play Baseball and the Rest of the World Plays Soccer

STEFAN SZYMANSKI

ANDREW ZIMBALIST

BROOKINGS INSTITUTION PRESS
Washington, D.C.

To our children,
Edward, William, and Kitty
Jeffrey, Michael, Alex, and Ella
Who, we hope, will be more proficient practitioners
of soccer and baseball than their fathers

ABOUT BROOKINGS

The Brookings Institution is a private nonprofit organization devoted to research, education, and publication on important issues of domestic and foreign policy. Its principal purpose is to bring the highest quality independent research and analysis to bear on current and emerging policy problems. Interpretations or conclusions in Brookings publications should be understood to be solely those of the authors.

The Library of Congress has cataloged the hardcover edition as follows:
Szymanski, Stefan, 1960–
National pastime : how Americans play baseball and the rest of the world plays soccer / Stefan Szymanski and Andrew Zimbalist.
    p.   cm.
ISBN-13: 978-0-8157-8258-2 (cloth : alk. paper)
ISBN-10: 0-8157-8258-6
1. Professional sports—Economic aspects—Cross-cultural studies. 2. Baseball—Economic aspects—United States. 3. Soccer—Economic aspects. I. Zimbalist, Andrew S. II. Title.
GV716.S99 2005
338.4'7796334—dc22   2005001160
            ISBN-13: 978-0-8157-8259-9 (pbk.: alk. paper)
            ISBN-10: 0-8157-8259-4

9 8 7 6 5 4 3 2 1

The paper used in this publication meets minimum requirements of the American National Standard for Information Sciences—Permanence of Paper for Printed Library Materials: ANSI Z39.48-1992.

Typeset in Minion

Composition by Cynthia Stock
Silver Spring, Maryland

Printed by R. R. Donnelley
Harrisonburg, Virginia

Contents

Preface to the
Paperback Edition

Since *National Pastime* was published one year ago, the owner of an American football team has taken over one of the biggest soccer clubs in the world, Major League Baseball has successfully staged the World Baseball Classic in imitation of the soccer World Cup, and the leading soccer clubs in Europe have threatened to form an independent league modeled essentially on the U.S. major leagues. In an era of globalization nothing is more parochial than sporting loyalty, but the forces of commercial logic are driving the organizers of the world's biggest competitions to adopt successful business models from sports about which they may know little.

We wrote *National Pastime* because we believed that while many people understand the business of baseball or the business of soccer, no one has ever tried to explain systematically how they compare in terms of histories, structures, and outcomes. To us this seemed important not only because both are so successful and important in their own right, but also because their structures are so profoundly different. Part of the joy of writing *National Pastime* was to learn from each other the mirror image of institutions we thought we had always understood. In the process we uncovered some striking parallels in the early development of the sports and even some hitherto unremarked connections between the founders of professional baseball and professional soccer.

Of course, not everyone is happy to see practices move from one sport to another. The takeover of Manchester United by the

Glazer family produced an outpouring of xenophobia, based on fears that American profit taking will undermine the integrity of the English league system. But much of this fear is based on ignorance of the way that American sports operate. If, for instance, soccer fans understood the emphasis that American leagues place on competitive balance, they might view the adoption of American practices more favorably.

The biggest sporting event of 2006 will be the FIFA World Cup held in Germany. The success of this competition stems from the universality of the sport and its appeal to nationalistic sentiment. At times the World Cup is a positive festival of international harmony, at others it becomes a proxy war. What is interesting about the World Cup is the way that it has been used by FIFA to build an international system, subsidizing weaker countries and using the enormous financial surpluses generated by the competition to maintain solidarity.

Yet all this is under threat from a court case currently before the Charleroi Commercial Court in Belgium. Clubs have always been obliged to release players to participate in international games, with no compensation and no right of refusal. The biggest clubs are now demanding a share of the income, which will fundamentally undermine FIFA and the governance of soccer if they succeed.

Meanwhile, U.S. baseball magnates are jealous of soccer's world market. During 2006 the International Olympic Committee bosses kicked baseball and softball out of the summer Olympics. Baseball was booted because MLB would not take a respite to allow its players to compete in the Summer Games. Whatever happened to the amateur Olympic ideal? No one seems to know why softball was also eliminated; presumably guilt by association.

But if baseball cannot have the Olympics to spread its legend, in 2006 it had the World Baseball Classic (WBC). Sixteen countries fielded teams during March, with games played in Japan, Venezuela, Puerto Rico, and the mainland United States. The television ratings outside the United States were impressive. Nearly half of South Korea's television households watched their national team lose to Japan in the semifinals. Even in the United States ratings were reputable: the matchup between Mexico and the USA drew 2.5 million viewers on ESPN, nearly double the network's average audience for NBA telecasts. MLB even turned a tidy profit. The next classic is planned for 2009.

Ours is a book about the two national pastimes that form the basis for the organization of sports across the world. Fans of either soccer or baseball are used to thinking of theirs as the only relevant model of sporting organization. Accordingly, some have read *National Pastime* with an eye only to what it says about their own sport. Yet some readers (most, we hope) have found in this book the doorway to a parallel universe, in some ways worse, but in some ways better than the one they know. In our view, it is almost inevitable that administrators in each sport will learn lessons, and there is plenty of evidence to show that this process is already at work. Globalization in sports is here to stay. National pastimes continue to become international.

Preface to the
First Edition

This is a book about two national pastimes, one that belongs to the United States of America and the other that has come to be known as the world's game. Baseball and soccer are merely games, but because of the interest they generate and the traditions they have created, they have become cultural icons. In almost every country of the world, the way that the national pastime is played is seen as a guide to national character and identity.

As economists, we set out to write this book to emphasize the ways in which the different traditions of each sport have generated different possibilities for their commercial organization and exploitation. But we also embarked on this enterprise in the belief that it would be constructive for the organizers and decisionmakers in each sport to study and, sometimes, to borrow from each other's experiences. This book is about the origin, evolution, and trajectory of the different sporting cultures that exist in the United States and the rest of the world. In it we endeavor to illustrate how the organizers of baseball and soccer have learned from each other in the past and how they can continue to learn from each other in the future.

We would also like to think that there is a broader lesson to be drawn from our book. We write at a time when, following the horrors of 9/11 and the war in Iraq, the divisions of opinion between the United States and the rest of the world seem greater than they have ever been. People may disagree for reasons grounded in objective realities, but they may also disagree merely because they see the same things through a different lens. It can sometimes be instructive to try on the other guy's spectacles.

We launched our project with a basic curiosity and faith that there would be fundamental commonalities and differences in the experiences of soccer and baseball that would enrich our understanding of the functioning of sports leagues. We were also motivated by the fact that no one had undertaken a cross-cultural comparison that sought to uncover the basic dynamics of business organization and evolution of sports leagues.[1] We, at least, were not disappointed with either the process or the outcome.

One theme that emerged from our research is that the traditions often held to be central to the identity of a particular sport were originally created for reasons that were accidental. Baseball could have evolved more like soccer, or soccer could have evolved like baseball. But some traditions, however venerable, create obstacles to the healthy development of a sport, or simply outlive their usefulness. In such cases, we argue, change is desirable; a slavish adherence to tradition is not in the interests of the majority of those who love the game they follow. John Maynard Keynes once wrote that "practical men, who believe themselves to be quite exempt from any intellectual influences, are usually the slaves of some defunct economist."[2] A similar kind of observation can be made in sports: those who uphold established traditions are often merely following the arbitrary rules established by long defunct administrators. By studying the rules of others, it might be possible to develop new and better ways to run things.

But we are not advocating the jettisoning of all tradition to adopt wholesale the approach of another sport. We propose no simple solutions; rather, in our concluding chapter, we suggest that there are approaches to problems that may be emulated. By studying the distinct methods of organizing team sports leagues around the world, we can get a better perspective on our own. In a sense, for an American to look at European soccer, or a European to look at American baseball, allows a more distant perspective than looking at one's own sport. It is not unlike the perspective that those in, say, the year 2030 may have when they look back at 2005.

There is yet another motivation for this effort. The current period is often referred to as the era of globalization. Commerce and capital are spreading around the globe. One consequence of the globalization of capital is that the same individuals (and companies) who invested in U.S. baseball are beginning to invest in European soccer. One such individual is

Rupert Murdoch. Murdoch began as an Australian newspaper heir, but eventually bought up papers in England and the United States. He then aggressively entered the world of satellite and terrestrial television. Murdoch started the Australian Rugby League to meet the programming needs of his satellite television company. He began the national Fox Network and the Fox regional sports networks (RSNs) in the United States. His Fox Network currently holds the primary national television contract with Major League Baseball (MLB), and his RSNs serve twenty-five of MLB's thirty teams in their local markets. Until early 2004 he also owned the Dodgers— a team he admitted that he bought in order to gain control over the RSN market in southern California. Of course, Murdoch also is the controlling investor in BSkyB in England and Sky Italia in Italy, satellite distributors that hold television soccer rights for the English Premier League and the Italian Serie A. Today, as Europe debates the creation of a pancontinental Super League, it is being lobbied by Murdoch's BSkyB, which would like nothing better than to obtain broadcast rights to such a league.

Another such individual is Malcolm Glazer, owner of the National Football League's Tampa Bay Buccaneers. For the past two years Glazer has been buying shares of Manchester United (the famous soccer team in England's Premier League). As we write in August 2004, Glazer owns nearly 20 percent of the team and has stated his intention to buy a controlling interest. Meanwhile, in 2003, Manchester United entered into a joint marketing venture with the New York Yankees.

With growing cross-fertilization, it is natural to expect that leagues will be increasingly influenced by each other. Rupert Murdoch undoubtedly has his own ideas about how a model league should be organized, and while we do not doubt that this will reflect his best interests, we are less sure that it will reflect the best interests of the fans. Rather than abandon the design of sports leagues to the Murdochs and Glazers of the world, we think that a public airing of issues that arise from a cross-cultural interpretation of sports leagues might be part of a wider debate on the reform of baseball and soccer. What follows, then, is our attempt to offer a perspective that we believe is rooted in the best interests of the fans—a perspective that is likely to differ from that of owners, many of whom are using sport teams as vehicles to promote their business empires.

We benefited from the advice and support of many people. Many academic colleagues and practitioners discussed related issues and commented on earlier incarnations of the chapters that follow. In particular, we would like to acknowledge Eleanor Abend, Sandy Alderson, Paul Alpers, Wladimir Andreff, Guido Ascari, Larry Baer, Allen Barra, Carlos Barros, David Begg, Rich Berlin, Dave Berri, Hal Biagas, Jean-François Bourg, Jim Bouton, Bob Bowman, Andrew Brunswick, Gene Budig, Tunde Buraimo, Bill Burdick, Brian Cashman, Jerry Colangelo, Bob Costas, Jim Duquette, Todd Durbin, Don Fehr, Steve Fehr, Bill Francis, David Forrest, Bernd Frick, Philippe Gagnepain, Jim Gallagher, Don Garber, Gary Gillette, Jean-Jacques Gouguet, Dorothy Griffiths, Sunil Gulati, Allen Guttmann, Fred Hanser, Jen Hughes, Brad Humphreys, Billy Hunter, Leo Kahane, Stefan Késenne, Jeffrey Kessler, Anthony King, Bill Kirwin, Klemens von Klemperer, Ron Klempner, Ruud Koning, Chuck Korr, Jonathan Kraft, Umberto Lago, Stephanie Leach, Randy Levine, James Lloyd Gates, Jr., Romilly Lockyer, Larry Lucchino, David Matthew, Marvin Miller, John Moores, Stephen Morrow, Gerd Muehlheusser, Phil Nielsen, Roger Noll, Gregory Papanikos, Doug Pappas, Alex Phillips, Didier Primault, Arne Rees, Toby Regner, Tom Reich, Stephen Ross, Allen Sanderson, Tom Shieber, John Siegfried, Rob Simmons, Peter Sloane, Tommaso Valletti, Wray Vamplew, Hans Vandeweghe, Dan Wasserman, Paul Weiler, Tom Werner, Mark Williams, and David Wolff. The excellent and friendly staff of the library at the Baseball Hall of Fame in Cooperstown, especially the library's director, Tim Wiles, were extremely helpful. Susanna Nutsford, the librarian of the Tanaka Business School at Imperial College London, tracked down a number of useful references, as did Mike Bondy; the staff of the British Library, at Colindale and St. Pancras, and the New York Public Library offered generous assistance. The acquisitions editor at Brookings, Chris Kelaher, provided much appreciated good cheer, encouragement, patience, and sound judgment. We were also aided by Anh Ta, Borislava Marcheva, and Yevheniya Hyrina, who provided able research assistance.

Finally, our families supported us and put up with our preoccupation and distractions for months on end. With our love and gratitude, thank you to Shelley and Hayley, Edward, William, Kitty, Alex, Ella, Michael, and Jeffrey.

CHAPTER ONE

Introduction

The Fields of Play

The rest of the world loves soccer. Surely we must be missing something. Uh, isn't that what the Russians told us about communism? There's a good reason why you don't care about soccer—it's because you are an American and hating soccer is more American than mom's apple pie, driving a pick-up and spending Saturday afternoon channel-surfing with the remote control.

Tom Weir, quoted at www.soccersucks.org

Another reason to hate soccer: The "accused" terrorist (who has already admitted to being sent into Belgium to drive a bomb into a U.S. Air Force base, and to "committing himself to becoming a 'martyr' for Osama bin Laden") is named Nizar Trabelsi. And he's a former European pro soccer player. You don't see any former NFL players or Major League Baseball players joining al-Qaeda, do you?

http://warliberal.com/mt/blog/archives/005321.html

When British soldiers in Afghanistan and southern Iraq wanted to befriend the locals, they played a soccer match. On Christmas Day, 1914, British and German soldiers in the First World War trenches did the same thing. For nearly 100 years soccer has united a divided world—apart from the world's hyperpower, the United States. You can buy a McDonald's Big Mac on the Champs-Elysées and anything from anywhere in the world on Fifth Avenue, but American sporting culture and the world soccer culture do not mix.

In his book *Take Time for Paradise*, former commissioner of Major League Baseball and president of Yale University Bart Giamatti wrote: "It has long been my conviction that we can learn far more about the conditions, and values, of a society by contemplating how it chooses to play, to use its free time, to take its leisure, than by examining how it goes about its work."[1] Sport reflects culture. If the culture of baseball is American, the culture of soccer has been largely fashioned in Europe. Soccer was formalized in England in the mid-nineteenth century and rapidly spread to Europe and South America. The dominant influences, however, have been European. The gulf between

European and American values is nowhere more evident than in the gulf between the cultures of soccer and baseball.

Soccer is the world's dominant sport, but only baseball has a World Series.[2] The Soccer World Cup draws an audience larger than the Olympics, but barely registers with American viewers. The antipathy that many Americans feel for the way soccer is played is matched only by the distaste of many Europeans for the American style of play. Many Americans scorn the fact that feeble teams can often win in soccer by concentrating only on defense (they see this as unfair), they snicker that one-third of games end in a tie (because every game should have a winner!), and they are appalled that star players like David Beckham are traded like horsemeat from one team to another, often leaving their home country (such players are disloyal). For their part, Europeans cannot believe that a national sport would change its rules to suit TV, permit lousy teams to continue in the league (even rewarding them with earlier draft picks), or dictate through the draft system which team a player can join. Americans and Europeans have absorbed the structure and rules of their sports into their psyches, turning the arbitrary rules of nineteenth-century administrators into a way of life.

Franklin Foer, in his acclaimed book *How Soccer Explains the World*, attributes American hostility to soccer (at least in some quarters) to globalization. Globalization is feared by many because it seems to force us to accept other people's cultures and values. In France, this phenomenon is represented by McDonald's; in the United States by soccer. As Foer writes, seen from an American perspective, "Soccer isn't exactly pernicious, but it's a symbol of the U.S. junking its tradition to 'get with the rest of the world's program.'"[3] Thus, even if many Americans have come to enjoy soccer as a game, at least when played by their children, when it is organized as a professional league it follows the American sports model rather than the established model of European soccer leagues.

But our national pastimes did not materialize out of nothing. Rather, they were shaped by the conscious decisions of organizers, albeit decisions made a very long time ago. No doubt some, if not most, of these decisions were made with the intent of promoting and developing the sport over the long term. But often these decisions were made in response to short-term problems that may no longer be relevant. Some decisions were not made with the interests of the game itself at heart at all, but purely for temporary personal gain. This book explores how two national pastimes, baseball and soccer, which developed out of the rule-making of each sport's administrators, came to be woven into the fabric of different national cultures.

To some, two economics professors writing about culture might seem a little incongruous. After all, economists are supposed to worship at the altar of the mighty dollar (or euro, or whatever), certain of the price of everything and the value of nothing, as the saying goes. While it is true that we consider economic incentives (and these include motives associated with the acquisition of political power) to be the driving force behind the decisionmaking in professional team sports, we also believe that the purpose of any economic or political institution is to serve the public. In sports, this means the fans, the people who watch the game. One distinctive feature of professional sports is that the interest of the public accumulates over time. Indeed, one of the most important elements in the attraction of a sport is the relationship between the stars of today and the history of the game. This means that, in a sense, the current generation of administrators and owners is no more than the trustee of an asset that must one day be passed on to the next generation. Moreover, the policies of those in positions of power should be determined by the long-term interests of the fans rather than short-term gains. It also means that there must be a willingness to adapt venerable institutions to the times in which we live, rather than clinging to tradition for its own sake.

In this book we highlight ways in which the distinctive institutions of baseball and soccer developed to deal with specific problems, and how these institutions then came to be part of the fabric of the national pastime. We also examine the extent to which the institutions of today are fitted to the needs of the present generation of fans, and of fans of the future.

Sports leagues in the United States are organized in a fundamentally different way than those in the rest of the world. Those in the United States are based on the model created by the National League back in 1876. Those in the rest of the world are based on the model created by the English Football Association (FA) and Football League (FL) in the 1880s and 1890s.

U.S. sports leagues are closed. Team owners carefully control the number of franchises and their locations. Generally, each team is granted a monopoly over a given territory. Teams extract substantial public subsidies for their facilities. When leagues expand, existing owners charge a handsome entry fee to the new owners. Limits are set on roster size. Leagues benefit from a variety of antitrust exceptions.

In the English model, leagues are open. In each country where soccer is played (save the United States), there is a hierarchy of leagues. Poorly performing teams from higher leagues can be relegated to a lower league, and strong teams from lower leagues can be promoted. New teams can enter leagues at the bottom of the hierarchy without paying an entry fee to existing owners and work their way up to the higher leagues.[4] Teams are not conferred territorial monopolies and usually cannot extort public subsidies from local governments to support facility construction. Roster size is not limited. Open leagues thus generate a number of desirable characteristics from the standpoint of the fans, but as we shall see, the operation of the promotion/relegation system in Europe has created significant incentive and financial problems. These differences in the way baseball and soccer are organized reflect each sport's origins and evolution. Baseball emerged in the 1850s as an upper-middle-class leisure sport, but it soon spread to the lower middle class. At first, elite baseball clubs were extremely conscious of the social status that membership conferred, similar to that of the English cricket clubs upon which they were modeled. Yet as the game became more popular, winning, rather than gentlemanly behavior, became more important. Clubs began to invite (and pay for) good ballplayers from the lower classes. At this stage the game divided. Those old-fashioned gentlemen who wanted to preserve the social exclusivity of baseball segregated themselves from the professional teams, while in the professional teams the white-collar members became the managers and the blue-collar players became the employees. Amateurs and professionals went their own ways.

The National League was formed in 1876 by one group of managers who thought that they could produce a better and more profitable competition by exercising control over the employment of ballplayers (who up until then had moved freely to whichever team would pay the highest price, a practice known as "revolving"). They also believed that they would be more likely to achieve their ends by limiting membership in the league to an exclusive elite. Their business model was so incredibly successful that it not only co-opted or destroyed effective competition, it also became the pattern for American sports leagues.

Soccer in England was also created by a status-conscious upper middle class, but unlike baseball, it never evolved into a purely business-oriented enterprise. Even when the leading clubs started to charge money to watch games and to pay players, they held on to the principle that they were first and foremost sporting entities, not profit centers. When businessmen started to involve themselves with the clubs, they might have gone down the same path as baseball, segregating amateur and professional. Instead unity was preserved through a series of messy compromises. These compromises meant that although an amateur might compete against the professional, the outcome was seldom in doubt. At the same time, the professional clubs accepted restrictions on their commercial activities and their freedom to make profits. As a result of these decisions, soccer preserved a unified governance over the entire game (amateur and professional), which was lost to baseball. Unlike professional baseball, which was free from such constraints, soccer has been slow to learn how to organize the business aspect of the game in ways that sustain financial stability. In short, baseball developed as a monopolistic industry with a tight focus on profit, while soccer developed as a broad federation of highly competitive clubs. Each system has its problems.

A good illustration of this point is the funding of stadium construction. The United States has witnessed an extraordinary boom in stadium construction in recent years. Between 1989 and 2001 there were sixteen baseball-only stadiums built for major league teams. During the previous thirteen years, there were no baseball-only stadiums built.[5] The total cost of the sixteen facilities constructed during 1989–2001 was $4.9 billion in current dollars, with an average development cost of $306 million. Of the $4.9 billion, $3.27 billion, or 66.7 percent, came from public coffers.[6] This is an enormous amount of public subsidy for what is supposed to be private enterprise, and must largely be understood as a manifestation of the monopoly power of the major leagues.

Major League Baseball (MLB), as it is now known, has maintained a tight grip over professional baseball since 1915, when its last real competitor, the Federal League, was driven out of business. Despite significant demographic changes in the United States that have created new demand for baseball in new locations, the team owners have managed the process of expansion and relocation to ensure that there is always excess demand for franchises from economically viable cities. With excess demand, MLB has been successful at getting cities to bid against each other for a franchise. The result is public subsidies far in excess of the economic and social benefits generated by a team.

As an example of public policy, this situation leaves much to be desired. Not only are the subsidies huge, crowding out social programs that might create jobs and rebuild local economies; they are also raised through taxes that are typically regressive, falling more heavily on the poor than on the rich. Moreover, there is now a substantial body of academic research showing that these subsidies bring negligible benefits in the form of jobs and business for the local economy.[7] It is, of course, possible that there are feel-good and other intangible benefits that accrue to a city from hosting a baseball team. The evidence on the size of such benefits, however, is ambiguous.[8] Ultimately, the monopoly power of MLB distorts the stadium economy at the expense of taxpayers.

A rather different picture emerges from the soccer world. The openness of soccer, with its system of promotion and relegation, enables any city, or town, or even village, to host a "major league" team, so long as a good enough squad of players can be assembled. This immediately neutralizes the relocation threat: no city needs to buy someone else's team to join the elite. Even so, municipal government may invest in a local stadium for reasons of public pride, but this motive is far less reliable than the fear engendered by the relocation threat. Moreover, because competition between teams is so intense, and a club's tenure in the top flight is so uncertain, the clubs themselves are often reluctant to invest their own money. This can lead to a problem of facility underinvestment, with often tragic consequences.

In May 1985, fifty-six fans were burned to death at the stadium of Bradford City after a dilapidated wooden stand caught fire. In April 1989, ninety-six fans were crushed to death in Sheffield, England, because the stewards and the police were unable to see that too many fans had been admitted into one part of the stadium where an FA Cup semifinal was being played.[9] As recently as 1990, most stadiums in England had been little altered since their construction in the first two decades of the twentieth century. Most clubs lacked the resources to invest in upgrading facilities, and municipal government was usually not allowed to support such investments. The gradual decay of stadiums in England was not just a safety hazard; it also discouraged supporters, and between 1950 and 1985 total attendance fell by more than half (from 41 million per season to 18 million). The audience for soccer became concentrated among young men on low incomes who were increasingly involved in violent confrontations with the fans of rival teams. By the mid 1980s, with most teams close to bankruptcy, the hooliganism problem was so pressing that Margaret Thatcher's government contemplated closing down professional soccer altogether.[10]

This sorry tale is not just an English one. As we detail in chapter 3, stadium disasters and crowd violence have been commonplace throughout the soccer world. In England, the trend was reversed in the 1990s after the government mandated stadium improvements. During the 1990s, the government earmarked £200 million (about $350 million) in subsidies for soccer clubs at all levels (most of the money was allocated to the 100 or so professional clubs in the United Kingdom) to help finance stadium redevelopment. However, once all teams were required to invest, most teams decided that it made sense to spend even more than the government required. By 2002 total capital investment in stadium redevelopment over a ten-year period amounted to nearly £1.5 billion (about $2.7 billion), mostly from funds provided by the clubs themselves.[11] In other words, a small public subsidy triggered a huge wave of private investment. During this period, soccer in England underwent a renaissance, drawing a larger and more socially diverse body of support than it had enjoyed for fifty years.

To be sure, soccer has its own monopoly excesses induced by the bidding to host the World Cup, which is held every four years. Nations are so desperate to host the event that they offer to build stadiums that have limited use once the event is over. For example, in hosting the World Cup, together with South Korea, in 2002, Japan invested about $3 billion to complete ten stadiums with an average capacity of about 40,000. This amounts to about $100 million for each World Cup game played in Japan. After the event the stadiums were handed over to teams in Japan's national soccer league, for which attendance is typically in the region of 10,000 per game.

The lesson we draw from these baseball and soccer examples is that an unrestrained monopoly will inevitably lead to the exploitation of fans and taxpayers, while a system of unrestrained competition will, as we will explain, lead to financial pressures that may threaten the health of the league. Sports are, in the business world, a special case because each team depends upon the others to play the game and provide an opposition. Without opponents, no team can produce anything at all. This situation demands a minimum of cooperation among the teams; otherwise chaos will ensue. In practical terms, the extremes of pure monopoly and unlimited competition are to be avoided, but plotting a course between them is not easy. Soccer has lessons to learn from baseball about how to create a degree of cooperation so that club level policies do not undermine the long-term future of the league. By the same token, baseball can learn from soccer that a degree of diversity and competition can limit some of the excesses of monopoly.

At the risk of oversimplifying, the object of this book is to set out how baseball and soccer have evolved into their current structures. Tracing this evolution, in turn, leads us to a diagnosis of baseball's and soccer's current problems and to identifying some solutions that are gleaned from each other's experiences. This analysis naturally draws heavily on the historical record. In chapter 2 we set out how the basic pattern of each game's administration developed in the crucial formative years of the nineteenth century. It will perhaps come as a surprise to some that baseball in America and soccer in England were quite conscious of each other's development. Not least, we use contemporary sources to show that the English authorities modeled the championship of the English Football League in 1888 on its forerunner, the National League in baseball, in significant measure because of the latter's commercial success. It may well be that other institutions, such as the system of controlling player mobility, also were copied by the soccer authorities from the baseball authorities.

In chapter 3 we turn our attention to the different ways in which soccer and baseball have been disseminated throughout the world. Although baseball is played and followed passionately in parts of the Caribbean and the Far East, neither it nor most of the other U.S. team sports have become particularly popular oversees.[12] In contrast, soccer is played virtually everywhere, and in many countries it is the leading team sport. Soccer's initial diffusion had much to do with the flow of international visitors to England and the foreign tours of English clubs that had become a regular feature of the game by the first decade of the twentieth century. These soccer exchanges were an outgrowth of Britain's expansive foreign trade and investment ties and the accompanying value system that sought to bring British culture to the rest of the world.

Another factor that accounts for soccer's spread is the existence of the Fédération Internationale de Football Association (FIFA), soccer's international governing body, and the policies it has pursued to spread the game, particularly in Africa in recent years. But perhaps the most potent factor has been the identification of soccer with politics and nationalism. While a significant contributor to soccer's vibrancy, it is also sometimes connected to the political and social excesses often associated with the game.

Without players, of course, there is no game. Although the players are the heroes of any sport, in baseball and soccer they were long bound, like servants, to their masters, the professional clubs. In Chapter 4 we discuss the evolution and functioning of the players' markets in the two sports. We show how the labor market in each sport has been controlled and how the players have eventually broken free, either through the power of organized labor, or, after Europe's Bosman judgment, through the power of the courts.[13]

In chapter 5 we treat the distinct business models that have prevailed in soccer and baseball, and compare the financial performance of baseball and soccer clubs. Notwithstanding claims that they are losing money, we argue that all the evidence points to baseball clubs as significant creators of profits. This follows from the monopolistic nature of Major League Baseball, an aspect of the game that has given rise to concern over many years.[14] In soccer, by contrast, we argue that the nature of the competitive structure of the game limits the ability of all but a small elite to generate profits.

In chapter 6 we turn our attention to broadcasting. Despite initial reluctance to broadcast its games, baseball has moved far faster than soccer to embrace, first, television and then new media. This is perhaps not surprising given the enormous wealth that TV can generate for a popular sport. Many administrators in soccer have resisted TV as a medium because they have believed, almost without regard to the evidence, that it will destroy the game. The facts seem to suggest the reverse: TV has done much to increase the appeal of both baseball and soccer by bringing them to wider audiences and creating new markets. Indeed, the eventual realization that this is true has brought the state of soccer TV broadcasting much closer to that of baseball in recent years. One problem, however, which affects the soccer world more than that of baseball, is the specter of monopoly—not at the level of the leagues themselves, but at the level of broadcasters. In recent years, European nationalized monopolies in public broadcasting have been replaced by monopolistic private sector suppliers of pay TV services, leading to relatively high charges for watching live soccer in Europe in comparison with baseball in the United States.

In chapter 7 we discuss one of sport's most complex problems: competitive balance. Every sport needs a degree of competitive balance to create uncertainty of outcome, without which the excitement and suspense that make a sport attractive are lost. The complexities of the competitive balance argument have to do with three issues. First, competitive balance is hard to define in a precise and measurable way. Second, it is hard to find conclusive evidence about how much it really does matter. Third, fixing a problem of competitive imbalance typically means allowing team owners to agree on restraints that further enhance their monopoly power. There is little doubt that competitive balance has been central to the debate over baseball's state of health in recent years. In European soccer, however, it appears that leagues are capable of withstanding levels of imbalance that would be deemed unacceptable in baseball. We discuss the compensating factors in soccer that make its fans more tolerant of imbalance.

In the final chapter we draw out the lessons that soccer can learn from baseball, and that baseball can learn from soccer. Each sport faces difficulties: in soccer, there is an immediate financial crisis; in baseball, there is a long-term challenge to protect and expand its fan base. Since the nineteenth century, soccer has been promoted very effectively throughout the world. Its fan base continues to grow and spread, even into the United States. But soccer's promotion-and-relegation system, its many virtues notwithstanding, has generated incentives that have led to its present financial dilemma. Compounding this problem, the mix of national and supranational competition has skewed the teams' financial resources even more sharply.

In recent years the European soccer leagues have had to deal with a number of new problems. The liberalization of the player markets following the Bosman decision in 1995, the recent decline in television rights fees, the antitrust ambiguities at the league and Union of European Football Association (UEFA) levels, the double league phenomenon for the leading teams, the inadequacy of revenue-sharing mechanisms, and the financial weaknesses of many clubs have all challenged the health of the leagues. The interaction of national and EU policy oversight has created an uncertain and interesting environment of institutional fluidity. The present system in European soccer needs reform, and it can learn from baseball.

In the United States, baseball has been slipping in popularity relative to football but holding its own relative to other sports. Outside the United States, the Caribbean, and Japan,[15] baseball has made few inroads into new countries and remains a distant third in popularity behind soccer and basketball in mainland China with its huge market of 1.2 billion people. More recently, it has had problems sustaining interest among America's youth as well as among African Americans. This marketing problem has been exacerbated by baseball's protected monopoly. Baseball's barons have been myopic and without an effective business plan for decades. Revenue inequality and unstable labor relations have continued to damage baseball in the United States, as have recent strategy decisions and public relations missteps by the commissioner's office. The game is groping for a direction and cries out for more effective leadership. Soccer's open and fan-friendly system has important lessons for MLB.

In the end, the organization of soccer and of baseball reflects the societies where they were created. Soccer and baseball will never be organized the same; nor should they be. As in most matters, however, open-mindedness and cross-cultural understanding can be powerful forces.

CHAPTER TWO

The Origins of Baseball and Soccer Leagues

Here lies poor Fred, who was alive and is dead,
Had it been his father, I had much rather,
Had it been his sister, nobody would have missed her,
Had it been his brother, still better than another,
Had it been the whole generation, so much better for the nation,
But since it is Fred who was alive and is dead,
There is no more to be said![1]

Frederick Louis, Prince of Wales, died on March 20, 1751, after the ball hit his head while he was fielding in a game of cricket.[2] Fred loved bat-and-ball games. Not only was he obsessed with cricket, but he is also on record as playing baseball indoors, something perhaps only the heir to a throne can get away with.[3] Had it not been for the prince's untimely death, his mad son George might not have ascended to the throne, the colonies might not have rebelled, and the world's two most popular sports, baseball and soccer, might not be what they are today.[4] Cricket was the first of the modern team sports to be formalized by a rule book (1744), a governing body (1787), the compulsive gathering of statistical information,[5] and a recognizable public following. It was the model for many team sports that followed, including baseball and soccer.

In this chapter we explore how baseball and soccer became established in the nineteenth century. But to do this we have first to explain how their common ancestor (in an organizational sense), cricket, came to be known as England's national pastime. Cricket is a sport that has always had an aristocratic air, and the development of cricket in the eighteenth century was

12

due largely to patronage.[6] Cricket evolved from the plethora of games involving bat and ball played by English children in the Middle Ages, games with colorful names such as cat & dog, stool-ball, hurling, club-ball, trap-ball, northern spell, and tip-cat whose rules are now mostly forgotten.[7] That cricket alone developed from these informal games into a national sport is an accident of geography. Cricket was most popular in the wealthy counties of Kent and Surrey around London, where aristocrats needed to assemble to be close to the court and to the King. The English nobility, along with poor Fred, took up the game and made it the center of English cultural life. Among the significant early patrons were the fourth Earl of Sandwich (inventor of the snack), the first Duke of Newcastle (secretary of state and advocate of noninterference in the colonies), the second Duke of Richmond (ambassador to Paris and noted patron of the arts), the third Duke of Dorset (paramour of Marie Antoinette, who once gave her a cricket bat as a present), and the ninth Earl of Winchilsea (who raised his own regiment to fight the colonists in the Revolutionary War).[8] These aristocrats not only provided the cachet necessary to make the sport fashionable; they also provided the means to maintain the cricket fields that sprang up in and around London. By the end of the eighteenth century, anybody who was anybody needed to belong to one of the country's exclusive cricket clubs.

The Commercialization of Cricket

From its very beginning, cricket was about money. The English nobility were inveterate gamblers,[9] and aristocrats like the Earl of Winchilsea might bet sums as large as 1,000 guineas (about $110,000 in today's money) on the outcome of a single game.[10] Winchilsea was a particularly important figure in the development of cricket. Having returned beaten from the Americas, he threw himself into organizing cricket matches in London and provided the financial backing for the laying out of Lord's cricket ground in northwest London in 1787.[11] Known ever since as the home of cricket, its importance as a cricket ground stems from the fact that it became the home of the Marylebone Cricket Club, the MCC. Thanks to the patronage of earls and dukes such as Winchilsea, the MCC has ever since been a club the membership in which signals one's arrival into the elite of English society. Like his fellow gamblers, Winchilsea was a cricket player too—albeit a pretty poor one—and put together teams for the purpose of betting. To give his side a better chance, he scoured the country for farm laborers able to bat and bowl (pitch) for his team. If they won the match, they were paid 5 guineas (about $525 in today's money). Not surprisingly with such large bets at stake, accusations of match-fixing began to spread. Stories of wickets bought and runs sold abounded.[12] According to one popular story, a batsman and a bowler each bet against themselves, resulting in a ludicrous stalemate where the bowler would not pitch the ball anywhere near the batsman's wicket, while the batsman refused to try to hit the ball. As this kind of publicity became common currency, the aristocratic version of the game fell into disrepute.

What saved cricket was the adoption of the game by the English public school movement.[13] By the beginning of the nineteenth century, new ideas about the education of children were talked about all over Europe. In England, reformers, such as Thomas Arnold, adopted the view that the development of children required a healthy body as well as a healthy mind. These educators saw sport not just as exercise, but as a moral example of behavioral rectitude and physical strength. The adoption of these values at schools such as Eton, Harrow, and Winchester had an enormous impact on Victorian values in Britain. This is best exemplified in the novel *Tom Brown's Schooldays* by Thomas Hughes, published in 1857 and set at the Rugby School. In the story, the eponymous hero struggles against Flashman, the school bully, to uphold a combination of Christian virtues, physical courage, self-reliance, loyalty, and patriotism.[14] Tom Brown stands for a generation of English gentlemen schooled through the love of sport to build and maintain an empire, endowed with attributes characterized simply as "muscular Christianity."[15]

If the educators saw cricket as the embodiment of the spirit they were trying to create, their championing of the game rescued it from the crisis of gambling that was endemic at the end of the eighteenth century. As the Industrial Revolution spread and the British Empire began to take shape, the growing upper middle class played and followed the game in increasing numbers. The playing of the game became increasingly systematized, treatises were written on the art of batting, and the business of making and selling cricket equipment became significant. In 1851 the first history of the game appeared, written by the Reverend James Pycroft. *The Cricket Field*, also published in Boston in 1859, provided both a detailed history and a paean to the supposedly English virtues cricket embodied: "The game of Cricket, philosophically considered, is a standing panegyric on the

English character: none but an orderly and sensible race would so amuse themselves."[16]

As cricket acquired a new moral context in the mid-nineteenth century, it also needed new ways to symbolize the social ordering. In the aristocratic days of the eighteenth century, the lord could mix socially with his tenant, who was paid to play cricket without any confusion on either side as to social standing. The new middle classes who played the game could not rely on these antiquated distinctions. Although professional cricketers were not excluded from the game, new names had to be invented to ensure that differences in status were properly understood. The term "gentleman" was applied to the leisured amateur, the term "player" to the hired professional.[17] Gentlemen and players might compete as equals on the field, but at dinner a firm social segregation was enforced. Cricket's hierarchy remained a thing of fine social distinctions well into the second half of the twentieth century. The aristocracy patronized Lord's and ran the MCC, which, as the longest-standing club, was acclaimed as the ultimate arbiter of the rules of the game, while the middle classes competed to climb the social ladder. The working classes, used exclusively as players and excluded from social gatherings, were kept firmly in their place.

The growth of the middle classes also created commercial opportunities. As well as being played, cricket was increasingly able to attract large crowds. Thanks to the railways, teams could move around the country to play matches. Undoubtedly there were many entrepreneurs who stood ready to exploit the commercial opportunities of cricket as a spectator sport, just as there had been in its gambling days. From its earliest days, there existed a great variety of formats for playing cricket, over periods of time ranging from a few hours to an unlimited number of days. Had commercial interests dominated in the nineteenth century, there can be little doubt that a short version of the game would have become standard. As it was, however, the format that came to dominate was one that involved playing the game over three whole days (cricket is the only sport in the world that includes breaks for both lunch and tea). Still worse, games were usually scheduled during midweek. For this reason, whatever its claims to being England's national game, cricket could never be a commercially successful activity.

By the mid-nineteenth century, however, it was catching on across the world. Cricket teams were to be found in every part of the British Empire— Australia, India, New Zealand, South Africa, and Canada—as well as in most of Europe and even in the United States. Cricket had been played in American colonies before the Revolution, but proper cricket clubs were not established until the 1830s. The St. George Cricket Club of Staten Island claimed to be the first established club playing according to the rules of the MCC, but in the next couple of decades cricket clubs sprouted along the eastern seaboard and, according to one contemporary newspaper, there were as many as a thousand clubs by the year 1859.[18] Along with regular matches between the leading clubs, an annual series between the USA and Canada was started in 1840, and in 1859 the best eleven cricketers in England were challenged to tour the United States and play a series of games. The most famous of these was played at the Elysian Fields in Hoboken, New Jersey, and drew a crowd of 24,000 over three days. (The Americans were soundly beaten.)

The Outgrowth of Baseball

Cricket was by no means the only game in town, however. At the Elysian Fields, cricketers had been playing alongside exponents of the new sport of "base ball" for almost twenty years. Like cricket, baseball can lay claim to an exotic menagerie of antecedents including rounders, barn ball, town ball, old cat, and baste ball. The identity of the game's immediate progenitor is of less importance than its parallel development with cricket between the 1840s and 1880s. Abner Doubleday to the contrary, the origin of baseball as we know it dates to the Knickerbocker baseball club of New York City.[19] Under the leadership of Alexander Joy Cartwright, the Knickerbocker club was formed in 1842 and codified the rules of the game for the first time (for example, nine contestants to each side, ninety feet between the bases) and provided for the first uniforms (though not the famous knickers, which were first introduced by the Cincinnati Red Stockings team in 1869). Cartwright thus supplied the first unifying basis for the game that previously had been played under different rules in each community.

Once a common set of rules became established, interclub and intercommunity contests became viable. During the 1850s, the game's popularity grew rapidly throughout the Northeast, even to the point that to limit attendance certain clubs began to sell tickets for special matches.[20]

Were a modern baseball fan to enter a time machine and attend a baseball game in the 1850s, she might have to strain to recognize it as the same game. Without stands, fans either stood on the sidelines or watched from the outfield, sometimes seated in a horse and carriage or in a tent to shield ladies from the sun. The field was all grass except for a narrow, forty-five-foot-long dirt patch from the pitcher's mound to home plate. The pitcher threw underhand, there were no called balls and strikes, the basemen in the field stood literally on top of their bases, and the catcher could usually be seen some twenty or thirty feet behind the batter, where he attempted to catch the pitched ball on one bounce. Fielders did not wear gloves (cricketers do not wear gloves for fielding to this day).

The games of these early years were not commercially motivated. Baseball was still a sport for gentlemen—much like cricket—played to establish one's proper social standing. Cartwright's rules included a prohibition against swearing. Baseball historian Robert Burk comments: "A club represented a select fraternity of like-minded men, a voluntary association of sober, respectable Yankees dedicated to healthful recreation, fellowship and public virtue.... In the way of a religious congregation, the Knickerbockers used dues ($5 annual, $2 initiation), fines, and punishments to help maintain their exclusiveness, finance their activities, and define their purposes."[21]

Cartwright not only wrote the rule book; he also umpired the first inter-club contest at the Elysian Fields in 1846 when he fined a player 6 cents for cussing.[22] Cartwright himself was soon to buy a covered wagon and be off to California on the Gold Rush. He eventually made his way to Hawaii, where he died in 1892.

In the early 1850s, baseball contests were usually followed by elaborate social affairs, where food and spirits abounded. One description of a postgame gathering hosted by the Knickerbockers for their opponents, the Brooklyn Excelsiors, read as follows: "[The Knickerbockers] entertained in splendid style, covers being laid for over 200 gentlemen. Dodworth's Band was in attendance to enliven the scene, and all the arrangements were exceedingly creditable to the taste and liberality of the committee who had charge of the festive occasion."[23]

The Knickerbocker club often began its social gatherings with a toast in verse to the visiting club. This toast gives a good sense of the spirit and meaning of the early baseball contests:

The young clubs, one and all, with a welcome we will greet,
On the field or festive hall, whenever we may meet;
And their praises we will sing at some future time;
But now we'll pledge their health in a glass of rosy wine.[24]

As the game's popularity grew in the 1850s, its social exclusivity was rup-
tured. The livelier pace of the game and the greater athleticism of the fielders started to draw much larger crowds than cricket matches, and baseball's
appeal as a spectacle spread rapidly across the classes. Moreover, from the
mid-1850s, workingmen's clubs were established to play the game, clubs
such as the Brooklyn Atlantic Club and the New York Mutuals. Even the
original gentlemen's clubs began a gradual self-transformation. As interclub
matches became more public and competitive spectacles, clubs took on new
members based on their playing ability. Formerly all-white-collar clubs
began to admit craftsmen as players, some of whom might even be paid
(illicitly) for their services.

Competition started to become more intense. In Brooklyn, the hotly contested rivalry between the Atlantics and the more venerable Brooklyn Excelsiors helped to promote interest in the game. In 1860 a crowd of 15,000
gathered to watch the decider in the championship series between the two
teams. So partisan was the crowd that day that the Excelsiors refused to finish the game, and despite the presence of a hundred policemen they had to
flee the scene under a barrage of stones and insults.[25]

The widening circle of baseball enthusiasts and the more intense competition did not meet with everyone's approval. The democratization of baseball gave it a somewhat harsher edge. In future years, many old timers would
look back nostalgically to the sport's antebellum era of fraternal amateurism. According to historian Robert F. Burk: "Increasing expressions of
concern by 'traditionalists' within the sport, and by reporters of similar cultural background who were beginning to cover it, reflected the realization
that the ballplaying fraternity was losing its exclusiveness. By the mid-1850s,
mirroring the shifting production structure and social mobility patterns of
antebellum cities and the influx of Irish and German immigrants, the game
was becoming both less Yankee and less preindustrial in its personnel and
guiding spirit."[26]

Burk asserts that whereas during the first half of the 1850s three-quarters
of club members were white-collar, by the latter half of the decade skilled
blue-collar and lower white-collar clerical participants were three-quarters
of membership. As the size and social diversity of club membership grew, so
did the spectator interest in the game, converting the ballfield from a venue
for the expression of social fellowship to one for contests pitting neighborhood against neighborhood, or one ethnic or occupational group against

another. By 1858 there were some fifty adult and sixty youth baseball clubs in the greater New York City area.

By this stage, however, there still was no organizational structure to baseball. Teams recognized each other by agreeing to abide by the Knickerbocker rules, but that was all. Inevitably, other clubs wanted to revise the rules; but who could force the Knickerbocker club to change? As the popularity of the game grew, newspapers and pundits started to agitate for a national association so that there could be "one game, peculiar to the United States."[27] They looked to the older clubs to take the lead, to "give the association of Base Ball Clubs of Manhattan Island a similar standing which the Marylebone Club of London exercises over the game of cricket throughout the British Islands."[28]

On March 10, 1858, the presidents of the Knickerbockers, Gothams, Empires, and Eagles clubs called the elite clubs of greater New York City together. The result was the formation of the National Association of Base Ball Players (NABBP). However, these baseball aristocrats viewed their purpose quite differently than the newspapers. The founders of the NABBP wanted above all to preserve the social values that they believed in and had little interest in fostering the expansion of the game. One of the NABBP rules, for instance, was that member clubs had to have at least eighteen members—to ensure that clubs were large enough that there would be a separation between players and managers, allowing white-collar members to control the administrative functions of the clubs. Other rules mandated upstanding player behavior, banned player compensation, and prohibited betting by players, umpires, and scorers. And in 1859 the NABBP proscribed postgame banquets because they had degenerated into rowdy affairs rather than decorous expressions of fraternal fellowship.

But, willy-nilly, baseball continued to grow. By 1860 the NABBP membership had expanded into New Jersey and Pennsylvania and included fifty-three clubs.[29] In 1860 *The Clipper*, New York's sporting newspaper, was able to state confidently that baseball "may now be considered the national game."[30] The Civil War then intervened, both to disrupt normal play in the Northeast and to spread the game to the South. While membership in the National Association fell during the war from over fifty to fewer than forty clubs, following the war it grew rapidly. In 1866, 202 clubs belonged to the association. And whereas member clubs in 1860 were all within a seventy-five-mile radius of New York City, by 1866 membership had spread across seventeen states. The number of association clubs jumped again in 1867 to over 300.[31]

By the end of 1860s, baseball clubs were forming in practically all states of the nation. The NABBP had neither the will nor the capacity to exercise any control over this development, and it is arguable that even a more forceful administration would have been hard put to do so during a period of such rapid change in all aspects of American life. And the power vacuum permitted all kinds of abuses to take hold.

The Commercialization of Baseball

One kind of abuse, at least in the eyes of the purists, was the taking of gate money. Even before the Civil War, a crowd of 5,000 was not unusual for a baseball game in Brooklyn, and after the war, crowds of 10,000 to 15,000 were attracted to the more popular games. Admission prices of between 10 and 50 cents were levied by the owners of baseball lots, which were enclosed for the purpose. The Knickerbockers refused to have anything to do with gate money, although they did eventually agree to play in contests where admission was charged.[32] Other clubs did not see it this way and demanded their share from the lot owners. Inevitably, the more entrepreneurially minded clubs saw a business opportunity. By 1868 the eight largest clubs registered a combined income of $100,000.[33] Other forms of income were to be found in the form of prizes offered by the newspapers to the winners of a particular series. The lure of gate money together with the emerging railroad system helped to establish the practice of the baseball tour, which did much to spread the game to the interior of the country.

As night follows day, so gate money leads to player payments. Since the NABBP rules prohibited player payments, teams resorted to paying players under the table. The first player known to have received illicit remuneration was James Creighton of the Brooklyn Excelsiors in 1860. Numerous tricks were developed to pay players, including the sale of souvenir tickets with a player's picture on each and the provision of soft jobs on the city payroll (the coroner's office was a favorite). Some clubs risked the NABBP's sanction and paid a salary outright, an early example being Al Reach of the Philadelphia Athletics in 1862.[34] The burgeoning practice of paying players reached Albert G. Spalding in 1867, when he was offered a job as a clerk for a grocery wholesaler at $40 a week, approximately ten times the normal wage for the job, as an inducement to pitch for the Chicago Excelsior team.

With gate money and player payments, some now started to use a word in association with baseball that no Englishman would have dared to apply to cricket: "business." Moreover, while the "old fogies" of the Knickerbocker Club might click their tongues, more progressive voices pointed to the advantages of the business ethic: it would ensure an adequate supply of baseball fields, which were rapidly disappearing in the big cities; it would raise the quality of play; it would generate surpluses that could be paid out to charitable causes; and it would price the rowdier elements of the crowd out of the ballpark.[35] No less an authority than Henry Chadwick, the doyen of early baseball writing, welcomed the transition to a business footing as early as 1868.

At the same time, a more sinister abuse seeped into the game. The first significant baseball betting scandal was recorded at a contest between the New York Mutuals and the Brooklyn Eckfords on September 28, 1865.[36] Gambler Kane McLaughlin paid Mutuals catcher William Wansley $100 to ensure the game was won by the Eckfords. Wansley, in turn, paid the team third baseman and shortshop $30 each, keeping $40 for himself, to blow the game. Wansley himself entered the game in the fifth inning with his team ahead 5 to 4. Wansley committed six passed balls and went 0 for 5 at the plate, as the Eckfords scored eleven times in the fifth inning, going on to win the game 23 to 11.

Gamblers were opposed to players being paid a salary because (a) it made players less vulnerable to the gambler's bait and (b) it made management care more about player behavior. Joining the gamblers were gentlemen amateurs (or "idle dilettantes," as baseball historian Lee Allen called them), who were concerned that paying players would result in skill (rather than social standing) determining who played. The church was also in the mix. Sporting spectacles on weekends stole attention from church activities. Juxtaposed to the mysteries of metaphysics, baseball's rational ordering through its rules and statistical cornucopia posed a threat to religion similar to the advance of materialist and capitalist values.[37] Perhaps some ministers also feared the potential for this compulsive sport to satisfy the emotional and spiritual needs of their parishioners in competition with the established religion.

Secretly paying individual players ineluctably led to paying entire teams overtly. The first fully professional baseball team was established in Cincinnati in 1869. Team backer Aaron Champion spent $9,300 on payroll for ten players ($800–$1,400 each)—a payroll that in today's prices would come to approximately $160,000. With this modest sum, the Cincinnati Red Stockings traversed the country, winning all fifty-seven of their games.[38]

The Red Stockings' average salary of $930 was topped the next year when the Chicago White Stockings were formed as a professional team and paid the players an average salary of $1,200. To lure the top players from the East, the White Stockings had to offer each player a $500 advance on their salaries. The president of the team was David Gage, who, according to an indictment brought against him in 1873, had embezzled over $100,000 from his company to finance the team.[39]

Of course, in order to become professional teams, the Red and White Stockings had to pull out of the NABBP. The New York Knickerbockers also pulled out of the association, but for a different reason. The Knickerbockers did not want to go professional, but in the Knickerbockers' perception, the amateur teams were not remaining amateur. As Ted Vincent put it: "Baseball as a vehicle for organizing and perpetuating elite social clubs was dying out; the status seekers had been in the game to gain fame; the professionals were monopolizing the fame; and the clubs that didn't go pro were losing their prime reasons for being in the game."[40]

As early as the 1868 season, the NABBP rules committee, acknowledging that the no-pay rule was mostly honored in the breach, recommended that the association split into two groups—one amateur, the other professional. The bifurcation finally occurred in 1871, but the tension had been building for some time. In November 1870 there was a heated debate at the NABBP's annual convention over the proposition that "the custom of publicly hiring men to play the game of base ball is reprehensible and injurious to the best interests of the game."[41] The motion failed, but amateurs and professionals both recognized that they would now have to go their own way. In early March 1871, thirty-three of the leading amateur clubs met in Brooklyn to plan their future. At the meeting, Dr. Jones of the Excelsior Club fondly remembered the times when amateur players from all social classes rubbed shoulders and roundly blamed the example of England's paid professionals for introducing the idea of pay for play on their cricketing tours of the United States.[42] The meeting concluded with an agreement to form the National Association of Amateur Base Ball Players (NAABBP). Meanwhile, executives from ten of the leading professional clubs met at Collier's Café on Broadway at 13th Street on March 4, 1871, to form the National Association of Professional Base Ball Players (NAPBBP). The former collapsed after four years, the latter after five years.

While neither can be considered a long-term success, the NAPBBP did leave a lasting mark on the structure of baseball. In conception, the association was an open players' league. It had little structure, but it marked the first effort at organizing a professional league. Teams were organized either as joint stock companies and paid players fixed salaries, or as co-operatives and shared gate receipts with the players. The association had several critical flaws, but it can claim one overriding distinction: it established the notion of a national championship. Before the NAPBBP, teams competed in ad hoc contests or championships. The NAPBBP had not quite invented a league, since teams were free to fix their own schedules, but it was an important precursor.

However, the creation of a national championship was not enough to save the NAPBBP from its flaws, one of which was rampant corruption: "Corruption was rife and the chief ingredients of life were bribery, contract breaking, and the desertion of players. . . . Discovering that their salaries represented only a fraction of what they could make by dealing with the gamblers, the players traveled from city to city like princes, sporting diamonds, drinking champagne at dinner every night, and ostentatiously paying the tab by peeling off folding money from the wads of the stuff that mysteriously reproduced themselves."[43] This was the era of the robber barons, and some players too wanted to stake their claim to the booty.

Henry Chadwick, the leading baseball writer of the time, commented in the *New York Mercury* after the 1872 season: "It would appear as professional clubs were no longer amenable to any influence save that of the betting and pool selling business. Hence the steady decline in the popularity and loss of that prestige of playing games on the square which is the very life of a professional organization . . . not one man who witnessed the majority of the games in October last can be persuaded that the contests were fairly or honestly contested."[44]

Another baseball historian, George Moreland, writes of the NAPBBP: "Bribery, contract-breaking, dishonest playing, pool-room manipulations and desertion of players became so shameful that the highly respectable element of patrons began to drop out of attendance, until the crowds that came to the games were composed exclusively of men who went to the grounds to bet money on the results. The money was bet openly during the progress of the game."[45] One section of the crowd at Brooklyn Atlantics games was reserved for bettors and came to be known as the "Gold Board," where action resembled that on the floor of today's stock exchange.

Indeed, the owners themselves were often entwined with the sordid city politics of corruption. The New York Mutuals were owned by William Marcy "Boss" Tweed. Tweed had taken over the team in 1857. The team for Tweed was a moneymaking venture, charging 10 cents for admission to its games in 1862 and 15 cents the next year. Reminiscent of the publicly financed stadiums in today's game, by the late 1860s Tweed had the city underwriting the growth of baseball. His aldermen voted for one appropriation of $1,500 from the city treasury to fund a prize for a local baseball tournament.

The Mutuals players were originally firemen, but were transferred to the city's street-cleaning department by Tweed. As city employees, the Mutuals had no problems skipping work for practice or games, so the team played a more extensive schedule than others. The Mutuals became charter members of the NAPBBP in 1871.

Tweed, himself a close friend of the infamous robber barons Jim Fisk and Jay Gould, ran and owned much of the city. Tweed had the city sign contracts with or purchase objects (chairs, desks, cuspidors, cabinets) from his companies and sometimes received city money for phantom goods or services. Tweed's control of the Mutuals faded after his first jail term during 1873–74. Tweed was found to have pilfered over $30 million from the city's coffers—a tidy sum back in the depression years of the 1870s.[46]

According to historian Ted Vincent, the Philadelphia Athletics were another of several teams laced with propitious connections to city government. Vincent writes that "an inordinate number of baseball club officials held office as city or county treasurer, tax collector, comptroller, assessor . . . or clerks and deputies working with city finances."[47]

In 1871 the Chicago team held first place for most of the season but was deprived of its quest for the flag by the great fire that ravaged the city in early October. Still recovering from the fire, Chicago did not even field a team in 1872. In 1872 the league started with eleven clubs and finished with only six. Of the finishers, four paid their players regular salaries and two operated as co-operatives, sharing gate receipts with the players.

The NAPBBP championship's last season was 1875, which began with thirteen teams and ended with seven. Over the league's five years, twenty-five different clubs participated, and eleven of them did not survive a single year. Lee Allen writes: "Drunkenness among the players in 1875 became so prevalent that it presented a problem almost as serious as the throwing of games."[48]

The drinking problem was only avoided by Harry Wright's Boston Red Stockings. Oddly, this compounded the league's difficulties because Wright's Boston team dominated the league, winning all but the first of the five championships. The teams organized as joint stock companies with the wealthiest backers were able to hire the best players. The average yearly salary of joint stock teams was $1,200, while that for teams organized as co-operatives was only $300. The Boston team, organized as a joint stock company, paid an average salary of $1,450 in 1871 and $2,050 in 1875. In 1875 the Red Stockings' pre-Bambino-curse record was seventy-one wins against only eight losses—an .899 win percentage! Baseball's competitive imbalance was not invented by Bud Selig's Blue Ribbon Panel in its 2000 report.

The result of these various deficiencies was that attendance fell during each year of the association's existence. The combination of falling attendance, corruption, inebriation, and competitive imbalance also meant that ownership squabbles were ever-present, but they were particularly acute between eastern and western clubs—the latter feeling repeatedly disadvantaged by association policies.

Historians have often referred to the NAPBBP as "Harry Wright's League," and Wright was in many ways its leading light. He later demurred at the title "father of the game" offered to him by William Hulbert, but he did nurse the ambition to introduce baseball into England. Wright himself was born in England, the son of a professional cricketer who emigrated to America, where both father and son were paid to play for the St. George Cricket Club of Staten Island. He was still a cricket professional in 1867 when he switched to try out the baseball code and played center field for Cincinnati in 1869.

In the spring of 1874, Wright sent the young Al Spalding to England to negotiate a tour of England for the Boston Red Stockings and the Philadelphia Athletics.[49] Spalding tells a delightful tale of how he managed to inveigle an interview with the "Dooks" of the MCC. In his version, this twenty-four-year-old stood before the club committee (whose luminaries included the Prince of Wales, the Marquis of Hamilton, and the Earls of

Dudley, Sefton, and Clarendon) and explained that whereas the English had been sending many fine cricketers to America for some years, the Americans had now invented their own game and would like to send over a couple of teams to show the English how it was played. In his enthusiasm, Spalding even suggested that some of the baseball players were familiar with cricket.[50]

Spalding was supported in his proposal by Charles Alcock. Alcock is a pivotal figure in the history of both soccer and cricket, and a man whom Harry Wright had appointed agent for the prospective tour.[51] As secretary of the prominent Surrey County Cricket Club, Alcock was a man capable of securing Spalding's entry into London's aristocratic sporting society. But what the American was suggesting and the Englishmen understood were not quite the same thing. The MCC issued an invitation to Wright's party to visit Lord's and play an exhibition of baseball, to be followed by a cricket match between an English eleven and the Americans. Imagine Wright's horror when Spalding returned with this offer, when no more than half a dozen of the eighteen tourists had played cricket before! Nonetheless, with the endorsement of the pinnacle of cricket's establishment, the tourists were able to arrange a full calendar of dates around the British Isles for the summer of 1874, including Sheffield, Liverpool, Manchester, Surrey, and Dublin, as well as Lord's.

The party docked at Liverpool on July 31 and departed on August 25, playing a series of fourteen baseball matches between the Red Stockings and Athletics, of which Boston won eight. As a means of promoting baseball in England, the tour was a hopeless failure. The English watched the games politely, but what they were really interested in was the Americans' cricketing skills. The high point of the tour was the exhibition at Lord's on August 3 and 4. The event is fully written up in *Wisden*, the cricketing almanac started in 1864 and to this day the ultimate authority for cricket statistics and commentary. On the first day, 3,580 people turned up and "the Americans surprised and delighted the company with a display of ball-throwing and catching abilities."

The cricket contest then began, with the MCC batting, reaching a score of 42 runs for the loss of four wickets when lunch was taken at five past two. After lunch came the baseball display, "but they had not proceeded far with the match before many of the spectators were impressed with the idea that they were witnessing a modernized, manly—and unquestionably an

improved—edition of that most enjoyable old game of their boyhood—
Rounders." Within two hours and ten minutes Boston had trounced the
Athletics by a score of 24 runs to 7.

The cricket then resumed at 6 p.m. and continued until MCC had
reached 88 for five wickets. Following a dinner hosted by the Marquis of
Hamilton, president of MCC, the cricket did not resume again until the following afternoon because of rain, and the Marylebone Cricket Club was
quickly finished off for a total of 105 runs. Harry Wright and his brother
George had done most of the damage, retiring eight batsmen between them.
In recognition of the Americans' lesser experience, they were given the
advantage of having eighteen players rather than the MCC's twelve. When
it came to batting, in the eyes of the English "the strangers went in for hard
hitting." Al Spalding was the star, thrashing twenty-three runs, almost the
highest score of the match, his stroke play drawing the approval of the MCC
scribe. Play was interrupted by a severe rainstorm that temporarily flooded
the ground, but when play resumed the game rose to a thrilling climax. The
Americans reached a score of 87 with seven wickets remaining and needing
just nineteen runs to win, a seemingly simple task. But three wickets fell on
87, and with only three runs required for victory the Americans had only
one wicket left. The visitors triumphed however, to general applause, for as
Wisden notes, "This MCC twelve was undoubtedly the best English team the
Americans met at cricket throughout this brief tour."

The Americans were justly proud of their achievements, and indeed they
did not lose a single match on their entire tour. The English frequently commented on the superior fielding skills of the baseball players,[52] and several
compared the admirable sobriety of the baseball players with the condition
of their usual beer-drinking opponents. Some even favorably compared the
greater speed and excitement of baseball with the stately progress of a
cricket match. Henry Chadwick, in his *Beadle's Dime Base Ball Player* for
1875, waxed lyrical: "The visit of the base-ball players has opened old John
Bull's eyes to the fact that we are not as neglectful of athletic sports as he
thought we were." But what, in the end, had the tour achieved? The English
notably declined to take on the Americans at baseball. Years later the Prince
of Wales seemed to sum up the British view of baseball: "Baseball is an
admirable game, for Americans." Spalding himself wrote many years later:
"Cricket is a splendid game, for Britons. It is a genteel game, a conventional
game—and our cousins across the Atlantic are nothing if not conventional.

They play cricket because it accords with the traditions of their country."[53] What the tour emphasized was that while Americans could put their hand to another sport, their own national game was baseball, or as Chadwick said in 1875, "What cricket is to Englishmen, Base-Ball has become to an American." In other words, in sporting terms, the two countries seemingly had little more to say to each other.

Meanwhile, back in Chicago in 1875, William Hulbert was made president of the White Stockings. Hulbert and other owners of the NAPBBP "western" teams felt that the "eastern" teams kept stealing the better players. Hulbert decided to take matters into his own hands.

A pivotal event for Hulbert was the association's decision in 1875 to resolve a dispute over a player contract between his White Stockings and the Philadelphia club in favor of Philadelphia. The player in question was Davy Force, winner of the batting title in 1872 with a .406 average. One baseball historian wrote that in reaction to the loss of Davy Force, "Hulbert . . . was so infuriated that he resolved to bring the Association to its knees. In another year, the Association was dead and Hulbert had fathered the National League."[54]

Hulbert's first step, with $30,000 of capital available, was to hire Boston's star pitcher, Al Spalding, for the 1876 season. With Spalding aboard, he went after three other stars of the Boston team by offering healthy pay increases.[55] Hulbert clearly violated the NAPBBP rules by signing these players and Cap Anson from the Philadelphia Athletics for the 1876 season before the completion of the 1875 season. Although the players agreed not to mention their new contracts, the news eventually leaked out.

Confronted with the possibility that he and his five new stars might be expelled from the NAPBBP, Hulbert hit upon the idea of starting his own league. With the assistance of Spalding and Harry Wright, Hulbert drafted a constitution for his new league and then contacted the backers of the St. Louis, Cincinnati, and Louisville clubs in the NAPBBP. These westerners, all resentful of the greater power of the eastern teams in the NAPBBP anyway, met with Hulbert on December 16 and 17, 1875, in Louisville and endorsed Hulbert's plan.

Before approaching the eastern teams, Hulbert persuaded Morgan Bulkley (a prominent politician and financier from Connecticut, owner of the NAPBBP Hartford franchise, and future governor and U.S. senator) to chair the meeting on the new league and eventually to serve as its first president.

Hulbert's next step was to hold individual meetings with the backers of the four eastern clubs in the NAPBBP to pre-sell his plan.[56] The fateful general meeting took place on February 2, 1876, at the Grand Central Hotel in New York. The resolution to start the National League (NL) was adopted unanimously.

An article from *The Daily Graphic* of February 4, 1876, could scarcely restrain its ridicule for the now defunct NAPBBP.

> The decline of professional base ball in public favor has hardly been less rapid than its rise. The very general conviction that players sold themselves out and "threw" their games has served to kill the interest. . . . One of the most flagrant abuses of the old association was the ease with which a player expelled from one club for misdemeanor could reinstate himself despite the knowledge of his misconduct.

Ironically, William Hulbert was born in 1832 in Otsego county, New York, just twenty miles down the road from Cooperstown, but his family moved to Chicago when he was only 2 years old. In his early adult years, Hulbert developed a profitable wholesale grocery business and became a successful coal merchant and member of the Chicago Board of Trade.[57] Hulbert was a great booster of Chicago and became actively involved in its civic affairs. His Chicago chauvinism is well represented in his brash comment: "I would rather be a lamp post in Chicago than a millionaire in any other city."[58]

Hulbert bought three shares of stock in the White Stockings in 1870 and was elected president of the team's board of directors in 1875. Albert Spalding, Hulbert's partner in building the NL, described Hulbert as "strong, forceful and self-reliant . . . and a man of tremendous energy and courage, [who did things] in a business-like way."[59]

Hulbert's National League appears to be the first example of a closed professional team sports league anywhere in the world. At least there are no known models from which Hulbert borrowed and no known preexisting leagues.[60] Rather than borrowing from someone else's model, Hulbert, as a successful capitalist with a good knowledge of commodity and financial markets as well as the emerging aggressive, competitive practices of the robber baron era, appears to have used the NAPBBP as an anti-model. He then added elements of what Alfred Chandler describes as the evolving rational business paradigm in the United States during the last quarter of the nineteenth century.

Of course, one element of that paradigm was owner control over the production process. Worker or player control would not do. Al Spalding portrayed Hulbert's vision as "reducing the game to a business system such as had never heretofore obtained. . . . It was, in fact, the irrepressible conflict between labor and capital asserting itself under a new guise."[61] The crucial building blocks of Hulbert's NL organization included the establishment of a league bureaucracy with team owners and a president, a secretary-treasurer, and a board of directors with undisputed authority to enforce rules and implement disciplinary measures. Again, the players were excluded from these management organs. The new rules tightly bound players to their contracts, limited franchises to cities with at least 75,000 inhabitants, granted teams territorial monopolies, mandated the completion of team playing schedules under threat of expulsion for missing contests, imposed uniform ticket prices at all ballparks, proscribed Sunday play, alcohol, and betting, and hired paid umpires.

Member clubs were to pay annual dues of $100, ten times those of the NAPBBP. Each team was to play ten games (five home, five away) against each other team between March 15 and November 15. The team with the most victories at season's end would be declared the champion and be awarded a pennant worth not less than $100.

Hulbert's White Stockings finished their first NL season with an .800 win percentage and apparently were the only team to turn a profit that year. The New York Mutuals and Philadelphia Athletics did not even finish their schedules and were summarily booted out of the league by the uncompromising Hulbert, leaving only six NL clubs for the league's second season.

Hulbert's strong and principled leadership was also evident after the Louisville scandal in 1877. The Louisville Grays began the 1877 campaign in convincing fashion, winning fifteen of their first twenty games. Their dominant play continued into early August, when they inexplicably went into a prolonged slump that lasted until September 30, the day Boston clinched the championship. Then the team suddenly came alive again, playing winning ball until season's end in mid-October. The involved players foolishly flamed suspicions by sporting new diamond jewelry. Hulbert ordered an investigation, wherein it was discovered that four leading players on the team had taken bribes to throw games. The players confessed and Hulbert immediately expelled them, then turned a deaf ear on their repeated emotional appeals for readmission.[62]

If Hulbert ever compromised his principled leadership, it was on behalf of improving the already dominant strength of his Chicago White Stockings. With its five new players for 1876, the White Stockings easily won the first NL championship with a 56 and 14 record.

As if to purposely adumbrate the leadership style of George Steinbrenner, Hulbert was always on the lookout for new star players. During the 1877 season, Si Keck, the owner of the Cincinnati NL team, was losing money and failed to pay its dues. He also refused to pay his team's expenses for an eastern road trip. In June, when Keck declared that he was disbanding his team, Hulbert opportunistically pounced on the chance to sign two of Cincinnati's stars. A few weeks later, a group of Cincinnatians bought the team and sought the return of their stars from Chicago. Hulbert at first refused, but after considerable public uproar, compromised and returned one of the two players.

Some objected to a different compromise—that Hulbert continued both to be president of the White Stockings and president of the National League. To these voices of protest, the *Chicago Tribune* retorted: "Who should boss the League if not Chicago?" and then added, reminiscent of Charles Wilson's famous defense of General Motors, "What is good for base-ball in Chicago is good for the League as a whole."[63]

Not surprisingly, those NAPBBP teams that believed players should be involved in management formed their own new league in 1877, the International Association of Professional Baseball Players. The International League (IL) had no restrictions on city size or on the number of teams that could enter the league. The only requirement was that each team pay the league entry fee of $10 and dues.

In its first year, 1877, the International League had twenty-four clubs. Most International League clubs were organized as co-operatives. Of the 129 identified club officers, eleven were players and thirteen were blue-collar workers. The notion that workers should have some control over the organization of their workplace had significant resonance in the political atmosphere of the 1870s—a time of numerous worker strikes, a large share of which were over shop floor control issues.

Including the IL, there were about fifty professional clubs outside the NL in 1877. These outside clubs periodically played NL clubs to generate extra revenue for both sides. All indications are that the level of play of the outside clubs was high, and sometimes higher than that of the NL clubs. NL teams played roughly half their games in 1877 with outside clubs, and the outside teams won at least seventy-two times.[64]

Hulbert's NL clearly felt threatened by the International League and the other outside clubs. The NL issued a decree prohibiting its clubs from playing International League clubs in NL ballparks. The NL also formed a league alliance with independent small-town teams outside the International League, promising alliance clubs playing dates with NL clubs and mutually agreeing to respect clubs' territorial rights.

The NL came under steady criticism for its philosophy of maintaining a small and closed league. Each year independent clubs sought membership in the NL but were turned away. In part to minimize the public relations fallout from its exclusive behavior, the NL added article 12 to its constitution for the 1877 season. Article 12, section 1, read in part as follows:

> As a token of good will and friendship for all base ball clubs not members of this League, and with a view of stimulating a proper rivalry among such clubs and of advancing public interest in the game of base ball, it is hereby declared that any club whose organization and conduct are not inconsistent with the objects of this League ... which shall have won from other clubs, during an entire playing season, the greatest number of games played under the rules of this league, in series so arranged as to afford a fair test of merit, shall ... be eligible to membership in the League at the ensuing annual meeting.[65]

This provision—which seemed to foreshadow an element of the promotion/relegation system that emerged a decade later in English soccer—actually led to the defection of some of the stronger International League teams to the NL. In 1878 Providence left the IL for the NL. The 1878 IL championship team from Buffalo left for the NL, along with runner-up Syracuse and Troy. And the 1879 IL champion from Worchester fled to the NL for 1880. The loose organization of the IL, the effective competition from the NL, and the country's severe depression of the 1870s, following the banking crisis of 1873, were sufficient to doom the IL by 1880.

Several of the IL organizers did not give up and became involved in the formation of the American Association (AA) in 1883. According to some reports, each of the AA team owners owned either a pub or a brewery. Little wonder, then, that the AA distinguished itself from the NL by allowing beer to be sold at the ballpark. Some referred to the AA as the "beer and whiskey circuit." The AA also distinguished itself by allowing play on Sundays and dropping the price of admission from 50 to 25 cents. Thus the AA aggressively sought a mass popular base—something that Hulbert eschewed, believing that it was monied classes who would best support professional baseball's reputation.

Hulbert wrote to an associate in 1881: "You cannot afford to bid for the patronage of the degraded, if you are to be successful you must secure recognition by the respectable. . . . The sole purpose of the League, outside of the business aspect, is to make it worthy of the patronage, support, and respect of the best class of people." Here one can see the vestiges of the sport's origins in the 1840s as a leisure time activity for the genteel classes, promoting good fellowship and reinforcing social standing.

Luckily for the sport's business future, Hulbert's elitist notions were put in check by competition from the American Association. The AA's policy break—cutting ticket prices, selling beer, and permitting Sunday play—encouraged mass participation in baseball as a spectator sport and helped to set the foundation for baseball's identity as the national pastime.

Hulbert, however, was a hard realist, and he knew that the NL needed to make accommodations with its competitors. Before his death in 1882, Hulbert initiated a mutuality pact with the AA to provide protection for each league's player reserve systems and recognition of each other's territorial rights.

Thus, by the early 1880s, professional baseball had reached a stage of development not far removed from that of "organized baseball," which defined the game in the twentieth century. At the same time, English cricket had also reached an organizational stage recognizably akin to cricket played one hundred years later. The main form of competition that had emerged by this time was County Cricket, involving a dozen or so of the major English counties. The status of this championship was rather like that which existed toward the end of the NABBP era, in that there was no formal structure. The newspapers kept records and constructed league tables based on matches won, and thus an annual champion was acclaimed (although newspapers often disagreed over the identity of the rightful champion). County players could be either amateur gentlemen or professional players, but the gentlemen, led by the MCC, were firmly in charge. Not that the gentlemen were averse to taking generous expenses when it came to touring or playing exhibition matches—the term "shamateur" was coined in the 1880s to refer to noted gentlemen cricketers such as W.G. Grace and their moneymaking scams. However, the road to a fully commercialized sport was barred by the insistence of the authorities that the game should properly be played over at least three days.

The Beginnings of Soccer

It is at this point in history that Association Football—soccer—reached the critical stage in its development that would shape the way the game is today played across the world. The game takes its original name from the Football Association (the FA), the governing body of the game in England to this day. The FA was founded in 1863 by a group of eleven football clubs, most of them based in and around London, with the purpose of establishing a common set of rules. This was a pressing need from the 1840s onward because of the way the games of football were spreading.

Almost every culture in the world has at some point had a game involving a ball that is kicked, and the playing of football in England is recorded from medieval times, largely thanks to laws prohibiting it. Edward III (1349), Richard II (1389), and Henry IV (1401) all passed statutes obliging English yeomen to practice their archery instead so that the monarch could engage in his traditional sport: attacking the French. The traditional form of football was played on Shrove Tuesday (before entering the rigors of Lent) and survived in many English villages until the early twentieth century. In 1801 Strutt described the game thus:

> When a match at foot-ball is made, two parties, each containing an equal number of competitors, take the field, and stand between two goals, placed at the distance of eighty or an hundred yards the one from the other. The goal is usually made with two sticks driven into the ground, about two or three feet apart. The ball, which is commonly made of a blown bladder, and cased with leather, is delivered in the midst of the ground, and the object of each party is to drive through the goal of their antagonists.[66]

However, he also says that the game had by this time fallen into disrepute, perhaps because it was "exceedingly violent." Like cricket, what saved the game from oblivion was its adoption by the English public school movement of the early nineteenth century. These schools recruited only the sons (not yet the daughters) of the wealthy elite and molded them for their imperial destiny. The violence of football became admired for the "manly virtues" it inspired, and the game was adopted as the winter pastime, to complement summertime cricket.

Eton, Harrow, Winchester, Shrewsbury, Rugby, and the other leading schools all developed their own versions of the game. However, the absence of common rules meant that trouble arose when graduates wanted to play against rival schools, either while attending university or when they moved to London to follow a career. A committee of students first wrote a set of rules for the game in Cambridge in 1846. Though followed at Cambridge, the rules were not universally adopted. It was not until October 26, 1863, that a group of gentlemen got together at the Freemason's Tavern in London's Lincoln Inn Fields, not only to draw up a common set of rules, but also to establish a Football Association (FA) for the purpose of promoting the game.

The association was immediately faced with a crisis, since the representatives of Blackheath, one of the founder clubs, refused to accept the outlawing of "hacking," the practice of deliberately attacking the shins of a player with the ball. After six meetings and much recrimination, Blackheath withdrew to found its association, the Rugby Football Union.[67] The game of rugby football is a close cousin of American football.

The leading light of the FA in its formative years was Harry Wright's London agent, Charles Alcock. Alcock was born in 1842 in Sunderland, in England's industrial north, into an upwardly mobile family.[68] His father had made his fortune by taking the family's small upholstery business and moving into shipbuilding, ship owning, and ultimately marine insurance. Thus from relatively humble beginnings the family was able to send Charles to the grand old school of Harrow (on the edge of London) to rub shoulders with the nobility. He showed little skill at sports in school. He played both cricket and the Harrow version of football, but then everybody had to, and he did not come near to representing the school eleven in either sport.[69] Neither was he a scholar, and he did not progress to the university, but instead went to the family's marine insurance business, which by then was based in London.

This business gave him plenty of time to play cricket and football, which he did throughout the 1860s and early 1870s. He still did not shine at cricket, where sporting talent abounded, but fared much better in the smaller pool of footballers. His elder brother, John, was also a keen player and was one of the founding members of the FA. Charles joined the FA Committee two years later and was involved with many of the initiatives that helped to spread the association game.[70]

The first of these was to reel in the northern football-playing fraternity, since the association was originally based entirely in London. Alcock played in the first match against Sheffield in 1865, the other major center of the game at that time. Sheffield formed its own association in 1867 and then joined the FA in 1870. In a similar fashion, other centers of football were cajoled into subscribing to the FA code: the Birmingham Association affiliated in 1875; Staffordshire and Surrey in 1877; Berkshire, Buckinghamshire, Cheshire, and Lancashire in 1878. By 1885 there were twenty-eight county associations affiliated with the FA, each controlled by the football clubs in their area.

During the 1860s, Alcock's involvement with marine insurance diminished as he became increasingly prominent as a sporting journalist. Record-keeping in cricket was an established obsession, and he contributed regularly to a competitor of the *Wisden* cricketing annual. In addition, he launched in 1868 the *Football Annual*, the first publication of its kind for the new sport. Alcock was to remain an influential journalist for the remainder of the century in both sports. Finally, he achieved positions of real prominence when he became secretary of the FA in 1870 and secretary of the Surrey County Cricket Club in 1872, positions he held for twenty-five and thirty-five years, respectively.

During his stewardship at Surrey, the county became once again preeminent in the unofficial national championship. The location of Surrey's field in the heart of London at the Kennington Oval also gave him the ability to create new fixtures.[71] We have already seen his role in promoting the baseball tour of 1874, which included a match at the Oval. He also used his influence to enable football matches to be played at the ground, as well as track and field, bicycling, and lacrosse. In 1880 he arranged for the first "test match" between England and Australia to be played at the Oval, initiating international cricket and one of the fiercest rivalries in world sport.[72]

But it was in soccer that Alcock's genius reached its apogee. He was the driving spirit behind two critical innovations. He instituted the first "international" match between England and Scotland in 1870, a process requiring the selection of the best players from their regular clubs. In the twentieth century it was international competition, exemplified by the World Cup, that helped to spread the game's popularity. Alcock established the firm principle that member clubs of an association were obliged to release their best players to participate in such contests. Without this ability to mandate the release of the top stars, it is doubtful that international soccer as we know it could have been established.

Alcock's other innovation was the creation of the FA Cup in 1871, an annual, single-elimination tournament open to all members of the FA. Seemingly modeled on the "house" competitions of the public schools (familiar to anyone who has read *Harry Potter*), this competition was an immediate and enormous success. In fact, it was so successful that the competition it generated quickly undermined the social equilibrium of the game. Like cricket and baseball before it, soccer was originally a pastime for gentlemen, in this case the products of the public schools, and gentlemen controlled the FA. It was probably inevitable that the game would spread lower down the social order, but the FA Cup did much to hasten that expansion. By the end of the 1880s, more than 200 clubs had affiliated to the FA, each of which wanted to compete for the Cup. Soccer reached into all sections of society, and it was by no means true that the best teams and players were drawn from the gentlemanly class.

Moreover, the Cup became a very strong draw for paying spectators and made soccer a very attractive commercial proposition for anyone who could organize a successful team. Having a successful team meant having the best players, and attracting the best players meant offering them money—that is, professionalism. As in baseball, these early payments were illicit, since the FA rules prohibited pay for play. But also as in baseball, illicit payments proliferated. The main offenders were the Lancashire clubs, which were being developed by mill owners and other local worthies as a way of promoting local pride and generating some profit. Losing teams brought this state of affairs to the attention of the gentlemen of the FA Committee, and in 1882 a subcommittee was appointed to investigate, dominated by Alcock and one N. L. Jackson. Jackson was a monumental snob, but also one of the great figures in the early development of soccer.[73] Like many snobs, he was genially tolerant of those he considered his inferiors, so long as he didn't have to mix with them. Alcock had no particular objection to professionalism, familiar as he was with it in cricket, and so the committee lamely reported in 1883 that it had insufficient evidence to comment.

But the matter was not allowed to rest there. Following a Cup match in January 1884, Upton Park lodged a complaint with the FA that Preston North End was paying players. At the hearing Jackson, who by then had decided that the importation of professionals from Scotland was undermining the playing prospects of true Englishmen, provided the FA Committee with evidence that Preston was indeed importing players from Edinburgh. The representative of the North End, one Major Sudell, decided to go on the offensive and admitted that his club hired professionals, largely because every other major club was doing the same. Faced with the charge of hypocrisy, the FA went into retreat. Alcock now urged the FA to accept professionalism outright, but many amateur diehards from the northern associations, whose clubs were most likely to be threatened by competition from local professionals, tried to fight it. The aristocratic Londoners, led by Jackson, saw no need to socialize with the professionals and were in any case confident of beating them. Hence they acquiesced to the necessary rule changes that legalized professionals in 1885.

Jackson, meanwhile, had set about to prove that gentlemen amateurs were the equal of any professional. In 1882 he founded the Corinthian Football Club, a peripatetic "scratch" team (meaning that it did not organize a formal playing schedule) of public school graduates that eschewed practice, formal competition (the Corinthians would not enter the FA Cup until 1919), and social integration. Their most famous matches were played against the leading professional teams of the day, all of which they beat. From 1882 until 1900 most of the England team was drawn from the ranks of the Corinthians. In the 1870s, England had a 27 percent win record against Scotland; for the remainder of the century this rose to 53 percent. Not content with these achievements, the Corinthians took it upon themselves to spread the game across the world. Between 1897 and the outbreak of the First World War, they toured South Africa (twice), Hungary, Scandinavia, Canada, the United States (twice), Germany (three times), the Netherlands, France, Spain, and Brazil (twice), raising the profile of the game wherever they went. It would be difficult to overstate the effect of the Corinthians on the international spread of the soccer code.[74]

The march of professionalism in England, however, was not to be derailed by a few toffs. Northern Britain was the industrial heartland of the country in the nineteenth century and had much more in common with the no-nonsense practicalities of Americans than with the southern gentlemen of the English establishment. Here clubs like Preston North End and Blackburn developed more athletic teams and more sophisticated tactics than most of the southern amateurs could muster, leading to their complete domination of competitions like the FA Cup. It was not long before the representatives of these clubs wanted a bigger say in the administration of the FA.

In 1886 the more numerous northern clubs voted many of the traditional southern representatives off the FA Committee and installed members of their own faction. Men like Alcock, unlike the amateurs of the NAABBP, tried to hold the ship together and agreed to compromise. This had enormous long-term consequences for the game, since it ensured an integrated administration for the game at all levels. It meant that administrators at the highest level felt themselves responsible not merely for the welfare of the biggest clubs, but for the whole of soccer. It meant that surplus funds generated by competition at the highest level could be appropriated by governing bodies (national associations like the FA, and in future years international bodies such as UEFA, the European association for soccer, and FIFA, the worldwide governing body). In American terms, it would be the equivalent of a person, such as the commissioner of baseball, being responsible for the health of the game at all levels within the United States, not merely the interests of the major league teams.

But for many this compromise went too far. Increasingly, men like Jackson withdrew from the FA. He, in particular, became embittered when the London Association that he had founded, and whose amateur purity he wanted to maintain, was obliged to accept professional teams as members.[75] One team, Arsenal from North London, had earlier withdrawn from the London Association so that it could play professionally against the northern teams. In 1902 the FA passed a resolution that no member association could deny affiliation to a club on grounds of professionalism. Egged on by Jackson, the amateur London clubs seceded from the FA to form the Amateur Football Association in 1907. However, the rest of soccer treated them as outcasts, and even in London there were many middle- and working-class clubs that wanted no part of this snobbery. At the same time, Jackson was losing his enthusiasm for soccer altogether, and increasingly concentrated on his other sporting interests, tennis and golf, where he could be much surer of mixing only with his own type. The Amateur Football Association rejoined the FA in 1914, and Jackson's influence over soccer was at an end.[76]

We have seen that gate money professionalism in baseball led quite naturally to a more structured form of competition, first in the NAPBBP championship and then in the stricter National League. In soccer, similar pressures to generate a stable income stream started to emerge after 1885. The initial success of the FA Cup had inspired all the member associations to start their own regional cup competitions, such that teams might compete in several such competitions all at once. Each association claimed the right to the gate revenues from the semifinal and final matches in each cup competition and therefore had a financial interest in the system. The clubs, of course, also welcomed the extra excitement that participation in the cup competitions generated.

By the mid-1880s, the cup competitions dominated the sporting calendar, as is illustrated by the following schedule from a sporting newspaper in 1888:

Oct. 13	Birmingham Cup, first round
" 13	Lancashire Junior Cup, second round
" 20	Staffordshire Cup, second round
" 27	Derbyshire Cup, first round
" 27	English Cup, second round
Nov. 3	Birmingham Cup, second round
" 10	Welsh Cup, second round
" 10	Staffordshire Cup, second round
" 10	Lancashire Cup, second round
" 10	Lancashire Junior Cup, third round
" 19	Derbyshire Cup, second round[77]

While cups produced excitement, because individual teams played in various cup competitions at the same time, the uncertainty they created for the scheduling of matches was becoming a problem. As one journalist wrote:

It must be tolerably clear to those concerned in the welfare of the Association game of football that we have reached a point in which there is too much "pot" hunting business introduced into the recreation. There are national, county, local, district, charity and town Cup competitions. When a club gets "into its cups" there is no knowing when it will get out of them. Ordinary fixtures, no matter how interesting, have to "go by the wind" and teams are in consequence often kept in a state of suspense until the middle of the week, and even later, before they are aware whom they will meet on the following Saturday.[78]

This structure of competition was not at all suited to the interests of professional clubs. According to William McGregor, "Usually a club like the Albion [one of the leading teams of the day] would enter four or five cups, and make provision for a reasonably long run in each. If they were thrown out in the first round they had blank days; if they kept in longer than they expected to remain, then fixtures already arranged had to go by the board. Spectators, too, became disgusted by the intermittent fare provided for them."[79]

McGregor called for a "fixity of fixtures" throughout the season. William McGregor was a Scot of humble background who emigrated to Birmingham (England's second city) around 1870, where he owned a small draper's shop. Not much of a footballer himself, he got drawn into the administration of Aston Villa, then and now a leading club of the English midlands. On March 2, 1888, he sent a letter to five other leading clubs (all from the midlands or the north) inviting them to a meeting to discuss forming a league of twelve clubs. The first meeting of club representatives took place in London (because club representatives were there to watch the FA Cup final) on March 22. A further meeting in Manchester on April 17 formally established the Football League as an organization. Plans were rapidly advanced, and the first league matches were played on September 8, 1888.

McGregor became known as the "Father of the League," and in later years he reminisced about how he came by this revolutionary idea: "A great many people saw the difficulty which football and footballers were in; I happened, luckily, to be the one man at that particular time who saw the way out. It appeared to me that a fixed programme of home-and-home matches between the leading clubs in the country, such fixtures to be kept inviolate, would produce football of a more interesting nature than the average game we then saw."[80] Later, official historians of the league and the FA would suggest that McGregor was inspired by the County Cricket Championship, an odd assertion since this championship was not formally established until 1890, and until that time there was no "fixity of fixtures" such as McGregor's league established. This version has been retold by most soccer historians, but a rather more obvious source for McGregor's inspiration can be found in contemporary accounts.

J. A. H. Catton was a sportswriter from the early 1880s onward and wrote several histories of soccer. In one, entitled *The Real Football* and published in 1900, he wrote:

> Some plan was urgently needed to sustain interest in the game as in the county cricket championship. A weekly periodical, the *Athletic News*, and its daily contemporary, *The Sporting Chronicle*, persistently advocated that the leading clubs must have the Saturdays for each round of the Cup Ties definitely named, so that the leading teams could play a tournament on the principle of an American handicap, in fact, the same as the baseballers of the United States.[81]

It is not unnatural to suppose that English sports enthusiasts were aware of developments in America, and we have seen already that leading figures in baseball, such as Chadwick, Wright, and Spalding, were in touch with prominent English journalists and administrators such as Alcock.

By 1888 English sports enthusiasts had heard of the success of the National League as a competitive structure. According to one contemporary source, "It is largely due to Mr. W. McGregor of Birmingham that the Football League was founded in 1888. Something of the kind had been talked of in a general way, and the idea of adapting the tournament system that prevailed among the baseball clubs in America was not novel."[82]

In fact, by the end of the 1880s, the English were beginning to show some interest in baseball. Sir Frances Ley, an English industrialist from Derby who fell in love with the game on a trip to the United States, set up an English baseball league in 1890. Not surprisingly, Spalding was involved in the plans, following his world baseball tour of 1888–89, which included an exhibition match at Alcock's Surrey Oval (although the Americans firmly refused to play cricket this time). The league itself consisted of four teams, each connected to a local soccer club: Derby County,[83] Preston North End, Stoke City, and McGregor's own Aston Villa.[84] We know that McGregor was connected with this baseball league, since he is listed as the honorary treasurer of the Baseball Association of Great Britain and Ireland in a book about baseball published in England in 1891.[85] An even more direct connection between the American invention and the Football League is drawn by the following quotation:

> Undoubtedly the most successful of the enterprises which were the outcome of professionalism is the Football League. This is a combination of clubs binding themselves to play a series of home and home matches, each with its best team. The club winning the most matches is the champion for the season. The system has flourished in connection with professional baseball in America for some years, and it was this that suggested it to Mr. W. McGregor, a gentleman well known in Birmingham football circles.

This quotation comes from another book on the state of football written in 1899 by none other than N. L. Jackson.[86] Jackson, of course, despised the league and all it stood for, and complained that the FA had allied itself too closely with commercial interests. There was no doubting, he asserted, "the obvious fact that the Football Association had turned from its original object of promoting sport and had adopted the care of the business of football."[87]

In the book, Jackson outlined his objections to the commercialism of professional sport. His view was that it destroyed local communities and inhibited the development of local talent because of the importation of foreign players. It promoted sport as spectacle, but discouraged participation, which he considered the more desirable way to develop a sport. Among spectators and players alike it encouraged unsporting behavior, as well as promoting both alcohol consumption and gambling. His final objections were (a) that the organization of professional clubs gave no voice to the professional player, who is forced to obey his masters under "servile conditions," and (b) that few of the clubs were financially stable, and only survived thanks to the financial contributions of wealthy patrons.[88]

These indictments of sport when treated as a business have surfaced over and over in the long-standing debates over the virtues of amateur and professional sport. Catton frankly observed that "the League has made football a business." McGregor himself preferred to talk of the league in purely cooperative terms. He initially advocated the equal sharing of all gate revenues and defined the league as a union founded on "the joint principles of self-interest and mutual advantage."[89] However, there was to be no doubting the amount of money that the league was able to generate. Catton illustrated the point using the example of McGregor's team, Aston Villa, whose revenue increased from £2,000 in 1889 to £13,753 by 1899.[90] Similar rates of increase were recorded by the other league clubs. Wage rates had not increased nearly as fast, having been limited by the FA rules to a maximum of £4 per week, a little over double what they had been in the 1880s. Clearly, there were large financial surpluses being created by the new system.

Baseball versus Soccer

Setting aside mere vanity, anxieties about the perception of the Football League as a vehicle for business interests may help to explain why McGregor was unwilling to acknowledge an American inspiration for his league. McGregor was no Hulbert. The two men may have shared humble beginnings, but Hulbert had risen to be a man of significant financial and political standing, while McGregor remained to the end of his life a small shopkeeper. Hulbert was a business leader first and a baseball promoter second. McGregor was first and foremost a soccer lover, who brought some of his small-business experience to the management of soccer clubs. Hulbert was a leader who demanded control and, in the case of his club, a significant ownership stake. McGregor went out of his way to state that he had no interest in challenging the supremacy of the FA and always argued that the Football League should be subordinate. He did not own the club for which he worked as secretary, and his personal financial stake in Aston Villa was negligible.

There is also little doubt that the business culture of the United States during this period differed significantly from that of Great Britain, and that these cultures molded what was and was not permissible. U.S. culture was being transformed in the second half of the nineteenth century, embracing values of self-reliance, the work ethic, and aggressive individualism. The period between the end of the Civil War and the launching of the National League witnessed a profound transformation in the country's infrastructural landscape. The U.S. railroad system had grown from a fledgling network to the world's most extensive. Industrial investment had practically doubled, and the nation was rapidly becoming urbanized. The 1870s and 1880s were decades of concentrating economic power, which met with little resistance. Virtually any action to ruin one's competitors was acceptable as long as it did not egregiously transgress the boundaries of the law. Ruthlessness in the economic sphere became a virtue.

Britain, by contrast, was already an industrialized nation approaching the peak of its imperial glory. Always a society in which distinctions of class and etiquette could be as influential as money, any innovation was required to fit into the social order, not least because that order was seen to be so successful. Napoleon's taunt that Britain was a nation of shopkeepers still rang true, an empire built on "small" rather than "big" business. Gentlemen capitalists in London might finance big business (including in the United States) but were more likely to be passive partners than active or aggressive principals. Anyone interested in breaking this social mold was more likely to emigrate than upset this domestic equilibrium.

These differences in personality and culture can account for the differences in the personality and culture of the leagues that they created. There were many similarities. Both leagues provided a stable framework for competition that had been lacking, and both triggered greater spectator interest in attending professional matches. As a result, both significantly increased the revenue streams of the biggest clubs. Moreover, in both leagues, as we will see in chapter 4, the league authorities took steps to control the player market so as to prevent a reasonable share of the money from flowing into the pockets of the players.

The most important difference was the decision of the Football League to remain within the governance structure of the FA, rather than assert its independence in the manner of Hulbert's National League. Accepting FA control meant accepting significant constraints, such as those the gentlemen amateurs of the NAABBP might have imposed if they had had a say in running the NL. In 1896 the FA imposed a rule that no member club could pay an annual dividend in excess of 5 percent of the invested share capital, and that no club director could be paid for services provided as a director. As the FA's official history put it in 1953, "Within the powerful organization of the Football League were banded together its clubs, employing professional staffs and now run on efficient business lines. . . . Yet these clubs existed only under the strictest adherence to the Rules of the [Football] Association. . . . Thus . . . a tight control was kept on the financial activities of the new-type Football Companies, whose shareholders, by and large, came to be the local enthusiasts of the game, men and women who received little enough return for the monetary support that they gave."[91]

Clearly, the FA imposed serious restraints on the freedoms of league clubs. But at the same time, we have seen that many amateurs felt aggrieved by the influence exercised by the professional clubs over amateur affairs.

The English system represented a classic English compromise, the American system was a classic example of American laissez-faire capitalism. While the National League set out to distance itself from nonmember baseball clubs, this was never the intention of the Football League, which from its inception aimed to include as many of the leading teams as could be accommodated. The founders of the Football League never imagined that membership was a privilege that could be bought and sold. There is a plausible case to be made that the league's managers were either naive or ineffective. Potential capital gains were passed up, as the surpluses described above were dissipated in the privately financed stadium construction boom that continued up until the First World War. However, setting aside the personalities involved, there were practical reasons why the Football League remained part of a unified structure of soccer governance when the National League chose an independent path.

The National League had no use for the teams that it did not admit to the league, and it had little interest in preserving relations with them (unless it was to extend their control of their labor market and protect territorial monopolies). It was a relatively easy matter for the NL to turn its back on the thoroughly discredited NAPBBP.

In contrast, until the Football League became established, its member clubs needed the income and prestige they obtained from participating in the FA Cup. Had the league gone to war with the FA in 1888, the latter would undoubtedly have won, its competition and influence being well established by that date. One accommodation to the FA, then, was that the FL developed a more inclusive structure. By being inclusive, it assured its legitimacy to the largest number of FA teams and thwarted competition from potential upstart leagues.

The most important manifestation of the inclusiveness of the Football League is the system of promotion and relegation. This is the rule whereby the worst-performing teams at a given level of league competition are demoted at the end of the season to play in the immediately junior league and are replaced by the best-performing teams from that league. According to the 1889 rules of the Football League, it was agreed that there should be two "classes," later to be known as divisions, each to be composed of twelve teams.[92] An additional rule stated that the bottom four teams in each class should be required to "retire" but could be considered for reelection. Various amendments to this system were tried out in the first few years, but in

1898 the standard system for promotion and relegation was adopted whereby both the demoted and promoted teams would be determined by the number of points scored (two points for a win and one point for a tie) during the season. Not only has this system been almost universally adopted in the soccer world, it has also been widely adopted in other sports, especially in Europe. Thus no lesser authority than the European Commission stated in 1998 that promotion and relegation is "one of the key features of the European model of sport."

There can be little doubt that this system makes a difference. Promotion and relegation increases competition and reduces the long-term monopoly power of the big clubs. Relocation threats are not credible under promotion and relegation. Giving up because the season is not going well is not credible under promotion and relegation (unless you want to exit the major league). It is a hypercompetitive system in comparison with a closed system, and it shows in the relatively higher profitability and lower frequency of financial failure in the U.S. majors than in the top European soccer leagues. The financial surpluses that the original members of the Football League enjoyed in the 1890s, when it consisted of only twelve teams, were rapidly eroded as the league expanded to four divisions of eighty-eight teams by 1922. Thus not only did the FA restrict formally the right of Football League club owners to appropriate profits generated by the club, it oversaw the establishment of a competitive system that limited the potential profitability of league clubs.

The coexistence of the league and the FA was inevitably a compromise, and an uneasy one at that, but it was also one that enabled both to survive and to project an image of a unified sport to the world. While the cost of this uneasy unity was a slowness to adapt to change, it provided a means by which the game could be spread around the world. Following the Spalding world tour of 1889, professional baseball largely gave up any attempt to spread the game internationally. The FA, funded in part by the activities of professional clubs, entered into a relationship with emerging football associations in other countries and began the process of creating a world game.

CHAPTER THREE

How Soccer Spread around the World When Baseball Didn't

The governing body of world soccer, FIFA, is a community of nations, like the Olympic Movement or the United Nations (UN).[1] All three were founded around the same time. The modern Olympics began in 1896, FIFA in 1904, and the League of Nations (forerunner to the United Nations) in 1919. Belonging to one has usually gone hand in hand with membership in the other. For example, nearly half of the founding members of the League of Nations (nineteen out of forty-two) already belonged to FIFA, and of the fourteen new members that joined the league in the succeeding seven years, nine also joined FIFA.

Today, FIFA boasts 204 members, two more than the Olympic movement and thirteen more than the UN. Most of those not belonging to the UN are dependent territories that have been allowed, for historical reasons, to field their own teams in international competition. The most prominent examples are the "home nations" of the United Kingdom: England, Scotland, Wales, and Northern Ireland. Other examples are Hong Kong and Macao, the Netherlands Antilles, the Faroe Islands, Puerto Rico, and American Samoa (which only

joined in 1998 and promptly recorded the world-record defeat in an international soccer match of 31-nil against Australia).[2]

A very small number of countries are members of the UN but do not
belong to FIFA. The principality of Monaco submerges itself into the French
Republic for the purposes of playing soccer but prefers to stand alone at the
UN, while a number of Polynesian islands and American dependencies have
made their way to the General Assembly without showing any sign of interest in soccer, notably the Marshall Islands, Micronesia, Vanuatu, and Kiri-
bati. Today, 180 countries belong to both FIFA and the UN, and of these
sixty-one joined FIFA before joining the UN, nine joined in the same year,
and another fifty joined FIFA within five years of taking a seat in New York.

Baseball is also played around the world, but to a far lesser extent than
soccer. The International Baseball Federation boasts 112 members, and
since 1992 baseball has been a full Olympic sport. This puts it roughly on a
par with sports such as cricket (the International Cricket Council has 89
members) and field hockey (the International Hockey Federation has 114
members). Moreover, the level of competition in most countries outside the
United States is low. A baseball World Cup has been played on and off since
1938, when only two teams entered—the USA and Great Britain; since
Britain won, one can only assume the Americans did not take it too seriously. To this day, the U.S. team has consisted of amateur players only. The
most recent edition was held in Havana, Cuba, in October 2003, with the
gold medal being taken by Cuba, silver by Panama, and bronze by Japan.
The USA came in fifth out of the eight teams competing, behind Taiwan but
ahead of Nicaragua, Brazil, and Korea.

In this chapter we examine how soccer spread at the end of the nineteenth century, initially through the medium of British expatriates and then
via local elites as they adopted the game. This process contrasts sharply with
the more inward looking and commercial development of baseball during
the same period. This difference can be accounted for both by differences in
the economic development of the United Kingdom and the United States
during this era and by differences in the organizational structures of baseball and soccer.

The greater internationalism of soccer has not necessarily made it a force
for international progress. Soccer's popularity has often led to obsessive fandom and excessive behavior. We illustrate the repeated use of soccer by

politicians to whip up nationalist hysteria and the level of violence that has become synonymous with the game. It is just possible that the limited spread of baseball has spared its fans some of the wilder excesses of soccer hooliganism.

The Diffusion of Soccer

Even before the founding of the Football Association (FA), Englishmen were to be found playing their game in other countries. In 1860 the Lausanne Football and Cricket Club was founded in Switzerland, and in 1876 the Grasshoppers, still the most famous Swiss club, was founded by an English student.[3] In 1872 the first French soccer club was founded in the port of Le Havre by employees of a British shipping company. The first recorded soccer match in Spain involving Spaniards took place in Huelva in September 1874, among railway workers employed by the British copper mining corporation Rio Tinto.

KB Copenhagen, the first Danish team, was formed in 1876 and is probably the oldest surviving football club in Europe outside the United Kingdom. To this day it offers its members the chance to play cricket. An English team playing in Portugal, Lisbon FC, is recorded in 1875, although the Portuguese date their soccer history from 1884, when students returning from England introduced a soccer ball. In the 1890s the English founded Vienna's two first soccer clubs, 1st Vienna FC and the Vienna Football and Cricket Club, and their first match was played in 1894. The first recorded soccer match in Hungary took place on November 1, 1896, and involved several Englishmen. In the following year the Viennese cricketers, with nine Englishmen on their team, visited Budapest for a match. The Genoa Cricket and Football Club was founded by a British doctor in 1893 (the club survives under this name to the present day), and one of Italy's most famous clubs, AC Milan, was founded in 1899 by three Englishmen as the Milan Cricket and Football Club. In 1894 the first Russian soccer club, Orekhovo Sports, was established by an English manager, Harry Charnock, for the benefit of employees of the Morozovsti mill outside Moscow.

In the Americas, the older, rougher version of football was known, and matches are recorded from the 1820s at Harvard. The Oneida Football Club was formed in Boston in 1862, making it one of the oldest clubs to be founded anywhere in the world, but exactly what kind of football they

Frederick Louis, Prince of Wales (1707–51), heir to the throne of England and father of King George III. He was a cricket fanatic, and his patronage did much to establish the game. In a letter written in 1748 he is recorded as also playing "base-ball" indoors. Base-ball was described and illustrated in the *Little Pretty Pocket Book* (London, 1744) and is recognizably a forerunner of modern baseball. (Photo reproduction courtesy of Romilly Lockyer)

A baseball match between the Boston Red Stockings, champions of America, and the Philadelphia Athletics played at Lord's cricket ground, London, on August 3, 1874. Lord's, founded in 1787 and at its present site since 1814, was as much a club for English gentlemen as a sporting institution, so it was a great honor for the Americans to play their game on its hallowed turf. (Fine Arts Museums of San Francisco)

Harry Wright, born in England, played professional cricket in the United States before turning to baseball. A star player and manager of the Boston Red Stockings, which dominated the National Association of Professional Base Ball Players (NAPBBP), Wright played a major role in organizing the association and its first tour of his homeland in 1874. (National Baseball Hall of Fame)

Charles Alcock, one of the greatest administrators in the history of sport, secretary of the Football Association from 1870 to 1895 and of the Surrey County Cricket Club from 1872 to 1907. He also invented the Football Association Cup and promoted international competition in both soccer and cricket. Less well known is his role as the London agent for Wright's baseball tour of England in 1874 and Spalding's tour of 1889. (Photo reproduction courtesy of Romilly Lockyer)

Albert G. Spalding, a star pitcher during the early years of professional baseball, first in the NAPBBP and then in the National League. He formed the Spalding Sporting Goods company in 1876, which tied his fortune to the popularity of baseball and gave him a direct incentive to promote baseball as the U.S. national pastime and spread the game abroad. He went on to become a team owner and publisher of the well-known *Spalding's Baseball Guide.* (National Baseball Hall of Fame)

William Hulbert, founder of the National League. Distressed by the problems of the loosely structured and corrupt NAPBBP, Hulbert adopted the concept of a monopoly when he created the closed National League.
(National Baseball Hall of Fame)

The Management Committee of the Football League, 1902–03. From left to right, William McGregor (founder and life member), W. W. Hart (Second Division), T. H. Sidney (vice president), J. McKenna (First Division), J. J. Bentley (president), H. S. Radford (First Division), J. Lewis (vice president), T. Charnley (secretary). Within fifteen years of its founding the league had expanded to thirty-six teams and rivaled the Football Association in its influence over the game. (Photo reproduction courtesy of Romilly Lockyer)

A 1920 portrait of Judge Kenesaw Mountain Landis (seated), commissioner of baseball from 1920 to 1944, in a courtroom in Chicago, surrounded by owners of baseball franchises. Standing in the background (left to right): Connie Mack (Philadelphia Athletics, AL), Phil Ball (St. Louis Browns, AL), Barney Dreyfuss (Pittsburgh Pirates, NL), Clark Griffith (Washington Senators, AL), Frank Navin (Detroit Tigers, AL), Jacob Ruppert (New York Yankees, AL), Sam Breadon (St. Louis Cardinals, NL), Charles Ebbets (Brooklyn Dodgers, NL), James Dunn (Cleveland Indians, AL), Charles Stoneham (New York Giants, NL), August Herrmann (Cincinnati Reds, NL), Harry Frazee (Boston Red Sox, AL), William Veeck (Chicago Cubs, NL), and Robert Quinn (St. Louis Browns, AL). (Chicago Historical Society)

Babe Ruth seated in front of the grandstand with his second wife, Claire Hodgeson, at Chicago's Comiskey Park during the 1930 season. Ruth's exploits on the field brought him huge financial rewards, unlike soccer stars of his era. (Chicago Historical Society)

There are no pictures of the soccer matches played between English and German soldiers during the unofficial Christmas truce of 1914, but this picture, which is believed to show German prisoners of war playing a game while being guarded by a French soldier (whose attention seems focused on the ball), illustrates soccer's international appeal by the time of World War I. (*Illustrated London News* Picture Library)

Olympic Stadium, Berlin, on May 14, 1938. At the height of appeasement, England played a "friendly" match against Germany. Traditionally, national anthems are played before the start of international matches. In what was widely perceived as a propaganda coup for Hitler, English players were instructed, under pressure from the British government, to raise their hands in a Nazi salute before the game. England won 6 to 3. (*Illustrated London News* Picture Library)

The Game of Unity, played at the Ghazi Olympic Stadium, Kabul, Afghanistan, on February 15, 2002, between a team representing the "International Security Assistance Force" (player on the left) and a team of Afghans under the name "Kabul United." The game was organized by the English Football Association to mark the return of Afghanistan to international soccer, which had been suppressed by the Taliban regime. ISAF won 3 to 1. (Allsport UK/Getty Images)

Real Madrid in Hong Kong on August 8, 2003. Tickets for the exhibition game against a Hong Kong team were sold out within six hours of going on sale. The team of "galácticos" includes some of the world's most famous, and expensive, soccer players: left to right, Claude Makelele, France, transfer fee $13.7 million; Luis Figo, Portugal, $63 million; Roberto Carlos, Brazil, undisclosed; David Beckham, England, $41 million; Michel Salgado, Spain, $12.5 million; Ivan Helguera, Spain, $7.6 million; Zinedine Zidane, France, $77 million. (Richard A. Brooks/AFP/Getty Images)

Alex Rodriguez being interviewed by a Japanese reporter before the Yankees' opening-day game against the Tampa Bay Devil Rays in Tokyo on March 30, 2004. While the Yankees signed a sponsorship deal with the Ricoh company for the series in Japan, no MLB team has worn company logos on its uniforms while in the United States. (Photo by Koichi Kamoshida/Getty Images)

played is unclear. Football, according to the less violent English Football Association rules, was played in a match between Princeton and Rutgers in 1869, and collegiate football might well have developed along Football Association lines had not Harvard insisted on the rugby code, which later evolved into American football.

In Palermo Park in Buenos Aires, a plaque commemorates the first soccer match played in Argentina, on June 20, 1867, between Englishmen on the grounds of the Buenos Aires Cricket Club. The Argentine Association Football League was founded in 1893 by a Scottish headmaster, Alexander Hutton, and retained English as its official language until 1903. Albion, the first soccer club in Uruguay, was founded in 1891 by William Leslie Pool, a professor of English literature, and Charles Miller, son of a British father and Brazilian mother, introduced soccer to the exclusive gentlemen's clubs of São Paulo in Brazil. In 1888 he persuaded the São Paulo Athletic Club, formed by British expatriates to play cricket, to add soccer to its list of regular sports.[4]

Clearly there were plenty of British expatriates around the world willing and able to play the game, but this is not enough in itself to make a game spread. Cricket was played just as much by British expatriates, but it failed to catch on in any of these countries, or indeed anywhere outside the British Empire. One reason is that the game is too slow, another that it is too complicated; a third is that everyone perceives it to be quintessentially "British," so that it makes almost no sense for any other nationality to play it.[5] Soccer, on the other hand, is sufficiently simple that it can admit to any number of styles of play, each of which can become the distinct property of a particular society. South Americans have been proud to develop their own distinctive style of play, decidedly different from that of the British.

At first, in most countries, it was the wealthy children of prominent citizens, often taught in British schools or by British schoolmasters, who adopted the game. As Lanfranchi and Taylor observe: "Football pioneers generally came from wealthy families and were particularly influenced by the British traditions associated with the industrial revolution. They would often go to England or Switzerland (or both) to complete their education, arriving home with a football."[6]

Moreover, as local teams started to gain more prominence, English players and organizers stood aside to allow indigenous soccer players to take control. Although many associations were founded by the English, quite soon they passed under the control of local citizens. By 1914 around forty national associations had been created, including those of Denmark, the Netherlands, Argentina, Belgium, Switzerland, Chile, Italy, Germany, Uruguay, Norway, Austria, Sweden, Haiti, Paraguay, Finland, Romania, Russia, Spain, the United States, Portugal, and Brazil.

Historians often accuse the British of being insular about their soccer and refusing to share their game with the world. This, however, is to oversimplify. Not only did the British play a significant role in spreading soccer through their expatriate communities; they also engaged in large numbers of international soccer tours. In the previous chapter, we listed the fifteen tours undertaken by the gentlemen amateurs of the Corinthian Football Club (a name adopted by one of Brazil's leading teams). Other gentlemen's clubs undertook their own tours. Indeed, as early as 1903 there were so many foreign tours that the Football Association (FA) was obliged to relax its rule requiring prior permission because of the administrative burden.[7]

Until the second half of the twentieth century, professional English clubs were widely accepted as the best in the world, and clubs from all over Europe issued invitations for them to tour. The professional clubs were prepared to travel if their hosts were willing to pay, and, of course, this was only possible if there were enough paying fans. The frequency of professional tours is evidence that, from the early twentieth century, soccer matches in Europe could attract large paying crowds. Consider the example of just one European city, Vienna: Southampton FC played there in 1900, followed by the Glasgow Rangers, Tottenham Hotspur, and Everton in 1905, Manchester United in 1908, Sunderland in 1909, Barnsley in 1910, and Blackburn Rovers, Oldham Athletic, and Glasgow Celtic in 1911.[8] Most other major European cities hosted visiting teams with similar frequency.

It was much easier for British soccer to reach the rest of Europe than it would have been for American baseball. But the British also traveled the long distance to South America. Professional touring teams were prominent in Argentina, including Southampton in 1904, Nottingham Forest in 1905, Everton and Tottenham in 1909, Swindon Town in 1912, Exeter City in 1914, Third Lanark in 1923, Motherwell in 1928, and Chelsea in 1929.[9] Again, large crowds and guaranteed payments made these off-season tours both pleasurable and profitable.

The frequency of these English soccer tours contrasts sharply with the history of U.S. baseball tours. While the English FA helped to promote participation in the game of soccer by accepting all comers as affiliates, and the amateur elites took the game with them to the British colonies and investment outposts around the globe, the promoters of American baseball were occupied with fashioning a successful closed monopoly sports league and incurring the attendant rent-seeking costs. If the United States had had colonies or any significant sum of foreign investment in the late nineteenth century, U.S. elites might have been more active in spreading the game to foreign lands.

During the 1840s, Great Britain, the world's richest economy, introduced free trade, and between 1850 and 1914 the British dominated the world economy. In 1870, for example, 25 percent of world merchandise exports came from the United Kingdom, not including its imperial possessions. Most of this merchandise, and the return cargoes, were carried on British ships. British capital, moreover, could find more business opportunities abroad than at home, and so Britain became the largest international investor. In 1914 about 42 percent of all overseas investment was owned by the British, whose interests reached to all corners of the globe.[10] British net foreign investment as a share of its GNP averaged 4.0 percent in the 1870s, 4.7 percent in the 1880s, and 3.4 percent in the 1890s. The United States did not become a net capital exporter until 1900.[11]

To administer these interests, a large network of British banks arose, together with political and legal services to promote British interests. British technical know-how was also much in demand during this period. British military personnel were busy administering these interests. From 1877 to 1897 there were between 250,000 and 375,000 British troops stationed outside the United Kingdom every year. (In contrast, over the same period, the United States had fewer than 50,000 troops abroad.) It is not surprising, therefore, to find that there were huge numbers of British expatriates around the globe, many of whom played English games, especially soccer and cricket.

The role of the gentlemanly amateur in this story was crucial. Soccer spread to a large degree because English gentlemen played their game with gentlemen from other countries. These gentlemen saw their sport as embodying the virtues of the nation and their class, and saw the spreading of their game as a kind of missionary work, as the historian of the Corinthians wrote in 1906:

> It may be claimed that they [the Corinthians] are, to use a well worn phrase "Missionaries of Empire." It is true that their labours in this respect have been for the most part indirect, and that they have not

been called upon to undergo the hardships and disappointments generally associated with missionary work. But none the less the Club has
played no inconsiderable part in helping to bring the Colonies and the
Mother Country closer together. There is no tie like that of sport, and
the friendly rivalry and good fellowship which the colonial tours have
engendered cannot but have done good.

Nor have their efforts in this respect been confined to the Colonies.
The Corinthians were one of the first English football clubs to visit the
Continent, and their frequent tours, of which some account will be
found in this book, have done much to popularise the British idea of
true sportsmanship.[12]

Such intercourse, of course, brought more than merely sporting benefits. Just
as golf today helps business leaders to clinch a deal, nineteenth-century soccer played between members of the business elite could help oil the wheels of
commerce. During the period in which soccer spread, Great Britain had both
a formal empire—India, Australia, Canada, South Africa, and the rest—and
an "informal" empire. The latter included the South American countries of
Argentina, Brazil, Chile, and Peru, among others. The informal empire was
not directly controlled by the British crown, but because of the importance
of British commercial interests, the British prime minister often held more
influence than the nominally independent governments.

Thus the spread of soccer was intimately tied to British imperial and
commercial power at the end of the nineteenth century, and to the role of
the English gentlemen amateurs. These individuals, who played a significant
role both in the governance of soccer in England and in the new associations founded abroad, were conspicuously absent from the development of
baseball after the decline of the National Association of Amateur Base Ball
Players in the 1870s. Men like Spalding, who dominated the game, gave it an
image that was purely commercial, so an American gentleman of this era
would have been more likely to take up golf or lawn tennis.

Baseball's Insularity

Between 1876 and World War I, baseball developed through expansion of
the organizational structures created by the NL until it came to be known
as Organized Baseball, *tout court*. As a business proposition, baseball had

fabulous potential: it could attract large paying crowds, it required limited capital investment, and it could be played anytime and almost anywhere. The one problem was that once the league became a commercial success, it was easy for others to try to copy that success. The more profits the NL made, the more tempting it was for rivals to set up in competition. But competition led to higher player wages and smaller crowds, with the result that profits would slump and clubs fold. To avoid this cycle of boom and bust, the leaders of the NL gradually created a network of teams and leagues that accepted contractual limitations on the movement of players and territorial exclusivity. Thus the great baseball monopoly was created.

Baseball's NL was first challenged in the late 1870s by the looser and more open International League. Several smaller and more regional leagues followed. Most of these early rivals were dispensed with without much difficulty. Some joined the NL alliance and accepted status as minor leagues. Procedures and fees (discussed in the next chapter) were agreed upon to allow the NL to draft players from the lower leagues. Unlike English soccer, where not only the players but also the teams moved up and down between leagues, in American baseball the teams stayed put, while only the players moved up and down.

Then in 1882 the American Association (AA) was formed by brewmasters looking to advance sales of their beer and develop a more popular base for baseball fandom. Not only did the AA introduce Sunday games, 25 cent admission, and the sale of beer at the ballpark, but in order to entice other teams to join its league, the AA allowed its teams to play non-AA clubs and hold exhibitions on off-days. And to lure the game's better players, it permitted released AA players to receive severance pay and sign immediately with another AA club.

Competition over player salaries led to players jumping leagues. This activity initiated open hostilities, and the NL and AA canceled their scheduled postseason tournament in 1882. According to Spalding's public listing, the average player salary jumped by one-third in just one year, from $1,375 in 1882 to $1,835 in 1883.

Although figures vary, several reports had the AA outdrawing the NL at the gate in 1882. After the NL installed a new president, the senior circuit opted for cooperation and collusion rather than competition with the fledgling AA. The two leagues agreed on a peace pact in 1883 that established an eleven-man reserve list for each team, mutual recognition of territorial rights for clubs, blacklisting of rebel players, and a championship series. This pact set an important precedent for the future development of Organized Baseball.

With the player reserve system and without pressure from a rival league, however, the NL and AA executives sought to reestablish control over the players' market. The player reserve was expanded to twelve per team, and a maximum salary of $2,000 per player (several hundred dollars below the average salary at the time) was set.

Meanwhile, the brewmasters of the AA presented a different kind of challenge when they began introducing their business ways into baseball. Apart from their beer sales at the ballpark, some team owners sold exclusive concession rights separately to vendors of peanuts, sandwiches, or soda. The Cincinnati AA club charged a $1,000 fee to a company for the right to sell scorecards at its games.[13] Telegraph companies paid teams for the right to transmit game information to pool halls and saloons.

With revenues rising and salaries falling, the mid-1880s proved to be fertile ground for the emergence of an incipient players' union. John Montgomery Ward, star pitcher and shortstop, led the formation of the Brotherhood of Professional Base Ball Players.[14] The Brotherhood had a long list of demands, including an end to the player reserve system and maximum salaries; an end to extra duties for players, such as taking tickets at the gate and cleaning the ballfield; and an end to player sales where one owner paid another for a player and the player himself received nothing.

In part due to pressures from the Brotherhood, salaries began to rise again in 1887. The owners responded with one of their favorite ploys. They changed the rules to reduce offensive statistics and diminish the salaries of star hitters. In 1888 the NL and AA agreed to cease counting walks as hits and to reduce the number of strikes constituting a strikeout to three. Batting averages fell by 32 points in 1888.[15]

This time the ploy was less successful than the owners had hoped. With salaries continuing their upward drift, NL Cincinnati owner John T. Brush proposed a classification scheme after the 1888 season. Players would be assigned to a skill category, from A to E, and each category would have a salary limit. The scheme was intended not only to lower salaries in the short run, but also to drive a wedge between players and weaken their solidarity. The owners slyly adopted the Brush proposal while Ward and several other Brotherhood activists were on the Spalding-organized baseball tour around the world. Ward got wind of the owners' decision and left the tour early to return to the States.

These ownership maneuvers and player suspicions inspired the launching of the Players' National League of Base Ball Clubs or the Players' League (PL) in November 1889. The PL would have eight teams. Each team would be run by a board, consisting of four players and four "contributors" (investors). Instead of a reserve system, players were signed to three-year contracts. No player could be released until the end of the season, and only then by a majority vote of the board. Gate receipts were split 50-50 between the home and visiting clubs.

Most stars jumped to the PL and, according to the *Reach Guide* of 1891, the PL outdrew the NL in 1890, with attendances, respectively, of 980,887 and 813,678. The salary bidding war, the split of fandom among three leagues, and new legal expenses, however, engendered over $325,000 in losses for the PL backers. PL backers were businessmen not idealists. They eagerly accepted Spalding's offer of either incorporation into the NL or a cash payoff. Within one year the PL was defunct.

The AA never recovered from its competition with both the NL and PL in 1890. After a destructive bidding war with the NL for former PL players, the AA and NL struck an accord following the 1891 season. Chris Von der Ahe, brewer, owner of the AA's St. Louis Browns, and the league's strongest financial force, agreed to a partial merging of the two leagues with the assurance that Sunday ball and beer would prevail. Under the accord, four AA teams joined the NL and the other five were bought out.[16] A two-person panel distributed the rights to players from the disbanded teams. Team reserves were extended to fourteen players, and roster limits were set at fifteen. Temporarily without competition and with the U.S. economy suffering, NL owners again began to slash salaries.

In 1894 sportswriter Ban Johnson was named president of the eight-team Western League (WL). The WL was a top-level minor league and signatory to the National Agreement that governed the drafting of players for a fee by the NL. Growing grievances over the NL's drafting practices, however, prompted Johnson to contemplate invading three of the NL's markets, in Chicago, St. Louis, and Cleveland. In 1899 the WL announced that it was changing its name to the American League (AL) and proceeding with its expansion plans. In September 1900 the new AL proclaimed its intention to seek major league status.

The AL's pledge to abjure salary caps along with its lucrative compensation offers lured some one hundred players to desert the NL. Among those enticed to sign with AL teams were Honus Wagner, Cy Young, and Napoleon Lajoie. When Lajoie left the NL Philadelphia club, where he was receiving the league maximum of $2,400, to play for the AL Philadelphia club, the NL club tried to stop the move with a court injunction. The trial court found against the NL club on the grounds that Lajoie's contract lacked mutuality (it obligated the player to the team indefinitely but permitted the team unilaterally to release the player on short notice). The case was appealed to the state Supreme Court, which reversed the decision, arguing that mutuality was established by Lajoie's salary. The court ordered Lajoie, who played in the AL in 1901 and set an all-time batting record of .422, to return to the NL in 1902. Eventually, it was agreed that Lajoie would be traded to the AL Cleveland franchise.[17]

Lajoie's on-field heroics in 1901 notwithstanding, the NL outdrew the AL at the gate by a small margin in that year. In 1902, however, the AL attracted 2.21 million fans to the NL's 1.68 million. The postseason salary wars initially intensified until a truce was signed between the two leagues in January 1903, creating the modern monopoly of baseball as we know it today.

Baseball owners were again in the driver's seat with no competition and the reserve system firmly in tow. As the urban share of the U.S. population grew from 40 to 46 percent between 1900 and 1910, major league attendance increased from 4.75 million fans in 1903 to 7.25 million in 1909. Reported operating income totaled $17 million over this period. Thanks to the reserve clause, however, player salaries languished, and as late as 1914 the average player salary was only $1,200.[18]

Once again a rival league emerged to take advantage of the opening. In 1913 the Federal League (FL) was started as a minor league, but in August of that year it announced its intention to pursue major leaguers for the next season. The FL offered long-term contracts in lieu of a reserve system. As many as 221 players jumped to the FL during 1914–15.

And true to form, major league salaries rocketed upward. Ty Cobb, for instance, had batted .420 in 1911, but his 1912 salary did not increase. It was not until the challenge from the FL that his salary more than doubled, to $20,000 in 1915 (despite batting .369 in 1914—50 points lower than in 1911). Overall, the average salary jumped to $2,800 in 1915, an increase of 133 percent in just one year.

The salary wars crippled each league financially. One estimate suggested that the two leagues together lost as much as $10 million.[19] Something had to give. The FL brought a lawsuit against Major League Baseball in January 1915 for denying access to its players' market. The presiding Illinois District Court judge, Kenesaw Mountain Landis, opined: "As a result of thirty years of observation, I am shocked because you call playing baseball 'labor.'"[20] Quixotic as always, Landis took the case under advisement and had not ruled for almost a year when MLB and the FL reached an agreement.[21] Some FL owners became MLB owners, and the others received unequal payments totaling some $600,000.

Preoccupied as they were with the business of establishing a closed monopoly league, the leaders of Organized Baseball showed little interest in taking their game to the outside world. After the 1874 visit to England mentioned in the previous chapter, Al Spalding returned to the fray in 1888–89 with his world baseball tour. Spalding's first problem was to choose players for the trip. He commandeered his own Chicago team, and to oppose them he picked out what he considered to be a clean-living selection of All-Americans from the National League. As we have seen, Spalding also happened to select several players who were active in the newly formed Brotherhood of Professional Baseball Players, including its leader, John Montgomery Ward. Veterans Cap Anson and George Wright (Harry's brother) also joined the party: the former as player, the latter as umpire. Firmly believing in the superiority of the European and Anglo-Saxon races, Spalding selected an itinerary starting in Honolulu; then across the British Empire to Auckland, New Zealand; and on to Melbourne and Sydney, Australia. Japan was not even considered. Honolulu was the home of Alexander Cartwright. Independent Hawaii (the country was annexed by the United States in 1893) banned Sunday baseball, and the tour party left the islands without playing a single game.

The games played in Australia drew large crowds. Unlike the English, Australian cricketers were prepared to try the American sport, although they were roundly beaten. Originally, the trip was to return to the States directly from Australia, but Spalding was persuaded that the distance home westward was no longer than returning via the Pacific. Egypt was the first stop on the return leg. The principal memento of the Egyptian visit is the famous photograph of the tour party draped across the Sphinx. In Europe, the tour proceeded to Rome, Paris, and then London. In Rome, ever the showman, Spalding tried to requisition the Coliseum for a game, but despite much haggling the Italian authorities were unwilling to permit such a desecration. The Parisians showed some interest, but once again it was the British that Spalding really wanted to convert.

Spalding reestablished his friendly relationship with Charles Alcock at a reception for the tourists held at the Surrey Cricket Ground, where a display was laid on for London society, with Spalding explaining the game as it unfolded to an enthusiastic Prince of Wales. According to Spalding, the two seem to have hit it off, but there was some tut-tutting when he went so far as to tap the prince on the shoulder in order to draw his attention to a particular play, and even dared to sit in the royal presence. More games were played in Bristol, Birmingham, Sheffield, Bradford, Glasgow, Manchester, Liverpool, Belfast, and Dublin, and as many as 60,000 in total witnessed these displays.

Spalding clearly held high hopes that the game would have some chance of competing with cricket, and competitions involving local teams did get started in both Australia and England following the tour, but the impact outside the British Empire was negligible. Moreover, even though Spalding continued to encourage and support English baseball, it never became anything more than a curiosity.

Toward the end of the century Spalding tried a new tack. He got himself elected president of the American Olympic Committee in 1900 and in that year escorted the American contingent to the Paris games. Having complained in Honolulu about the ban on Sunday games,[22] in Paris he led American protests to exempt American athletes from running heats on a Sunday.[23] Spalding was closely involved in the 1904 St. Louis games, which turned into something of a circus.[24] Baseball exhibition matches were included, and Spalding even proposed a match between the National and American Leagues for the Olympic championship.[25] The idea was rejected, although some exhibition games of baseball were played.

At the London games of 1908, the British did not contemplate the playing of baseball. Even cricket, which was played at the 1900 games, was never again to be played as an Olympic sport. Soccer, though, was played for the first time in the 1908 Olympics, with eight teams entering the tournament.[26] Baseball was played at the 1912 games in Stockholm, and Spalding and George Wright were reunited for one last time as coaches of the U.S. team. However, only one team could be found to oppose the Americans, a Swedish club that took one look at the Americans practicing and declared that they could not compete. Even with the loan of a catcher and a pitcher, the Swedes went down 13-3. The lack of credible opponents meant that baseball also disappeared from the Olympics. It reappeared in 1936 in Berlin, but once again there were no foreign teams to compete with the Americans. After 1945 baseball was played as a demonstration sport but generated little interest, and it was not initiated as a full Olympic sport until 1992. The United States has only fielded teams of amateur players because MLB, true to its commercial purpose, is unwilling to disrupt its championship season. Promoters of sports that are played more widely in the rest of the world (such as rugby) still lobby to have baseball replaced—an idea to which International Olympic Committee (IOC) president Jacques Rogge seems favorably disposed.[27]

The last great attempt to spread the game via a baseball tour occurred in 1913–14, when Charles Comiskey, owner of the Chicago White Sox, and John McGraw, manager (and soon-to-be minority owner) of the New York Giants, decided to take their teams around the world. The tour opened in Ohio and made its way through the midwestern states of Kansas and Oklahoma, into Texas and Arizona, on to Los Angeles, San Francisco, and Portland, and finally up to Seattle. There they boarded a steamer to Japan. The Japanese were delighted to receive two such famous teams, since by this time baseball could truly be said to be a national obsession. As well as putting on exhibition games, an American nine also took on the Japanese champions from Keio University. Even though beaten 16-3, the Japanese did not show their disappointment, and the crowd of seven thousand erupted with applause when the game ended.

In Shanghai, no game was played because of the weather, disappointing the large expatriate community. In British-controlled Hong Kong, they had not expected much interest but were in fact greeted by a crowd of around seven thousand, including a large contingent of rowdy British sailors who had never seen a game of baseball before. The event was fairly chaotic: the converted soccer ground was poorly laid out; there was not even a pitcher's mound; and the spectators, who didn't understand the meaning of the foul lines, were constantly encroaching on the field. It was the first game of professional baseball, and possibly the last, played in Hong Kong. The touring players had a happier time in the American-controlled Philippines, although they were still pursued by the rains. From there they sailed to

Australia and, like Spalding, were delighted by the reception they received in Sydney and Melbourne.

The next stage of their tour, in Sri Lanka, brought them into contact with Sir Thomas Lipton, the tea magnate, with whom the tourists struck up a great friendship.[28] From there, the party made its way to Egypt for the compulsory picture (now a movie) of the players in front of the Sphinx, and on to Rome, where they met the Pope but were again unable to play ball.

Rain dogged the tour in France, but the grand finale in London was at least a success. This time the visitors hired out the home of the Chelsea Football Club at Stamford Bridge in London, and King George V himself agreed to attend the exhibition, sitting behind home plate. Before the game he was introduced to the managers and told them, "I am delighted to see you gentlemen here with your ball teams," and afterwards he sent a message saying, "Tell Mr. McGraw and Mr. Comiskey that I have enjoyed the game enormously." So, it seems, did the crowd of 20,000 that turned up with the king; nonetheless, the British press remained firmly of the opinion that "baseball is just rounders, played hard."

On February 28, 1914, the tourists boarded the *Lusitania* for the journey home. Like the previous tours, this one achieved essentially nothing in promoting the sport. The greatest draw of the tour, in fact, was Jim Thorpe, the great Native American multisport athlete.[29] Thorpe's principal claim to fame is winning both the pentathlon and the decathlon in the 1912 Olympics, where he also was a member of the U.S. baseball team. However, he was later stripped of his medals by the IOC when it was discovered that he had played semi-pro baseball and therefore did not qualify as an amateur. Nonetheless, during the baseball tour people from all over the world came to see the athletic phenomenon.

Comiskey and McGraw tried to organize another tour in 1924, this time of Europe alone, but managed only to get as far as Paris when they abandoned it. By then international soccer was in full swing. Never again before the 1990s did Americans put any serious effort into spreading their sport, and for the most part, foreigners showed little or no interest in learning about it.

Outside the United States, the best-known baseball-playing nations are probably the Caribbean and Central American countries (such as Cuba, the Dominican Republic, and Venezuela) and Japan. The southward spread of baseball is easily understood as a consequence of U.S. economic and cultural connections with these countries.

Baseball was being played in Cuba in the 1860s. Not only is the Cuban capital, Havana, only ninety miles from Florida, but Cuba had a rather modernized economy in the late nineteenth century. Cuba had the railroad before its colonizer, Spain. Spain had opened Cuban ports to trade in 1817, and within decades trade in Cuban sugar, cigars, and rum flowed copiously. Taking advantage of its long coastline, traffic in contraband and tourism also flourished. U.S. businessmen were selling a panoply of industrial accoutrements to Havana, operating sugar mills, and running American clubs. Some cigar factories were transferred to Key West and Tampa to get around the Spanish trade monopoly. The emerging Cuban elites resented Spain and were especially open to learning the ways of U.S. culture. They frequently sent their children to be schooled in the United States. Some returned with baseball bats and balls in the early 1860s. By the 1870s, baseball clubs were springing up across the island, and the first professional league—Liga de Beisbol Profesional Cubana—was inaugurated in 1878.

During the country's first war of independence against Spain, 1868–78, many Cubans fled the island to the east, arriving on Hispaniola (the island that is shared by Haiti and the Dominican Republic). With them they brought the latest techniques for cultivating sugar, and they also brought baseball. The die was cast.[30]

The Japanese story is more exceptional. The introduction of baseball to Japan is usually credited to Horace Wilson. Wilson was an American missionary and professor of English and history who taught at Tokyo University in the early 1870s, twenty years after Commodore Perry forced the country to adopt free trade at gunpoint. During this period, the Japanese sent numerous commissions around the world to ascertain the best practice in every field. They copied the French model in the education system, the German model for the army, and the British model for the navy. The sporting curriculum was heavily influenced by the Americans, and in 1878 a gymnastics institute was established under the directorship of Dr. George A. Leland, a graduate of Amherst College.[31]

While the Japanese had the opportunity to learn baseball from American businessmen and sailors who set up their own matches, the large British community played cricket. A struggle ensued at the Yokohama Athletic Club over which sport should be played. Only in the 1880s, when Americans came to outnumber all other expatriate communities, did baseball become the club's official sport. During this period, baseball was adopted as an intercollegiate sport by Japanese enthusiasts, and in 1891 the Japanese champions, the Ichiko Club, challenged the Yokohama Athletic Club to an "international match." Refusing to accept that the Japanese could be social equals, and questioning their physical capacity for the game, the Yokohama Club refused to play.

The Ichiko Club did not give up and continued to offer the challenge until eventually, in 1896, the Americans agreed to play. When the Japanese entered the field, they were jeered by the American spectators who expected the home team to register an easy victory. The crowd was quickly silenced by the quality of the Japanese play, and the Yokohama Athletic Club was humbled by a 29-4 defeat. The Americans immediately offered a return match, played two weeks later, and were once again thrashed, 32-9. If the Americans were shocked, the Japanese were ecstatic. The victories were written up in the national press and held up as proof that the Japanese were no longer inferior. From that moment, it was clear that the Japanese would take to America's game.

This story illustrates three key elements required for the widespread diffusion of a sport in the era before television. First, expatriates who play the sport among themselves can help bring it to the attention of and teach it to the local population. Second, the local population, particularly the local elite, must feel a desire to emulate these sporting achievements on the field. Third, spectators must be excited by the possibility not only that their countrymen play the imported sport, but also that they even exceed the inventors at their own game. This was true of baseball in Japan, but it was not true of baseball in most countries outside the United States. Soccer, by contrast, was everywhere communicated by the British elite to the local elite and in this way passed into national cultures. Other sports such as cricket, rugby, ice hockey, and basketball (before television) made some international inroads, but none achieved the dominance of soccer.

Sport, Diplomacy, and Violence

Despite the fact that many Englishmen played such an active role in spreading soccer, the British international sporting bureaucracy has always had an uneasy relationship with other countries. Even today, the British tend to view soccer as "their game," making it difficult to meet with other nations as equals. Britain's relationship with FIFA illustrates the problems.[32] When a group of nations, led by France, invited the FA to participate in establishing

FIFA in 1903, the FA delayed its response for so long that those countries went ahead without the British, forming FIFA on May 21, 1904. Finally, in 1905, the FA agreed to join, and in 1906 an Englishman was persuaded to accept the presidency. If the British were cautious, the rest of the world was both patient and deferential.

After World War I, when the other European nations wanted sporting contact with the defeated powers to resume, the British refused to play against them and withdrew from FIFA. Britain got over it in 1924 and rejoined, only to fall out again over the definition of amateurism. To the British the definition was clear: an amateur was someone who did not receive any remuneration for playing. Within the British class system this meant a gentleman, and every Briton knew the difference between a gentleman (a man of means) and a player (a working man). To the rest of the soccer world, where a less rigid sense of class distinction prevailed, one might still be poor and an amateur. To ease the burden of poverty, FIFA was prepared to tolerate "broken time" payments. To be sure, in the hands of the unscrupulous such a ruling was easily abused (most notably by the "amateurs" of the Soviet bloc after the Second World War), but by that time most national associations were more interested in international success than in class distinction. England, Scotland, Wales, and Northern Ireland once again withdrew from FIFA and did not return until 1950.[33] Among other things, this meant that British representative teams failed to appear in the World Cup, instituted in 1930 and played every four years, until after World War II, and were generally seen by all the other countries' soccer associations as being difficult and aloof.

Absent the British, international soccer took its own path. Some sociologists have argued that the development of modern sports is indicative of the civilizing process of social control in modern societies.[34] In this view, as societies have evolved they have introduced increasing levels of control over violence; and the formalization of a sport such as soccer, involving physical contact, represents one means by which "rough play" has been civilized. Many would make an even stronger claim: that sport itself can bring nations together and be a force for peace in the world. In 2001 "the game of football" was nominated for the Nobel Peace Prize, only to lose out to the United Nations.

In reality, the diffusion of soccer in the twentieth century was closely associated with social conflict, sometimes in positive ways, but arguably more often in negative ways. One of the most poignant stories in the history of soccer relates to the First World War and the Christmas truce of 1914. On Christmas Day, in the middle of one of the most gruesome and senseless wars in history, German and British soldiers in the trenches crossed No-Man's Land to share a drink and exchange sausages for plum pudding. Saxon and Scottish infantrymen mixed freely, and soon talk got round to a discussion about soccer.

Several British soldiers recorded in their memoirs the stories of Germans who had played while living in England before the war. Lieutenant Stewart of the Sutherland Highlanders was presented with a photograph of the 133rd Saxon Regiment's prewar team. In more than one sector of the front a match was proposed. Whether any matches were actually played, and under what conditions (given the size of the foxholes created by the incessant shelling), is less clear, but several eyewitnesses suggest that some kind of rustic free-for-all took place using rolled up papers or old tin cans for a ball. The official history of the Lancashire fusiliers claims that "A" Company won a match against the Germans, 3–2.[35] For many people this story symbolizes the potential for sport to overcome barriers and focus on our common humanity.[36]

Throughout the twentieth century there have been other examples of soccer matches creating a temporary escape for participants in more serious conflicts. In 2002 British soldiers in Afghanistan set up a soccer match in Kabul against a local team as a gesture of normalization, and the Football Association sent out personnel and equipment for the Afghans. Even where people are divided by language, politics, and culture, they usually find common ground in soccer. American soldiers in Iraq have being trying to start up local soccer, rather than baseball leagues.[37] By May 2004 the U.S. Soccer Federation had sent 60,000 soccer balls to Iraq. *Spirit of America* called for donations to help supply Iraqi children with "the items they need—school supplies, flying discs, and soccer balls."

But the negatives seem to weigh much more heavily than the positives for two seemingly unconnected reasons: the association of soccer with nationalism and the long history of violent conflict between rival soccer fans. Soccer's popularity led to fan intensity, which when transferred to the international scene often meant it served as a banner of nationalist sentiment, subject to political manipulation.

The most egregious examples of the connection between soccer and virulent nationalism concern the fascist regimes of Italy, Germany, and Spain.

Of the three infamous fascist dictators, only General Franco of Spain seems to have actively enjoyed soccer. According to one biography, watching soccer on TV became an obsession for Franco in later life:

> Having been delighted by the introduction of television into Spain, he also spent increasing numbers of hours watching the many sets placed around the Prado. His favourite programmes were movies and sport, particularly football. The revival of Spanish football since the arrival of Hungarian refugees like Ladislao Kubala, Ferenc Puskas, and Sandor Kocsis had enthused Franco who saw the triumph of Real Madrid and of the Spanish national team as somehow his own. He began to do the pools (*quiniela*)[38] every week. . . . He won twice. It is difficult somehow to imagine Hitler or Mussolini doing the pools.[39]

Hitler showed no interest in the game, even though it was by then very popular in Germany. German fascists preferred what they considered to be domestically produced games over foreign imports, particularly from a country such as Great Britain, which they considered decadent. Instead they favored the *Turnen* (gymnastics) movement, invented by Friedrich Jahn during the Napoleonic wars. Jahn attributed the defeat of Prussians by Napoleon to their lack of fitness and devised gymnastic exercises (using the parallel bars and the pommel, among others) to rectify this.[40] The movement grew throughout the nineteenth century alongside Prussian and then German military power, and the movement's objectives were perfectly suited to the purposes of the Nazis. Moreover, these skills served the Nazis well in the Olympics.

Hitler's aversion to soccer may also have been connected to the fact that the one and only match he attended was played against Norway in the 1936 German Olympics. The result was a 2-0 victory for the Norwegians, which eliminated the Germans from the tournament, much to the Führer's disgust.[41] Nonetheless, the publicity potential of soccer was not lost on the Nazi regime. On coming to power in 1933 Hitler promised to stage a lavish Olympic Games, no matter what the cost.

International opinion at the time was still divided on the nature of the regime, and so the staging of a soccer match in London against England represented a chance to show that Nazi Germany could behave itself. Germany lost the match 3-0, and the 5,000 German fans who attended took their defeat in a sporting manner. Although outside the grounds trade unions and Jewish organizations protested noisily against the Nazis, the British government and the sporting authorities were favorably impressed. At the banquet after the match Sir Charles Clegg, president of the FA, made a speech denouncing the protesters:

> This TUC [Trade Union Congress] have thought fit to interfere in a matter which is none of their business . . . before they start to tell a sporting organization what to do and how their members should behave, they should see that their own members responsible for rowdyism are kept under control . . . the TUC seems to forget that this is a sport free of all political interference.

To which Sir Walter Citrine of the TUC replied:

> Sir Charles Clegg does not bother to inform himself of the nature of sport in Germany. If he did so he would realize that football there is nothing more nor less than part of the Nazi German regime.[42]

That comment seems amply borne out by the Olympics of 1936. Ironically, the unwillingness of some sports administrators to acknowledge the political dimension of international sport has constantly left them prey to the schemes of politicians. In 1938 the FA agreed to a return match in Berlin, and this time the British Foreign Office went so far as to press the England team to perform the Nazi salute before the match. The British ambassador, Sir Neville Henderson, informed the representatives of the FA: "When I go in to see Herr Hitler I give him the Nazi salute because it is the normal courtesy expected. It carries no hint of approval of anything Hitler or his regime may do."[43] Thus one of the most notorious photographs in the history of English soccer shows eleven English players making a full Nazi salute before a crowd of 110,000 in the Berlin Olympic Stadium. England won the match 6-3, but the propaganda victory went to the Germans.[44] Only after the occupation of Czechoslovakia in 1939 did the FA break off sporting relationships, on the advice of the Foreign Office. Sadly, Sir Charles Clegg did not live long enough to see the connection between sport and politics so clearly revealed.

Mussolini, like Hitler, showed little interest in soccer and seems, in fact, to have positively disapproved of it. Like their German counterparts, the Italian fascists preferred indigenous sports, of which they were imaginative inventors when the need arose. In the late 1920s, Augusto Turati, national party secretary, reconstructed what he considered to be a classical, and therefore indigenous, version of football called *volata*, and hundreds of teams were organized under the fascist sport and cultural organization, the Dopolavoro. But this effort proved an embarrassing failure largely because young Italian men were so obsessed with soccer, and after 1933 *volata* disappeared, all reference to it being erased from party records.[45]

Mussolini was also motivated by a desire to excel in the Olympics and devoted huge resources to the Comitato Olimpico Nazionale Italiano (CONI), the supposedly amateur national Olympic association. Through CONI he controlled every sporting federation in Italy, including soccer. Until 1930 the fascists used their power to increase sports participation among Italian men (women were discouraged from participating in sport) with a view to engendering a martial spirit. After 1930 the focus shifted to achieving international recognition of Italian athletic, and implicitly, military, prowess.[46] This policy bore fruit in the form of impressive medal counts both in Los Angeles in 1932 (where Italy won the second highest number of medals behind the USA) and in Berlin in 1936 (where the Italians ranked third behind Germany and the USA). The Italians, like the Germans, also invested heavily in sports stadiums, which could be used to stage fascist rallies.

Mussolini came to power in 1922, just as Italian soccer was starting to become a national obsession. The Federazione Italiana del Football had been founded in 1898, when the sport was dominated either by English expatriates or by Italians who had spent time in England. By 1909 the sport had spread more widely and the association was patriotically renamed Federazione Italiana Gioco del Calcio (FIGC), after the Renaissance Florentine game of Calcio, which slightly resembles soccer. Thus the Italians and the Americans are the only two nations today not to use the name "football" to denote the Football Association game.[47]

During the 1920s, the popularity of soccer in Italy had grown enormously as clubs came under the influence of tycoons prepared to subsidize teams to achieve success. The most notable example was the acquisition of Juventus of Turin in 1923 by Giovanni Agnelli, founder of the Fiat car company, a relationship between team and company that persists to the present day. By 1926 the distinction between professional and amateur was recognized. In 1930 a single championship division for the whole of Italy, the Serie A, was established.[48]

The fascists effectively took control of soccer in 1926 when Leandro Arpinati, an undersecretary of the Ministry of the Interior, became president of the FIGC (he was also head of CONI from 1931 until 1933). According to de Grazia:

> Under fascism professional sports became big business, absorbing both public funds and private investment. The regime created a very favorable environment for professional sports and their big-time promoters. It underwrote the great public football stadia at Rome, Bologna, Turin and Florence. It granted generous tax incentives to sports impresarios. The travel of professional teams was heavily subsidized. ... All the way down the fascist hierarchy there appear to have been close ties between party officials and local sports promoters, ties that inevitably resulted in the diversion of public funds into professional sports.[49]

Arpinati's home team was Bologna.[50] His successor at CONI was Giuseppe Marinelli, a supporter of Lazio, one of Rome's two principal teams. The apogee of fascist football came in 1934, when Italy hosted and won the World Cup. The Italians had not attended the first World Cup in 1930, when only four European teams had been willing to make the journey to Uruguay where it was staged. But in Italy, supported by the government, the FIGC assured FIFA that no expense would be spared to stage the most splendid competition possible. The finals were boycotted by the Uruguayans, who had won on their own soil and were offended that only four European teams had turned up; the British teams also refused to participate, for reasons ranging from a megalomaniac sense of superiority to a paranoid fear that foreigners were trying to steal their game.

If the finals were staged with full fascist splendor, the fascists spared no expense to make sure that Italy won. The players themselves were thoroughly prepared and "reduced to a state of infantile purity; they were mentally focused on the single thought of the World Cup and the ethical responsibility placed upon them."[51] According to the soccer historian Bill Murray, Mussolini "had promised rich rewards to the Italian players if they won the cup and dire punishment if they lost."[52] Jingoistic motivations notwithstanding, the Italian team included four Argentines who played in the Italian league. While all of them had Italian names and ancestors, many Argentines felt their best players had been stolen. The Buenos Aires press sarcastically remarked, "If the Italians want good football like ours or the English variety, they should work at it themselves, rather than going out to buy it."[53]

When it came to the matches themselves, "The Italian team fought its way to the Final with a style that was a fitting tribute to the regime it represented."[54] The Italians, early on, defeated the U.S. team, 7-1. The game against Spain resembled more a battlefield than a soccer pitch, with seven Spaniards and four Italians seriously injured. Though the match ended in a draw, Spain was barely able to field a team for the rematch and was easily beaten. In the semifinal, Italy then disposed of Austria, the most talented team of the era, and went on to meet Czechoslovakia in the final.[55] The same referee officiated in both the semifinal and the final, in preparation for which he was given a personal audience with Il Duce. More violence in the final went unpunished, and the Italians were victorious 2-1. They were handed their medals by Mussolini, appropriately enough, given the opinion of the president of the FIGC that the triumph stemmed "from a unique inspiration: Il Duce."[56]

While Hitler and Mussolini saw sport as a means of fashioning a militaristic spirit at home and a powerful reputation abroad, the dictators of Spain and South America have tended to use soccer as a distraction. Of course, this strategy was hardly limited to soccer and twentieth-century dictators. The ancient Roman poet Juvenal used the phrase "bread and circuses" to describe the strategy of corrupt Roman emperors who provided cheap daily bread and circuses (comprising chariot races and gladiatorial and other violent spectacles) for their subjects. The intention was to appease and distract them from the abuses of the political world. In the same spirit, twentieth-century baseball barons argued to the U.S. government during each of the world wars that players should be given a special draft status so they could continue their patriotic duty of entertaining and distracting the population from the ravages of war.

Franco's fundamental political objective was to maintain the unity of the centralized Spanish state ruled from Madrid against the regional separatism manifested most notably by the Basques and the Catalans. In this he was quite brutal, forbidding the use of regional languages and dialects in public and using his secret police to find and punish offenders. He showed little interest in soccer in the early years of his rule, but after the Second World War, as the game became more and more central to national life, he started to take an interest.

Until then, the most successful teams in Spanish soccer had been Barcelona, based in the Catalan capital, and Athletic Bilbao, in the capital of the Basque country. Supporters of these two teams commonly accused Franco of setting out to humiliate them by deliberately building up the fortunes of Real Madrid. In fact, however, it appears that Franco only started to become interested once Real had been established as a successful team in the early 1950s. During the late 1950s, Real became the dominant team not only in Spain but also in Europe, where the European Cup quickly became the most prized competition for European clubs. Real won the Cup the first five times it was played, between 1956 and 1960. The association of the team with Franco's support, however, has been enough to ensure that the rivalries within Spain have been not merely intense but also bitter.

Franco also tried to use international sport to pursue his political agenda, famously refusing to allow the Spanish team to play the Soviet Union in the 1960 European Nations Cup, much to the dismay of Spanish soccer fans. However, he soon reversed his policy and persuaded UEFA to let him hold the 1964 finals in Spain, once again with the result that the home team won and a fascist dictator was able to bask in the reflected glory.

The nations of South America, especially Brazil and Argentina, have been blessed with great soccer players and plagued by dictators. Time and again, success on the soccer pitch has been hijacked by regimes eager to play down the suppression of human rights and poor economic performance. In the 1930s the Brazilian dictator Getulio Vargas gagged the press, banned political parties, granted the police arbitrary powers, and subsidized the most popular soccer clubs. From the 1950s onward, military regimes ensured generous funding for sports facilities, so that, by 1978, Brazil—its meager per capita income notwithstanding—boasted seven of the world's ten largest stadiums.[57]

Many would argue that the greatest soccer team of all time was the Brazil team that won the 1970 World Cup, led by Pele. President Emilio Garrastazu Medici, a general who took power in 1969, made sure that this victory belonged to him. One of his first acts on taking power was to remove the national team's coach, João Saldanha, who had failed to include the president's favorite player on the team. On being asked why he hadn't picked this player, Saldanha commented, "I don't choose the president's ministry, and he can't choose my front line." This was an error of judgment.

Following victory, Medici, who was a true soccer fanatic, went into over-drive. Addressing the nation he gushed:

> I feel profound happiness at seeing the joy of our people in the high-est form of patriotism. I identify this victory won in the brotherhood of good sportsmanship with the rise of faith in our fight for national development. I identify the success of our [national] team with . . . intelligence and bravery, perseverance and serenity in our technical ability, in physical preparation and moral being. Above all, our play-ers won because they knew how to . . . play for the collective good."[58]

The day the team returned from the finals in Mexico was declared a national holiday, and Medici was photographed congratulating the players. In a fit of liberal-mindedness, he even opened the presidential palace to the public.

In Argentina, where the passion for soccer reaches some of its greatest extremes, the frequent dictators have usually known how to exploit soccer for their cause. In 1975 FIFA awarded the 1978 World Cup to a democratic government only to find it replaced the following year by a military junta. On taking power, the junta suspended all programming on radio and TV and replaced it with the repeated playing of military marches. The one pro-gram they permitted was the match being played between Poland and Argentina: "Everything was prohibited except football."[59] Some 10 percent of the government budget, at a time when the country was bankrupt, was devoted to staging the championship. National hysteria was whipped up by the censored press. Remarkably, Argentina won and the nation exploded with joy. Richard Halac, a playwright, expressed the bittersweet emotions that many who opposed the regime felt:

> The military men wanted to use the *Mundial* [World Cup] but they also wanted us to come out champions. Many Argentines who cele-brated did not like the military, but we also wanted to be champions. What could we do? Not dance? Boycott the *Mundial*? Do dictatorships pass away, do Cups remain? We went, we won and we danced.[60]

It seems that the junta might also merit a measure of credit for the out-come. In its last qualifying match, Argentina needed to beat the fairly strong Peruvian team by at least four goals. In the event, Argentina won 6-0, with the Peruvians missing opportunities that one would not have expected them to miss. Stories circulated after the World Cup of secret gifts to Peru: according to one story there was a shipment of 4 million tons of wheat,[61] and of $50 million of credits in another.[62]

It is not enough, however, to note that dictators have used sports for political ends. All politicians seek to take credit for the success of the national team. When France won the World Cup in 1998, President Jacques Chirac was on hand to distribute the medals, claiming, "This is a France that wins and is, for once, united in victory." The team was later awarded the *Légion d'honneur*, the country's highest distinction, in a special ceremony at the presidential palace. German Chancellors Helmut Schmidt in 1974 and Helmut Kohl in 1990 both benefited from the aura surrounding German victories. British Prime Minister Harold Wilson once quipped that his greatest achievement was winning the World Cup in 1966, his party's reelection in the same year being commonly attributed to England's success. In 1970 Wilson's Labour Party led by twelve points in the polls leading up to election day on June 18. On June 14, England was defeated in the World Cup quarterfinal by West Germany, having squandered a 2-0 lead. The Conservatives rode to a narrow victory following a dramatic late swing in the polls. In 2004 U.S. President George W. Bush took credit for the success of the Iraqi Olympic soccer team in one of his campaign ads. The Bush campaign ignored the wishes of the Iraqi team to pull the ad, who felt their success was being used inappropriately for political purposes. Apparently, the U.S. Olympic Committee agreed with the Iraqi team. To no avail, the USOC too asked the Bush campaign to scrap the ad, stating: "It is the responsibility of the USOC to manage Olympic marks, teams and images in the U.S., and also to remain apolitical."

Even before World War I it was apparent that politicians of all nations, including the democracies, were not above using sport as a tool of diplomacy and national aggrandizement. The Olympic Games is a case in point. The first few games attracted little interest, and the overwhelming majority of participants in the St. Louis games of 1904 were Americans. The 1908 games in London were the first truly international games of the modern era, with over two thousand participants, twenty-two nations, and the beginnings of a media circus. However, the bickering over results between the British and Americans caused them to be dubbed "the battle of Shepherd's Bush."[63] Things began badly when, at the opening ceremony, there was no U.S. flag flying in the stadium, alongside the flags of the other competing nations, causing consternation among the American athletes. Once one had been found, the Americans refused to dip their flag as they marched past King Edward VII, in the style of all the other teams, to the outrage of the British.

The events themselves were the source of endless complaints—about fixing the draw for heats, unfair disqualifications, and bias in favor of the British athletes—charges mostly levied by the Americans. In the 400-meter race, two Americans finished first and second, with the British favorite third, but at an inquiry the British officials stated that the Americans had obstructed the British athletes and ordered a rerun. Disgusted, the Americans refused to take part, and the British athlete took the gold medal after ambling round the track. The British press criticized the Americans for their "win at all costs" attitude, and American competitors were jeered by spectators. At the games' conclusion, Britain had won 141 medals out of 321 awarded, more than double the number of the United States in second place. James Sullivan, secretary of the U.S. Olympic Committee, accused the British of cheating: "They were unfair to the Americans. They were also unfair to every athlete except the British, but their real aim was to beat the Americans. Their conduct was cruel and unsportsmanlike and absolutely unfair."[64]

When the Americans swept the board at the 1912 Olympics, with Great Britain ranked only fourth, *The Independent* newspaper observed: "The modern Olympic meet is chiefly regarded as a contest between nations. Here the disappointment of the English is especially humiliating, because they were the first to insist that success in sports is a measure of national greatness."[65] After the 1912 games in Stockholm, the next Olympiad was awarded to Berlin, in the hope that the sporting festival might calm rising tensions and military posturing, especially between Britain and Germany. But three years before the games were scheduled to begin, the British press was stressing the need to win medals for reasons other than the promotion of world peace:

There is also the consideration that the national reputation is more deeply involved than perhaps we care to recognize in the demonstration of our ability to hold our own against other nations in the Olympic contests. . . . Whether we took the results very seriously or not, it was widely advertised in other countries as evidence of England's decadence.[66]

At the same time, Carl Diem, secretary general of the German Olympic Association, said:

> What is taking place here on behalf of the Olympic Games is in the best interest of the army itself. . . . We are aware of the fact that we are not as much accepted abroad as we deserve. The knowledge of the importance of German economic life and industry, but also of Germany's military power has not spread fast enough. The Games of 1916 will be and are supposed to be a medium to convince the people of our worldwide importance.[67]

The Berlin games were fated never to take place, but if they had, it seems unlikely that the spirit of the Christmas truce would have been much in evidence. George Orwell emphasized the belligerent emotions evoked by sporting contests in his 1945 essay "The Sporting Spirit":

> Nearly all the sports practised nowadays are competitive. You play to win, and the game has little meaning unless you do your utmost to win. On the village green, where you pick up sides and no feeling of local patriotism is involved, it is possible to play simply for the fun and exercise: but as soon as the question of prestige arises, as soon as you feel that you and some larger unit will be disgraced if you lose, the most savage combative instincts are aroused. Anyone who has played even in a school football match knows this.

But that is just the players.

> As soon as strong feelings of rivalry are aroused, the notion of playing the game according to the rules always vanishes. People want to see one side on top and the other side humiliated, and they forget that victory gained through cheating or through the intervention of the crowd is meaningless. Even when the spectators don't intervene physically they try to influence the game by cheering their own side and "rattling" opposing players with boos and insults. Serious sport has nothing to do with fair play. It is bound up with hatred, jealousy, boastfulness, disregard of all rules and sadistic pleasure in witnessing violence: in other words it is war minus the shooting.[68]

Violence and soccer have a long history of companionship. Many fans today imagine that hooliganism only became a problem at the end of the

1960s, but rowdyism of all sorts has accompanied the sport from its earliest days. In 1895 police had to use batons to clear the pitch after a riot followed the referee's decision to abandon the match at Liverpool's Everton.[69] On April 17, 1909, a Scottish Cup final between arch rivals Celtic and Rangers ended in a draw, at which point the fans expected the teams to play extra time to decide a winner. When it became clear that this would not happen, six thousand angry fans invaded the pitch, and when policemen attempted to stop them they were savagely beaten. The fans then proceeded to vandalize the stadium, tearing up goalposts and making bonfires, until a larger force of two hundred police eventually dispersed the crowd. Over one hundred people needed hospital treatment.[70]

"Hooliganism" started to achieve prominence in the media during the 1960s, a period of rapidly increasing wealth and diminishing social barriers and taboos. Increasingly aggressive behavior could be observed both at the stadiums where matches were played (with highlights shown on TV) and, perhaps more important, in the streets of the city centers where most clubs are located. As time passed, this behavior moved from high spirits to vandalism and finally to outright thuggery. Gangs of fans set out to attack each other as much as innocent passersby, and the impression of lawlessness terrified a large fraction of the population. Stanley Kubrick's 1971 movie "A Clockwork Orange" explored the logic of the soccer hooligan to its limit in portraying the calculated sadism of the antihero Alex de Large and his gang of droogs. Yet Kubrick was so alarmed by the evidence that hooligans were starting to copy the droogs that he prevented the movie from being screened in the United Kingdom until after his death.

From the 1970s onward, policing at British soccer matches grew more and more sophisticated. Fans were segregated in the grounds, visiting fans were bused in, only fans registered with clubs were permitted to travel to away matches, and alcohol consumption at soccer grounds was restricted and then banned altogether. By the mid-1980s the number of arrests at soccer grounds had reached the level of about five thousand per season, or about three per match played. After a concerted government effort, by the end of the 1990s this figure had been halved.

Yet even at its peak, there were few recorded deaths in the United Kingdom due to soccer hooliganism. The disasters at Bradford in 1985, when fifty-five people died in a fire that started in a wooden stand, and in Sheffield in 1989, when ninety-six fans were accidentally crushed to death, dwarf the domestic hooliganism issue.[71]

Nonetheless, hooliganism came to be known as the "English disease," largely because of the growing importance of competition with other European clubs. European police forces were seemingly unprepared for English soccer fans who traveled to away matches and caused havoc in the capitals of Europe. The most horrific atrocity occurred in 1985 at the European Cup final between Liverpool and Juventus in Brussels. A crowd of English hooligans chased some Italian supporters, who ended up tightly packed against a brick wall with no escape. The brick wall collapsed under the pressure, and thirty-eight Juventus fans died. As a result, English soccer clubs (but not the national team) were banned from competing in Europe indefinitely. They were only reinstated in 1990. Since then, the most visible hooliganism in England has been associated with the national team, whose fans have engaged in pitched battles with police in the 1992 European Championship in Sweden ("The Battle of Malmo"), the World Cup 1998 in France (most notably in the streets of Marseille, where they smashed up shops and bars), and at Charleroi during the 2000 European Championship in Belgium. Yet when England hosted the European Championship in 1996 there was almost no violence.

England's reputation notwithstanding, soccer violence is to be found in almost every country where soccer is played. According to Hubert Dwertmann and Bero Rigauer, "Fights before matches, spectators interfering with play, the abandonment of matches and attacks on the referee were all common forms of behavior" in German village soccer in the 1950s.[72] Even before this, a pitch invasion in 1931 at a match between Hertha Berlin and Fuerth resulted in a severe injury to a visiting player.[73] Widespread concern about hooligans at German matches started to emerge in the late 1970s. Most of the major clubs attracted their own hardcore group of thugs who fought pitched battles on the day of a major match. Traditionally, Germany's greatest soccer rivalry was with the Netherlands, and disorder usually followed any match between the teams. In German domestic soccer, a fan was shot dead in a battle between Leipzig and Berlin supporters in 1991, and 268 fans were arrested before a relegation decider between Cologne and Bayer Leverkusen in 1998. One study estimated that 10 percent of all German fans are involved in soccer violence.[74] At the 1998 World Cup, German fans brutally assaulted a French policeman and left him with brain damage.

In the Netherlands, hooliganism has followed a similar pattern, first noticed in the 1970s and increasingly organized since then. The technology of combat has been advanced with the arrival of cell phones, which rival gangs have used to set up fights away from the police:"[One] fight took place on a day that no game was planned, it had nothing to do with winning or losing a match, it was orchestrated only to fight and to show which team had the 'best fans.' The fans decided where and when to fight over their mobile phones and by the time the police arrived it was already too late; one Ajax-fan was killed."[75]

In Italy, disturbances at soccer matches have a long history. Pitch invasions, forcing matches to be suspended, have been known since at least the 1960s. At the end of the 1960s, hardcore groups of supporters known as "Ultras" began to emerge. These fans occupied a particular area of the stadium, specialized in noisy and aggressive support of their team, and soon acquired a reputation for violence. By the 1970s, stabbings had become a regular feature, and in the 1979 Rome derby a fan of the Lazio team was killed by a firework aimed at him by a Roma fan. Murders continued in the 1980s, mostly in matches between local rivals, but the numbers diminished during the 1990s.[76]

One of the most notorious and destructive provocations of soccer-related violence occurred following the World Cup qualifying playoff between Honduras and El Salvador in July 1969. The political backdrop to this conflagration was that El Salvador (with a population density eight times that of Honduras) had increasing numbers of emigrants living in Honduras. The Honduran economy was struggling, and unemployment was high. Many Hondurans believed that the 300,000-odd Salvadoran immigrants were taking their jobs.

The three-game playoff began in Tegucigalpa, Honduras, with the Honduran team prevailing 1-0 on a last-minute goal. The second game was played in San Salvador, El Salvador. The night before the game, the hotel where the Honduran team was sleeping was set on fire. The team was transferred to a new hotel, only to be greeted by all-night serenaders beneath their windows. Needless to say, the Salvador team took the second game, but Hondurans took out their frustrations on some of the Salvadoran immigrants living in Tegucigalpa.

The rubber match was played in Mexico City, where the Salvadoran team went ahead in the game's last moments. A violent riot ensued on the streets of Mexico City and military skirmishes broke out on the El Salvador–Honduras border. Soon Salvadoran troops penetrated into Honduras, and four days of heavy fighting followed. The Organization of American States persuaded each side to sign a cease-fire, but not before 2,000–3,000 people had been killed and more than double that number wounded. Over 100,000 Salvadorans were expelled from Honduras, the border was shut, and hostilities lingered on.

South America is also not immune to the disease of soccer violence. On May 13, 1998, Judge Victor Perotta suspended all matches in the premier division of the Argentine Football Association after three fans were killed in a shoot-out with the police outside a stadium in Buenos Aires. According to the newspaper *Clarin*, there had been 137 recorded football fatalities, eighty of them in the previous five years alone.[77] Rioting at a soccer match is recorded in Argentina in 1916, when a match between an Argentine and a Uruguayan team had to be discontinued. Murder is recorded as early as 1924, when, following defeat in the South American Championship, an Argentine fan killed a Uruguayan fan.[78]

In more recent times, the cult of violence is associated with the "Barras Bravas," found mainly in Buenos Aires. These are paramilitary groups of soccer fans whose aim is to disrupt matches, primarily with the intention of intimidating opposition players, fans, and the referee. A large proportion of soccer deaths in Argentina have been attributed to the Barras Bravas, including "accidents" such as the crushing to death of seventy-four people on a stairway whose exit had been closed at a match between River Plate and Boca Juniors on June 23, 1968. The Barras Bravas get results, and for this reason many believe that club directors themselves pay off the leaders to create the conditions that will allow their teams to win.[79]

The greatest loss of life at any single soccer match occurred at a Peru-Argentina Olympic qualifying match on May 24, 1964, in Lima. Two minutes before the end of the game the referee disallowed a Peruvian goal, and two people tried to attack the referee; the police threw gas to contain disturbances, but 328 people died in the ensuing panic as the crowd tried to escape from the stadium.[80]

The litany of soccer violence is as tedious as its consequences are unpleasant. But two features stand out. First, outside England the violence is concentrated on local opponents rather than international rivals. This cannot be said to be a consequence of internationalist sentiment among soccer fans. One explanation advanced by scholars is that in most countries the local fans hate each other so much that they are incapable of uniting against a common enemy. Second, in most instances the number of deaths due to a violent incident is usually magnified by disrepair of the stadium: walls and stands collapsing, exits too narrow so that fans are crushed, fires started for some reason or other that turn into a conflagration. All of this testifies to the relative neglect of the facilities by soccer authorities in most countries. It is hard to disagree with Orwell's analysis of soccer as a promoter of animosity. The political exploitation and violence are clearly a byproduct of the intense passions that the "the world's game" excites.

In retrospect, there are probably many reasons that explain why baseball failed to spread when soccer did. Yet it is tempting to argue that the spread of soccer, its use as political tool, and its descent into violence are all connected. By contrast, baseball may have benefited from remaining largely an American phenomenon.

There is no reason to think that there was anything inevitable about the spread of soccer. Soccer's success may simply have been a function of timing: between 1870 and 1910 the overseas presence of the British was so great that people in practically every city of the world were exposed to soccer. Had American economic dominance materialized forty years earlier, then perhaps baseball rather than soccer would have become the world's sport. Moreover, had the Americans spent less time trying to persuade the British to play the game (the British never put much effort into converting Americans to either cricket or soccer) and concentrated on other countries, it might have spread further.

In any event, apart from episodic evangelists such as Spalding, until recently Americans have never seemed to be much interested in the spread of their games. Britain is a small island, and most of British history involves contact of one kind or another with other peoples. The American melting pot is a world unto itself. In the realm of culture, it is generally more concerned with its own comings and goings than with the wider world around it. If other nations wanted to play baseball, then that was up to them. Certainly if there was a business opportunity, then team owners were interested. But the tours of 1874, 1889, and 1914 showed that no significant business opportunities existed.

By contrast, during the period that soccer spread, the British elites had a strong interest in building friendly ties with the wealthy and powerful elites of the countries with which they did business. Sport proved a successful medium for building these ties. The British elites were not interested in building soccer as a business, and so had no need to make a profit from playing the game. Indeed, they wanted to keep money out of it altogether.

Not that the sport as it developed was exactly what the English gentlemen had in mind. When they played "international" sport, they tended to think more of competition between ethnic groups.[81] The rise of nationalism at the end of the nineteenth century in part contributed to the outbreak of World War I, after which many new nations were created out of the old empires, including some new and unstable combinations (for example, Yugoslavia and Czechoslovakia). The identity of ethnicity with nationhood and state-hood raised the stakes in international sporting competition. Winning became an important part of national and political self-esteem, betraying the internationalist ideals of de Coubertin and his followers. That soccer has held such a grip on the peoples of the world reflects in part its capacity to give flesh to national rivalries: Netherlands versus Germany, Argentina versus Brazil, Spain versus Portugal.

Just as such matches are capable of representing underlying international tensions, so the violence of soccer can reflect genuine local rivalries. Some of these are regional and linguistic (Real Madrid for the Castilians, Barcelona for the Catalans, and Athletic Bilbao for the Basques). Sometimes the rivalries reflect the power struggles between particular cities (such as Marseilles and Bordeaux in France), other times between districts within cities (Boca Juniors and River Plate in Buenos Aires). Some soccer rivalries reflect religious rivalries, as between Glasgow Celtic (Catholic) and Glasgow Rangers (Protestant). Everywhere soccer has come to be a powerful symbol of conflict. In the context of the conflicts where soccer has become a symbol, it does not seem surprising that it has become synonymous with violence.

If soccer has not yet become a popular spectator sport in the United States, why didn't the society's conflicts invade baseball stadiums? There is, in fact, a modest history of crowd disturbances at and around baseball games, but nothing on the scale seen at soccer matches in the rest of the world.[82] It can hardly be said that the United States is a less divided or less violent society: the crime and homicide statistics testify otherwise. One explanation may have to do with the location of soccer stadiums and ball-parks. In most of Europe and South America stadiums are located in the centers of big cities, often in areas that have become run-down and crime-ridden, deterring many traditional fans, especially families, from attending and leaving the field clear for young men, overwhelmingly the perpetrators of soccer violence. During the 1960s and 1970s, when many of the same trends were seen in American inner cities, many ballparks were moved to the edge of town, away from the run-down areas and into spaces that would attract a desirable clientele. Since 1992, when stadiums began returning to urban centers, many have been built in redeveloped areas. Moreover, through extensive construction of classy luxury suites, club seats, and lounges, they have catered to high-income fans and executives.

Baseball has always been a business, whereas the owners of soccer clubs have often been motivated more by social and political goals. For most soccer fans, winning has always been more important than the surroundings at the stadium, and owners have been more concerned about investing in players than in facilities. The contrast between the quality of seating, food, and beverage at a baseball game and a typical soccer match is breathtaking. While the owner of a ballpark maximizes the opportunities for spectators to spend, the owners of soccer stadiums seem almost to have minimized such opportunities. Food and drink are not usually served to spectators in their seats, and anyone foolish enough to get in line for a drink or hotdog at halftime is likely to miss the opening ten minutes of the second period.[83]

The very fact that a baseball park is a place of business means that owners would be very unlikely to allow any serious violence to enter the game, any more than Sam Walton would have stood by if hooligans had chosen Walmart for their Saturday night punch-up.[84] With only limited interest in the moneymaking opportunities, many owners of soccer teams found little reason to discourage hooliganism, and as we have described, some may have actively encouraged it.

As in so many things, the United States is the exception. Baseball is mostly a peaceful business unfractured by violence, and largely unsullied by international competition. It is tempting to suggest that this insularity is the greatest guarantor of peace in baseball. For in the end, all Americans know that while they might earnestly desire their team to win, and even heartily long for the defeat of their rivals at the hand of any other team, it is ultimately a game played primarily by and for Americans, one nation, under God, indivisible.

CHAPTER FOUR

Pay for Play

The Development of the Baseball and Soccer Labor Markets

Alex Rodriguez and David Beckham have a lot in common. Both were born in the summer of 1975 and both were precocious talents, A-Rod debuting for the Seattle Mariners at age 18, while Becks first played for Manchester United at age 17. Of course, both are prodigiously skilled athletes. But in addition, both have film-star looks and squeaky-clean private lives, which make them among the most attractive billboards in advertising.[1] Both earn sums of money that are almost unimaginable to their fans. Rodriguez signed a world-record ten-year $252 million deal (plus bonuses) in December 2000 and is currently said to make over $50 million a year, including endorsements. Beckham was estimated in 2004 to be the highest-earning soccer star in the world with an annual income of around $30 million.

And in 2003 both played for clubs that decided they no longer wanted them. The Texas Rangers couldn't afford to keep up the payments on A-Rod's contract and, after an extended but ultimately unsuccessful courtship with the Red Sox, traded him to the Yankees on February 17, 2004. By contrast, Manchester United, which generated more revenue than any other team in the world that year, could easily afford to pay Beckham's relatively modest $8 million salary. There were, though, a number of reasons for wanting to offload him. He had had several well-reported bust-ups with the team's manager, Sir Alex Ferguson, who had even benched Beckham for several games; his celebrity wife, former Spice Girl Posh (Victoria Adams), was reported to want to move away from Manchester; and some said the quality of his play did not match his superstar image. But another reason was that the Manchester United business wanted to cash in.

On June 17, 2003, it was announced that Real Madrid had done a deal with Manchester United that could end up yielding $45 million for the English soccer club. According to newspaper accounts, Beckham would receive the same $8 million salary he had been getting. So what was Manchester United being paid for? In soccer, unlike baseball, when a player is traded the old employment contract is torn up and a new one is signed.[2] At the transfer date in 2003, Beckham had nearly two years to run on his old contract, and the transfer fee was compensation to Manchester United for tearing up this contract. To anyone who has grown up with the soccer system this is normal business, but to a baseball fan this must seem peculiar.

For a start, it's not obvious that Manchester United needed any compensation. Sure, the team lost a great player, but when the contract was torn up, so was its obligation to pay him his salary. Certainly, neither Manchester United nor any other soccer club would admit to paying players less than they were worth. Yet the logic of the transfer fee as compensation to the club giving up the player suggests just this: the player must be getting paid less than the value he produces. Players over the age of 23 now have freedom of contract in soccer, so when they sign a deal the only way they can get paid less than what they are worth is if they have a lousy agent, which no one has ever said of David Beckham.[3] Moreover, Manchester United's directors were willing to trade Beckham and made no great play of wanting to keep him, so it's not clear how they thought they were losing out.

A different way of looking at the question is to ask why Real Madrid was willing to pay so much to Beckham's former employers at Manchester United. Beckham's new contract is for four years and so is worth about $32 million—just over 40 percent of the total value of the deal. Why wouldn't Barcelona, a club that was desperate to buy Beckham, offer him more money and offer less to Manchester United? As owner of the contract,

Manchester United might sue if Beckham joined another club without its agreement. Then Manchester United could take an action for breach of contract, but what kind of compensation would a judge agree to?

In practice, the court would be likely to examine the value of the benefit to Manchester United of employing Beckham and the cost in salary. If, following lengthy expert testimony by sports agents and economists, it was agreed that there was a gap between Beckham's value and his remuneration, it would likely be small. It is hard to imagine damages of more than $10 million, and certainly nothing like the $45 million transfer fee paid by Real Madrid.

Yet another way to think about it is to ask why Beckham didn't just wait out the two years on his contract and then sign as a free agent. Granted that soccer careers are shorter and more injury-prone than baseball careers, it still seems hard to imagine that Beckham would not be worth at least $50 million in 2005,[4] which, added to the salary he would have continued to draw at Manchester United for two years, would amount to about twice what he actually got.

At the very least, the remarkable contracts of baseball's and soccer's poster boys raise a lot of questions about how the labor markets function in these two sports. In this chapter we examine how the labor markets in baseball and soccer have developed and how they operate. Many of the most important features of player labor markets can be traced back to the origins of professional play. In baseball, the moguls of the National League and its competitors set out to create a system that would give the owners control over player careers and limit player earnings. Only in the last quarter of the twentieth century was the players' union able to win the concessions that have led to the enormous player earnings we see today. A similar story emerges in soccer, and there are strong parallels between baseball's reserve clause system and the control of labor contracts in soccer. Like baseball players, soccer players have won something akin to free agency in recent years, due more to the operation of competition policy in the European Union than to strong labor unions. While player remuneration in baseball and soccer at the highest level is now roughly comparable, some differences continue to exist in the way each system operates, as the above example of player trading shows.

The Development of Baseball's Labor Market

Fans often grow so accustomed to their sport's institutions that there is a tendency to think that they were born as they are in nature. In baseball, as in soccer, the labor market rules were imposed by each sport's administrators in response to the exigencies of the period.

The Reserve Clause and Minor Leagues

When the National League was founded in 1876, there was no formal division between "major" and "minor" league baseball. The International League, for instance, although organized on mutualist principles, thought of itself as playing at the same level as the NL. Generally, however, the NL had teams in larger cities and with deeper financial backing than the teams in other leagues. When a National League owner was informed of a star player in another league, he would try to lure the star to his team. Sometimes, after the objection of the other league, the NL would enter into an alliance agreement that recognized each league's reserve rights over its players. In these instances, the NL owner would compensate the owner from the other league for his "reserve" rights (that is, presumed property rights over the player.) One way or another, the better players found their way to the NL (or the American Association), and the distance between the "major" (top-level) and "minor" (lower-level) leagues grew.

We have already seen how the magnates of the National League sought to gain control over the labor market for player services during its early years. From the institution of the reserve clause in 1879, when five players per team were put on reserve, to 1887, when the reserve list was expanded to fourteen, the owners began to curtail labor market freedom and thereby artificially suppress salaries and limit player mobility. Occasionally a rival league emerged that temporarily gave players competitive options and paid higher salaries. In each instance, however, the NL was successful in either defeating or merging with its competition, and player salaries fell back to earlier levels. In the early 1890s, after the defeat of the Players' League and the American Association, the NL's reserve list was expanded again to include all of the players on the major league roster. While all NL clubs had at least sixteen players under reserve, many had more, and Cincinnati had as many as thirty-three.[5]

With an expanding number of players under reserve and without an active rival league in the early 1890s, the NL teams, along with cutting player salaries, were able to reduce the number of players on their active rosters to thirteen. The nonactive (major league) reserve players were placed with minor league clubs, paid only minor league salaries, and made available when the need arose to replace an injured or poorly performing player. From the perspective of the minor league clubs, however, this practice was an abuse of their relationship with the majors. The minor league club, having no reserve rights on such players, received no buyout payment when these play-ers went to the majors and had to endure excessive roster shuffling.

In addition to restocking the existing major league teams, the minor leagues were also the potential source of players for new rival leagues. In the late nineteenth and early twentieth centuries, the prospective threat from competing leagues was real, and periodically this gave the minors significant leverage. Thus it was in the NL's, and after 1900 also the AL's, interest to reach a peaceful accommodation with the highest minor league circuits. This led to a series of agreements over the years that were often honored in the breach.

The major league clubs were interested in (a) having nonactive reserve players so they could keep at a minimum the number of players to whom they paid a major league salary; (b) having as much flexibility as possible at the lowest possible cost to move players up and down; (c) having access to rising star players; (d) controlling as much of the potential talent pool as possible to prevent the emergence of a rival league; and (e) gaining a com-petitive advantage over the other clubs.

The minor league clubs, in contrast, were interested in (a) having stable rosters during each playing season; (b) having more reserved players on their teams whom they could sell to major league clubs; (c) getting the best possible price for their reserved players; and (d) keeping their payroll costs as low as possible.

These contrasting goals, of course, created conflict between the major and minor leagues.[6] The 1892 agreement between the NL and the minor leagues provided that the NL would respect the reserve lists of the minor league clubs in exchange for the right to draft players from these lists at a fixed price at season's end. The agreed price was $1,000 for a player from a top Class A league and $500 for a player from a Class B league. Class A was also given the right to draft from Class B. Below Class B minors, reserve lists were not recognized.[7]

Some Class A teams, however, sold their players off before the season ended to get a better price (higher than the stipulated draft price) for their best talent. Yet some NL teams avoided the purchase of minor leaguers altogether through unwritten "working agreements" that allowed for on-loan players to move up and down. Other NL clubs entered into cross-ownership agreements with each other, in part to avoid competing over minor league talent.[8]

Still another strategy was followed by John T. Brush. Brush contemporaneously owned the NL Cincinnati club and the minor league Western Association's Indianapolis team and frequently juggled their rosters to his competitive advantage. Brush sent his major leaguers down to Indianapolis to thrash the competitors of his minor league club, then brought them back up, along with some Indianapolis players, to defeat Cincinnati's NL opponents.

These schemes notwithstanding, the 1892 agreement provoked little conflict between the major and minor league for nine years. Then, before the 1901 season, Ban Johnson's American League (AL) declared its intention to be a major league—that is, to hire the top player talent and establish its own deals with subordinate leagues. Competition for players between the AL and the NL heated up. Since the AL had never signed an agreement with the minors, it felt free to ignore their reserve lists and raid their teams. The NL felt compelled to follow suit. The minors not only lost players, but they had to raise the salaries of the remaining players in an effort to retain them. Finally, in September 1901, the NL formally repudiated its agreement with the minors.

The beleaguered minor leagues responded by coming together to form the National Association of Professional Baseball Leagues (commonly referred to as the National Association) in late October 1901. The new National Association called for the recognition of its teams' reservation rights as well as team payroll limits for each of its circuits.

The 1903 National Agreement between the NL and AL also included the minor leagues (although the minors were not represented on the new governing body, the National Commission, which consisted of the president of the NL, the president of the AL, and one "independent" commissioner). As a concession to the National Association, this agreement banned "farming," meaning the binding transfer of on-loan players between major and minor league teams. The farming ban was intended, on the one hand, to limit the ability of rich teams to hoard player talent and, on the other, to enable minor league teams to fully benefit from the sale of their reserved players.

Major league clubs increasingly found ways around the farming ban. One method was to use "optional assignments" or "options." Options allowed a major league team to sell a player to a minor league team and then repurchase the player at a later time. The optional assignment was controlled by waiver rules, which allowed a player to be claimed by another major league club before he was optioned to the minors. In 1907 the National Commission allowed a particular player to be optioned only once per year and limited a team to eight optioned players per year. In 1908 the commission set a minimum repurchase price of an optioned player at $300.

In 1905 the New York Giants pioneered another loophole in the farming ban: the so-called working agreement. The working agreement usually provided a minor league club with financial assistance and help assembling its roster. In exchange, the major league club gained the right to exercise fixed-price options at season's end. The National Commission judged the working-agreement relationship to be compatible with the no-farming rule.

Another way around the no-farming rule was for the major league club to draft and put on reserve increasing numbers of players. By 1909 most teams had more than forty players on reserve, and eight teams had more than fifty. In 1912 a new National Agreement limited the number of reserved players to thirty-five per team, and to only twenty-five in mid-season between May 15 and August 20.

These various restrictions led two major league clubs, the Brooklyn Dodgers and Cleveland Indians, to follow John T. Brush's example and purchase minor league teams. But in 1913 the National Commission banned this practice as well.

The decade between 1901 and 1911 was a good one for the minor leagues. The number of minor league circuits grew from thirteen in 1901 to forty-nine in 1911: of these, five were at AA (highest) or A level; eight were at B; ten at C; and twenty-six at D (lowest). The advent of the Federal League during 1914–15, however, produced a new raid on minor league rosters and higher salaries. One player affected by these raids was Babe Ruth.

Ruth's story is illustrative. Jack Dunn owned the minor league Baltimore Orioles of the International League. Unlike other minor league owners, Dunn ran his team to win games and pennants, not to sell off his stars to the major leagues. By reputation, Dunn paid his players major league salaries and would not sell them to a major league club, if at all, until the twilight of their careers.[9]

Then along came the Federal League (FL). The FL had a team in Baltimore. Because of its major league status, the Baltimore FL club handily outdrew Dunn's Orioles. On April 22, 1914, in fact, there were 100 people in the stands at the Orioles game, while the FL club attracted some 5,000 fans to its game. The Orioles' pitcher that game was 19-year-old Babe Ruth, making his first professional start. Ruth, who had been signed by Dunn out of Baltimore's St. Mary's Industrial School earlier that year for $600, pitched a six-hit shutout that day.

Despite the Orioles' strong performance in 1914 (forty-seven wins and twenty-two losses through July 4), the team was eclipsed in popularity by the FL Baltimore club. In financial difficulty, Dunn began to run his team like other minor league operators. Dunn sold Ruth and two other players to the Boston Red Sox for $18,000. The Federal League was gone after one more year. Ruth, of course, remained.

The pressures on Jack Dunn's Orioles were felt throughout the minors, and the number of minor league circuits fell to twenty-eight in 1914. More pressure was put on the minors during World War I, when the AL and NL again raided their talent in order to replace major leaguers who had been drafted into the armed forces.

Teams found ad hoc ways to acquire players, and there were often disputes. One key dispute was over minor league pitcher Scott Perry. In August 1918 the NL Boston Braves arranged with Atlanta of the International League to purchase Perry for $2,800 on a thirty-day trial basis, with a down payment of $500. Perry, however, did not report to the Braves, but instead jumped to an outlaw league (a nonsignatory to the major-minor league agreement). The National Commission ordered Perry to return to the Boston Braves, but the Atlanta team made a new deal, this time with the AL's Philadelphia Athletics. The Athletics' Connie Mack, with the blessing of AL president Ban Johnson, refused to send Perry to the Braves. The NL president, John Tener, resigned in protest, and the National Commission seemed to have lost its authority.

Disorganization only grew when players returned from the war for the 1919 season. When the minors demanded higher prices for their drafted players, the AL and NL refused. The National Association responded by unilaterally suspending the majors' draft and optional assignment rights.

Meanwhile, with the exercise of effective authority by the National Commission on the wane, gambling at the ballpark proliferated. Gamblers were making overtures to the players to fix games. With salaries deflated by the reserve clause and the absence of competition from a rival league, several players found the allure of gamblers' payoffs irresistible. To be sure, it was not only their stagnating salaries, but also their sense of mistreatment that led some players to rebel. Players had no job security and paid for their own travel when they were demoted to the minors. Their incipient union, the Players' Fraternity, had been defeated by the owners in 1917.

In relative terms, perhaps the worst-treated players were on the Chicago White Sox. Their owner, Charles Comiskey, was a notorious penny-pincher. White Sox player salaries were below those on other teams. Joe Jackson, one of the best hitters in baseball history, was purchased by the White Sox from Cleveland for $65,000 but never made more than $6,000 a year.[10] Comiskey even made the players wash their own uniforms. Eliot Asinof in *Eight Men Out* tells the story of pitcher Eddie Cicotte being promised a $10,000 bonus if he won thirty games in 1917. When Cicotte reached twenty-nine wins, according to Asinof, Comiskey had him benched.[11]

The White Sox players were primed for a bribe when they reached the World Series in 1919. Players were offered between $10,000 and $20,000 to lose key games. Although the players were acquitted in a jury trial, baseball's new commissioner, Judge Kenesaw Mountain Landis, was determined to clean up the game and enforce a level of discipline that the National Commission never was able to attain. Landis banned the eight accused White Sox players, including Joe Jackson and Eddie Cicotte, from the game. Landis then went on to ban fourteen others before 1927.

Whereas Landis was successful in cleaning up baseball's image in the 1920s, he proved less effective in implementing his vision for the minor leagues. Following the minors' suspension of the draft in 1919, prices for minor leaguers rose quickly. The NL and AL owners responded by suspending the no-farming rules, which, among other things, allowed major league team owners to once again acquire minor league clubs. Then, in 1921, they reinstated the draft. The new draft raised the top price to $5,000 and permitted individual minor league clubs to opt out of the draft system; that is, they could protect their own reserved players from the draft if they agreed not to select players from lower classification levels. Three minor league circuits chose to opt out of the draft on this basis, and the sale prices for their players skyrocketed, with the top prospects commanding prices in the $70,000–$100,000 range for the rest of the 1920s.

With the escalation of prices for drafting or purchasing minor league talent and the abolition of no-farming rules, the St. Louis Cardinals' Branch Rickey went to work developing baseball's first extensive farm system.

Rickey's idea was to extend the working arrangements and cross ownership that existed between the majors and top classification minors down to the lowest classification levels. By establishing a vast scouting and player development system, Rickey's strategy was to allow a relatively poor club like the Cardinals to procure top talent more cheaply, as well as to develop strong prospects to sell or trade to other teams. By 1928 Rickey's Cards owned five minor league teams and had working agreements with many more. By 1937 the Cards' farm system peaked at thirty-three clubs, controlling almost 700 players.

The Cards' increasing success at the major league level led other clubs to attempt to emulate Rickey's system. By 1929 major league franchises owned twenty-seven minor league teams. During the 1930s, both the Dodgers and the Yankees built extensive farm systems, though they never became as large as the Cardinals'.

Commissioner Landis was not a fan of large farm systems.[12] As an old trustbuster, Landis believed that farming had inherent monopolistic tendencies because it imposed severe restrictions on the labor-market mobility of young prospects. Landis proposed a universal draft that would allow any team to pick an attractive minor league player, preventing him from getting trapped in one team's system because of the presence of a star player at his position on the major league team. Landis's protestations and recommendations, however, got nowhere with the owners.

After the disruptions of the Great Depression and World War II, the market for minor leaguers and amateurs took off once again. By 1951 total amateur signing bonuses had risen to $4.5 million, or 14 percent of combined Major League Baseball revenues. At these prices, Rickey's farm-system model proved too expensive. Baseball's minor leagues, which had grown to fifty-nine circuits and 464 clubs by 1949, began to cut back, first to 324 clubs in 1952 and then to 147 clubs by 1961.[13] Complementing the cost factor, minor league contraction was also fostered by (a) the spread of television, which allowed many fans to stay at home to watch their favorite major league team, and (b) suburbanization and the spread of the automobile, which made it easier to travel to the big-league ballpark.

MLB also tried to forestall the bonus wars among teams for amateur players. Various rules passed to this end in the 1950s had only negligible effect. In 1965, however, MLB introduced its reverse-order amateur draft, which granted exclusive rights to a single team to sign its drafted amateur.

Without competition to sign players, bonuses stagnated. The highest sign-
ing bonus in 1964 was $205,000, paid by the California Angels to Rick
Reichardt. This sum was not to be exceeded until 1980, when the New York
Mets signed Darryl Strawberry for $210,000.

As salaries exploded with free agency after 1976, amateur signing
bonuses also increased. Top bonuses today reach as high as $10 million.
Although teams do not compete for a drafted player, the player can sit out a
year and reenter the draft. This gives the player and his agent some bargaining leverage.

The Reserve Clause and Free Agency

Another crucial piece to baseball's labor market, of course, is the evolution of its reserve clause and the eventual introduction of free agency. For
several decades, baseball's reserve clause was protected by its judicially conferred exemption from the nation's antitrust laws.

Baseball's antitrust exemption dates back to 1922, when the U.S.
Supreme Court in *Federal Baseball* held that baseball was not involved in
interstate commerce and therefore not subject to the Sherman and Clayton
Acts. Antitrust laws are intended to foster open markets and competition. As
a monopolist, Major League Baseball has acted to restrain open competition
in a number of ways, such as granting teams territorial monopolies and
reserve rights over players. Such restrictive practices by MLB are shielded
from legal action by its presumed exemption from the antitrust laws. Baseball is the only professional team sport in the United States that carries such
an exemption.[14]

The exemption has been challenged in several legal cases over the years,
two of which rose to the Supreme Court. The first was the George Toolson
case. Toolson was a minor leaguer who refused an assignment to report to a
new team and filed suit. He claimed that the club's order under the reserve
system violated antitrust laws. The lower courts, basing their arguments on
the Supreme Court's decision in 1922, ruled against Toolson. Toolson
appealed, and in 1953 the Supreme Court reaffirmed its 1922 decision,
though it left open the question of the wisdom of its earlier ruling. The
Court's one-paragraph ruling in *Toolson* read in part: "We think that if there
are evils in this field which now warrant application to it of the antitrust
laws it should be by legislation. Without reexamination of the underlying

issues, the judgments below are affirmed on the authority of *Federal Baseball*." The Court seemed to be suggesting that it was the duty of Congress to undo the damage that was done originally by the Court.

The Curt Flood case was the second to make it to the Supreme Court, in 1972. Flood was a good-hitting, slick-fielding centerfielder from the Cardinals who resisted a trade to the Phillies late in his career. He asked baseball's Commissioner Bowie Kuhn to intercede and disallow the trade. Kuhn refused and Flood sued, arguing that the game's labor markets were not free and that he was being treated like chattel. The court voted 5 to 3 to uphold *Federal Baseball*, arguing *stare decisis* (let the old decision stand). In effect, too many long-term commitments had been based on the assumption of baseball's exemption to overturn it. Nonetheless, the Court called the 1922 decision "an aberration," and Justice Blackmun's rendering of the decision created ambiguity as to the scope of the exemption. This ambiguity, in turn, has led to disparate judicial interpretations in cases since the early 1990s, and the issue of whether the exemption applies to all or only parts of the baseball business remains unresolved.

That said, until 1998 it was always clear that the exemption's principal purpose was to protect baseball's reserve clause.[15] Curt Flood's challenge to the reserve clause came but three years after Marvin Miller had taken over as the head of the baseball players' association and begun to fashion it into a strong union.[16] Miller had managed to sign an agreement with the owners in February 1968 that established a formal grievance procedure, an increase of the minimum salary from $6,000 to $10,000, and a joint study group on the future of the reserve clause. More important, the union supported Flood's suit and began to focus on gaining free agency.

A few months after the June 1972 Supreme Court decision in the Flood case, the union was back at the bargaining table. The players now tried to win in collective bargaining what the courts would not grant them. The owners offered a compromise: they would grant free agency to players with either (a) five years major league experience if their team offered them less than $30,000 in salary or (b) eight years of service if their team offered them less than $40,000 in salary. Although this offer was far from acceptable to the union, the principle of free agency had been established on the bargaining agenda. Rather than accept the owners' paltry offer on free agency, the players bargained for a system of salary arbitration to take effect after the 1973 season.

Under the system of final-offer arbitration, a neutral party decides between the last offer of the owner and the last offer of the players. The arbitrator has to pick one salary or the other; he cannot pick a compromise figure between the two. This system, which still prevails today in modified form, is intended to give each side an incentive to make a reasonable offer, lest the arbitrator pick the offer of the other side. More often than not, the two sides reach agreement before the case ever reaches arbitration. At the time, players gained arbitration rights after two years of major league service.

Catfish Hunter was an All-Star pitcher for the Oakland Athletics. In 1974 he signed a contract with team owner Charles Finley that called for half of Hunter's salary to be paid into an annuity. When Hunter discovered that Finley had failed to make payments into the annuity during the 1974 season, breaching his contract, Hunter filed a grievance. Arbitrator Peter Seitz ruled that Finley's violation had voided the contract and declared Hunter to be a free agent. Hunter then signed a lucrative multiyear contract with the Yankees, making him the only player in MLB with a multiyear deal in 1975.

Hunter's victory emboldened Marvin Miller to essay another assault on the reserve clause, this time with pitchers Dave McNally of the Montreal Expos and Andy Messersmith of the Los Angeles Dodgers. McNally and Messersmith were dissatisfied with their 1975 contract offers and refused to sign new contracts. The clubs then exercised their rights and signed up the two players for an obligatory option year without the players' signatures. But when the 1975 season ended, McNally and Messersmith claimed they had played out their option year and were no longer under reserve. This unprecedented challenge to the reserve system went before arbitrator Seitz, who found in favor of the players. After firing Seitz, the owners brought suit first in federal district court and then in federal appeals court. Each court rejected the owners' appeal, the last in March 1976.

Four months later, the owners and players reached a new collective bargaining agreement that introduced professional team sports' first system of unrestricted free agency. The fundamentals of the system provided that after six years of major league service a player attained free-agency status; that is, if his existing contract were up, he could offer his services to any team and thereby receive competitive bids. Between two and six years of service, a player had salary arbitration rights. Before two years, the player was essentially under reserve and captive to his team.[17]

While the details have been tweaked over the years, the fundamentals of the system have remained intact. Average player salaries have risen steadily, from $51,501 in 1976 to $2.37 million in 2003.[18] In 2004, however, average salaries fell by 3 percent to $2.30 million—the first time they had dropped since 1995 and only the second time since 1976.[19] The decrease in 2004 is attributable to a number of factors that were introduced in the 2002 collective bargaining agreement, including increased revenue sharing;[20] a new luxury tax on high team payrolls; a new rule limiting team debt; a requirement that all deferred salaries be fully funded within eighteen months of the year in which they are earned; and a new rule that gives a team unable to sign its first-round draft pick a replacement pick in the same spot the following year.

After baseball introduced free agency, the other major team sports in the United States followed. But free agency in football and basketball are circumscribed by a salary cap, and unrestricted free agency in hockey does not occur until a player turns 31 years of age.[21] As we shall see, European soccer began to practice its own form of free agency after the Bosman decision in December 1995.

The Internationalization of Baseball's Labor Market

The final piece of baseball's labor market is its rapid internationalization. While a few Latin American ballplayers (some of whom were dark skinned) played in the National League in the nineteenth century, Major League Baseball did not integrate until 1947, with Jackie Robinson, and did not include significant numbers of Latin American ballplayers until the 1950s and 1960s.[22]

One factor that accelerated the employment of Latin American players was the introduction of baseball's amateur draft in 1965. The amateur draft applies only to players who reside in the United States, Puerto Rico, or Canada. Players from elsewhere in the Caribbean and the Far East have never been subject to the draft. They have entered MLB through competitive recruitment efforts of individual teams.

Thus, after 1965, MLB teams had free reign to scout, sign, and develop players only from outside North America. Teams began to put extra resources into this effort and to bring along new Latin ballplayers. These efforts began expanding in the 1990s as teams opened up scouting bureaus and training camps in the Dominican Republic, Venezuela, and elsewhere, and hired special assistants to work at finding and developing Latin talent.[23]

At the beginning of the 2004 baseball season there were 227 major leaguers who were born outside the United States. The two largest sources of these players were the Dominican Republic with seventy-nine players and Venezuela with forty-five. Major league rosters included twenty-five players per team plus eighty players on the disabled list on opening day in 2004. Thus foreign-born players constituted 27.3 percent of the 830 major league players. This figure is expected to rise in the coming years. Of the 6,117 minor league players at the beginning of the 2004 season, 47.6 percent were foreign-born. These players are the source for future major leaguers.

Of the foreign-born players on major league rosters in 2004, ten came from Japan and four came from South Korea. Although these numbers are small, ten years ago there were no players from either country in the major leagues. The first such player was Hideo Nomo, who signed with the Dodgers in 1995 and was selected as rookie of the year. In Japan, players don't earn free-agency status until after nine years in their professional league (Nippon Professional Baseball, or NPB), and even then there are a variety of restrictions. Nomo gained the right to sign with the Dodgers because, following a salary dispute with his Japanese team, he signed retirement papers.

Nomo's early success led MLB scouts to pour into Japan searching for the next bargain. In 1996 the Chiba Lotte Marines of the NPB reached an agreement with the San Diego Padres for annual player exchanges and other forms of cooperation. Fireballing righthander Hideki Irabu was to be the first player to move to the Padres. Irabu, however, insisted on going to the Yankees, and after extensive wrangling, Irabu's wish was granted.

Two years later, native Dominican Alfonso Soriano left the Japanese league to sign a contract with the Yankees. Soriano's agent, Don Nomura, arranged for Soriano to use the retirement loophole in the Japanese reserve clause. It allowed a player to retire from Japanese baseball and then enter professional baseball in another country.

Japanese baseball soon closed the Soriano loophole, but MLB interest in other Japanese players persisted. In December 1998 MLB and Japanese baseball systematized a player exchange system between the two leagues.[24] The so-called posting system provided that Japanese teams offer a list of eligible players and that interested MLB teams submit a bid for the exclusive right to negotiate with an individual player. If the team with the highest bid reaches an agreement with the player, the bid amount is paid to the Japanese team. Thus, as we shall see presently, similar to soccer's player transfer system, some of the transferred player's value is paid to his former team, and the balance goes to the player.

The Development of Soccer's Labor Market

Generally, professional soccer players the world over have been less well rewarded for their efforts than professional baseball players. One of the most striking contrasts is provided by two famous players who met in London in 1935, Babe Ruth and William "Dixie" Dean. At the time, the Bambino was returning from a baseball tour of Japan, and although he didn't play in England, he was pleased to discover that he was a celebrity in the land of cricket. He even agreed to take some cricket batting practice and discussed the finer points of the two games. The British were aware of Ruth's 1927 sixty-home-run record, and that was the reason for introducing him to Dixie Dean.[25]

Dean was as prodigious a goal scorer as Ruth was a batter. In total, he scored 377 goals in 431 league appearances, principally for the Everton Football Club, between 1925 and 1937, and eighteen goals in sixteen appearances for the England national team between 1927 and 1931. In 1927–28 he set the English record of sixty league goals scored in a season, a record that still stands today and seems unlikely ever to be beaten.[26] Yet when he met the Babe he was earning a mere $2,000 a year, while Ruth's annual salary was in the region of $70,000.

We can explain this difference in several ways. An obvious factor is the relative size of professional soccer and baseball teams at the time. In 1929 the Yankees generated a gross operating income of $1.3 million, while Everton, who won the Football League Championship in his record-breaking year, had an income of only $255,000.[27] New York is about twenty times the size of Liverpool, and both cities divided their loyalties: between two teams in Liverpool and among three teams in New York. This difference in size of the major clubs has a lot to do with the geography and politics of the two sports.

As we have seen, soccer spread around the globe in the early part of the twentieth century, but the dominant form of competition has remained, until the present day, the national league championship. There are almost as many national leagues as there are members of FIFA. In the areas of fan interest and financial muscle, the European leagues of Italy, Spain, England, and (more recently) Germany have tended to dominate. Mid-sized leagues, such as those of the Netherlands, Argentina, and Yugoslavia, have produced both some of the world's greatest players and, from time to time, dominant teams. Even small national leagues, such as those of Norway, Turkey, and Colombia, have produced teams that could compete on a world stage. However, while baseball has a World Series, there is no world club championship in soccer. In recent years FIFA has started to promote the idea of a World Club Championship, and the first such event was held in 2000, amid much fanfare. However, thanks to the opposition of national leagues and associations, the second championship, originally slated for 2001, has been postponed more than once and is currently scheduled for the end of 2005. To this day, almost all club competition takes place at the national level. Although FIFA harbors an ambition to make the World Club Championship an equal to the World Cup, as the world governing body it is also constrained by the interests of its member national associations. In the end, therefore, it will always support the balkanized system of local league monopolies.

The nearest comparison in baseball would be to imagine that the National League had started with teams located in New York State, and then all the other states had created their own leagues under a national system dedicated to the preservation of all fifty state leagues. Of course, in reality the National League grew by expanding its coverage within the world's richest nation. Had soccer developed along the same lines, there would have emerged a single European league and a single South American league, which might one day have merged to create global major league soccer. Instead, the leading clubs of each nation have remained firmly entrenched within their domestic professional leagues. Clubs like Manchester United and Real Madrid that have achieved global recognition are compelled to compete against very small local teams and are deprived of the opportunity to face their foreign peers in regular competition. (As we shall see in the next chapter, however, there are signs that this focus on domestic competition for leading clubs is beginning to break down.)

Again, to make the comparison with baseball, it is as if the Yankees were compelled to play their regular-season games against twenty teams from New York State and the Red Sox against twenty teams from Massachusetts. By forcing the big teams to remain rooted in national competition, the national authorities in soccer have benefited the smaller teams at the expense of the larger rivals. In addition, these restrictions have tended to depress the potential income from soccer in general (by denying or limiting the opportunity for big clubs in different countries to compete) and therefore to limit the funds available to pay players.[28] This argument amounts to saying that soccer clubs could not afford to pay American wages to the star players because the number of fans watching the top teams were generally smaller and the average ticket prices were lower.[29]

Yet there was more to the difference in wages between Babe Ruth and Dixie Dean than scale or wealth. In dollar terms, the Yankees paid out $366,000 in salaries in 1929, while Everton paid out $63,000. Even if we allow for the difference in scale, Dean was as big a star in English soccer as Babe Ruth was in baseball. Ruth received nearly 20 percent of the Yankee payroll, but Dean was paid only 3 percent of Everton's payroll. Had he been paid the same share of the total payroll as Ruth, the soccer player would have been making nearer $15,000 than $2,000. Ruth himself could hardly believe it: "What a racket that is! What's the chances of me buying into one of those football or cricket clubs?"[30]

The difference was the English maximum wage rule. In England, the governance of soccer resided with the Football Association, which claimed jurisdiction over all aspects of the game, including the Football League. The Football League acknowledged the primacy of the Football Association but claimed autonomy over commercial issues. Perhaps not surprisingly, their relationship was uneasy.

Between 1900 and 1960 the English Football League was able to control player salaries by fixing an agreed maximum wage, and that maximum never went far above the earnings of a skilled manual laborer. The story of how the maximum wage came to be imposed is a peculiar one. We have already seen how the gentlemen amateurs of the Football Association resisted or obstructed the rise of commercialism in soccer. Once professionalism was recognized in 1885, player wages rose rapidly, and by the early 1890s the clubs of the new Football League were looking for ways to control them. There is no documentary evidence that they explicitly copied baseball's reserve clause, but the system they invented bore some remarkable similarities. The motivation was certainly the same: preventing clubs from inducing players from other clubs to join them for inflated wages. The first professionals in 1885 earned no more than 10 shillings per match (around

$2.50) for a season of no more than thirty matches, producing an annual income of $75. By the mid-1890s, the top players could earn £4 ($20) per week for the full year, yielding an income of over $1,000. Still not a wage that would compare with a good clerical job, but much better than most manual laborers in Britain could expect.

The Football League rules of 1888 stated that permission was required for a player to transfer from one club to another within the same season.[31] In 1890 the league introduced a rule that threatened expulsion for poaching and passed a resolution blacklisting any nonleague team found guilty of the same offense.[32] In 1891 the clubs proposed a maximum wage but then dropped the idea,[33] and as early as 1892, clubs started to circulate lists stating how much compensation they would require in order to release a player.[34] In 1893 the league proposed a system whereby players could be transferred for a fee to be determined by the Football League Committee, but the clubs voted it down.[35] Unofficially, large sums of money were starting to pass between the clubs for the release of a player, and the first recognized transfer fee payment was made in 1895 by Burnley to Aston Villa for the services of James Crabtree.[36] The sum was £300, nearly 50 percent more than Crabtree's annual salary (£208).[37]

By this date, therefore, the league clubs had settled on a system whereby a team could only hire a player with the consent of his existing club, at a fee to be agreed between the clubs, while wages were to be agreed between the player and his employer. To facilitate the operation of this system, at the end of each season a club would list those players that it intended to *retain* and who therefore could not be approached by other clubs, and those it would place on the transfer list, along with a price for consenting to the transfer— hence the system's name: retain and transfer. By this system a player, once contracted, had no right to move to another club unless the club that owned his registration consented.

If ever a system could have been designed to offend the gentlemen amateurs of the FA, this was it. Not content with turning the game into a business, these Football League upstarts had now taken it upon themselves to decide who could and could not play football and for whom. This system was not only a direct challenge to the administrative authority of the FA but also an affront to the rights of all free-born Englishmen. In 1889 the Committee of the FA demanded that all transfers of professional players should take place only if countersigned by the secretary of the FA and in 1894 declared bluntly: "No club shall be allowed to receive or pay any sum of money as consideration for the transfer of any player." But the league and its clubs simply defied the FA. In 1899 a conference was held to try to reach an enforceable agreement. The FA even invited the players' union, formed in 1897, to participate. At the meetings, the union expressed the desire that the FA should determine the labor rules to govern professional players, and once again the FA issued a proposal that transfer fees be abolished. The conference broke down, and the FA issued a memo stating that "the practice of buying and selling players is unsportsmanlike and most objectionable."[38]

At this point, perhaps to show an evenhandedness between the players and the clubs or as a last ditch attempt to prevent soccer becoming a full-fledged business, the FA imposed the rule that no player could be paid more than £4 per week. Interestingly, two of the larger clubs, Liverpool and Aston Villa, opposed it, preferring a free market in players. In fact, for the next four years the FA was petitioned over and again by the large clubs to rescind the rule. In 1904 the FA decided that it had had enough of all this haggling and conceded control of financial rules relating to professional players to the Football League. The FA made one last attempt to regulate the transfer market, imposing a maximum fee of £350 in 1908, but since a fee of £1,000 (nearly $5,000) had been paid as early as 1905, the ruling was doomed to fail and was withdrawn within three months. The gentlemen had thus not only abandoned the players to their fate; they had also permitted that fate to be exclusively determined by the Football League and its clubs. A new players' union was formed in 1907. More radical than the first one, the union attempted to affiliate with the national trade union movement in 1909, to the horror of both the league and the FA.[39]

In 1912 it was agreed among all parties that the transfer system should be tested in the courts. The specific case related to a player named Lawrence Kingaby. Kingaby had been purchased for £300 by Aston Villa from Clapton Orient in 1905–06. After playing on the first team for only two months, Villa tried to sell him back to Clapton for half the price, but Clapton refused. Villa then put him on the retained list at no wages and with no contract. Rather than sit idly by, Kingaby got a place on the Fulham team that then played in the Southern League. At that time, the Southern League did not recognize the Football League's retain-and-transfer system. However, in 1910 the Southern League did reach an agreement with the Football League; by then Kingaby was playing for a team called Leyton, also in the Southern

League. With an agreement now in place, Aston Villa asserted that Kingaby was still contracted to them and that anyone wanting to hire him would have to pay a transfer fee of £350, a ridiculous sum for a player near the end of his career.

In fact, even without the fee, Leyton no longer wanted his services. Instead, Kingaby was offered employment by Croydon Common Football Club conditional on his being given a free transfer from his official club, Aston Villa. Aston Villa refused (seemingly more out of a sense of retribution than with any hope of making money), and so Kingaby, with the support of the players' union, sued.

This should have been an easy case for the players' union to win since it makes little legal or economic sense to permit a business to deny an individual a livelihood once the contract between the individual and the business has expired, particularly when the denial can bring no direct benefit to the club. The only rational argument from the club's position would be that the rule enabled it to monopolize the careers of its players, a position tantamount to slavery and hardly defensible at law. But Kingaby's lawyer made the mistake of attacking Aston Villa's motives rather than the inequity of the retain-and-transfer system as a whole. When the judge decided that there was no proof that Aston Villa had acted maliciously, the case was dismissed, without any consideration of the fairness of the system.[40]

The union was forced to pay the substantial legal costs and survived only thanks to the goodwill of the league and the FA, both of which took the opportunity to mold the union into a pliant, toothless servant. Of course, this meant that the union lost credibility with the players, something it was only able to rebuild fifty years later. Until then, the players, thanks to the retain-and-transfer system, remained the chattel of the clubs and, thanks to the maximum wage, badly paid chattel at that.

If English players had been placed in a particularly subservient position, it cannot be said that players in other countries were much better off. Player wages elsewhere were not in general much higher than those paid in England. In most countries the league clubs conspired to keep wages low, often using the excuse of the amateur "ethic" exported by gentlemen of the FA. The last significant league to turn professional was the German Bundesliga in 1963, by which time the country had already won the World Cup (in 1954). While nominally amateurs, many players received payment and did nothing else but play soccer for a living, even as their national association refused to acknowledge that the league was professional. For one thing, at this time professionalism often meant exclusion from the Olympic Games, and therefore a missed opportunity to vaunt national sporting pride. For another, few countries outside the United Kingdom had a formal split between the responsibility for the national association and the national league, and hence no clear split between amateurs and professionals.

Another important factor in the process was the politicization of soccer discussed in the previous chapter. Even when businesses took an interest in a club (such as Fiat in Italy [Juventus], Phillips in the Netherlands [PSV Eindhoven], Bayer in Germany [Bayer Leverkusen]), they were more interested in building ties with the local community and corporate promotion than in running the soccer team as a business. Most clubs were run by the social elite, often elected by club members who paid an annual subscription. Rich men might fund the acquisition of players, and local government might find ways to subsidize the team through stadium construction or other contributions. Against this background, few were interested in adding to costs by declaring their activities to be a business outright. Governments were usually prepared to accept this on the grounds that the role of sport, especially soccer, transcended mere commercial transactions.

Thus it is impossible to state precisely when, for example, the Italian league became professional. Although the amateur/professional distinction was recognized in 1926–27,[41] there is little doubt that players were paid before that date, or that members of the gold-medal-winning Italian Olympic team of 1936 were financially rewarded for their efforts. The Lega Nazionale Professionisti was not established as the official body controlling the top two leagues in Italy until 1959. In this context, we know that professional leagues existed as early as 1925 in Czechoslovakia, 1926 in Austria and Hungary, 1929 in Spain, 1930 in Argentina, 1932 in France, and 1933 in Brazil. Northern Europeans, by contrast, were among the later converts; along with Germany in 1963, the Netherlands did not turn professional until 1954, Belgium in 1974, and Denmark not until 1985.

While the informality of this system meant that some players could on occasion be offered large salaries, the clubs kept the wages of football workers at levels that had more in common with manual labor. In 1928, for example, the salary paid by Juventus to Raimundo Orsi, the Argentine star, was 100,000 lire per year, equivalent to about $5,000, plus a Fiat car; better than Dixie Dean, but still hardly a ransom by American standards. (Babe

Ruth's salary in 1928 was $70,000.)[42] In the late 1950s, a number of British soccer stars went to play in Italy. For example, Eddie Firmani, an Englishman with Italian roots, was transferred from Charlton Athletic to Sampdoria in 1957 for a fee of £35,000. He received a signing bonus of £5,000 but was paid only £1,000 (about $2,500) per year during his Italian career, despite going on to play for Inter Milan and the Italian national team.

Wage suppression depended in part on the creation of a tight web of contractual agreements among clubs not to poach players. As we have already seen, the Football League entered agreements with other leagues in England; they established similar agreements with soccer clubs in Scotland, which has always provided a significant fraction of league players in England. The international diffusion of soccer naturally created opportunities for players to play abroad. For example, during the 1920s a number of players crossed the English Channel to join French clubs, not least because of the more generous terms on offer. In order to control this trade, the English obtained an international agreement with FIFA in 1926 that no player should be permitted to transfer from one country to another without the explicit agreement of the national association of the country the player was leaving.

In practice, however, this permission was granted as long as the affected club was content with the terms of the deal. Virtually every country in soccer followed the English FA's rules, requiring that all players be registered with a club, as either a professional or an amateur, for the entire season, and that professional players at the end of each season could be either retained or transferred. Until 1995 the club holding a player's registration (whether or not his contract had expired) was entitled to receive a fee before any transfer could take place. Thus while sporting competition took place largely at the national level, the labor market rules were truly international.

The international transfer system helped to keep down wages by preventing players from marketing themselves. Players were not permitted to instigate negotiations, even when out of contract. Any club not willing to let a player move could simply specify an unrealistically high transfer fee. Moreover, many of the national associations, particularly in the wealthier soccer countries, also used the rules to control entry into the labor market. Until 1978, for instance, the English were unwilling to admit players from outside the United Kingdom or from former colonies. Italy instituted bans on foreign players between 1926 and 1945 (Argentine players with Italian ancestors were considered Italians) and again between 1966 and 1980. Foreign players did not appear in the German Bundesliga until the 1990s.

Despite this, player mobility between clubs has been a crucial part of the soccer system, because of promotion and relegation. Promoted teams need the opportunity to raise the quality of their roster to the standard of competition they are entering, while relegated teams need to offload talent since lower-division teams generate smaller revenues. Star players for relegated teams also want the opportunity to move to a club that is in the top flight. Further, unlike major league baseball clubs, the big clubs in soccer have not been permitted by the governing bodies to acquire farm teams to develop talent. This is largely because promotion and relegation would risk the possibility that a farm team could be promoted to the same division as the parent team, leaving two teams with a common owner to compete against each other.[43] Most major clubs have their own talent development schools, which provide training for young talented players in parallel with their normal schooling. They also run "reserve" teams with their own competitions, but the function of these competitions is purely for training, and only a handful of spectators turn up to watch. Rather than a fully developed farm system, the big clubs have relied on their ability to buy emerging stars from smaller clubs (especially those in lower divisions) in the transfer market. It is not surprising that clubs have also looked to the international market to acquire talent.

The first great movement of players internationally started in the 1920s. In the early 1920s, Italian clubs competed for the services of Austrian and Hungarian stars, until the ban on foreigners was imposed. After that they imported players from South America, especially Argentine, Uruguayan, and Brazilian "Italians." At first, the Italian clubs did not have to pay transfer fees since South American players were officially amateurs, a fact that rapidly promoted professionalization in South America. Also, during the 1920s and 1930s a number of English players moved to play in France (in 1932, 12 percent of players in the French league were British), but English players found it hard to adapt to living conditions abroad (something that has remained true to the present day).

With wages held down by the clubs at home and international transfers under the control of the national associations, one of the few options for players looking for a competitive salary was to find an "outlaw" league. Predictably, there has usually been one to be found in the USA. The first professional soccer league outside England was organized in 1894 by none other than the owners of baseball's National League. The American League of Professional Football adopted the same institutional structure that had been so successful in baseball, not least the reserve clause (perhaps this was an inspiration to the Football League, which was developing its system at precisely this time). As far as the owners were concerned, the principal attraction of soccer was to find a use for their baseball fields in the winter season and to keep baseball on the minds of the fans;[44] the soccer players were even coached by baseball managers. In the end, six teams played a grand total of twenty-three games in 1894, drawing crowds as large as 8,000 for some matches, but the season was suspended once the U.S. government announced its intention to investigate Baltimore's importation of British professionals. Though there were plans to revive the league in 1895, these too were shelved and the league was eventually forgotten.[45]

A second professional organization, the American Soccer League, was founded in 1921 and had its heyday in the 1920s. From the beginning it signed up a number of players with professional experience in Britain, mostly from Scotland rather than England. The ASL was a well-organized league, based in the Northeast, with eight teams in its first season each playing a schedule of twenty-eight games. The ASL had expanded to twelve teams by 1930. The league drew well, with match attendance often in excess of 10,000.

The ASL also deserves an honorable mention in the history of women's soccer. The story began in England, where women played cricket as far back as the eighteenth century and the first recorded women's soccer match took place in 1895.[46] During this period, middle-class women in Britain participated in a wide variety of sports, such as field hockey, tennis, golf, and lacrosse. However, it was working-class women who were at the heart of one of the most remarkable episodes in English soccer. During the First World War, women were hired by businesses such as the Dick, Kerr Works in Preston, which produced locomotives, to replace the men who had enlisted.

Most factories had a men's soccer team, and at some point during the war, the women challenged the Dick, Kerr Works men's team to a game. The result is unknown, but the women continued playing, initially to raise money for the war effort. As the team became more experienced, they attracted both more opponents and bigger crowds. In April 1920 they played the first women's representative game against a French eleven, and then, on December 26, 1920, they played in front of a sell-out crowd of 53,000 at the Everton soccer field in Liverpool against their rivals St. Helen's. This was a bigger gate than almost any men's game could attract at the time.

The outraged patriarchs of the FA stepped in. As far back as 1902 the FA had issued instructions to affiliated organizations not to permit matches against "lady teams." They now passed a resolution:

> Complaints having been made as to football being played by women, the Council feels impelled to express their strong opinion that the game of football is quite unsuitable for females and ought not to be encouraged. . . . For these reasons the Council requests the clubs belonging to the Association to refuse the use of their grounds for such matches.[47]

Staggeringly, this ban on women's competition lasted until 1971, when the FA finally acknowledged the right of women to play soccer. The FA's ban failed to put an end to the Dick, Kerr Ladies team, which continued to play until the mid-1960s, with a career record of won 758, tied 46, and only 24 lost.[48]

Having shown that they could draw a crowd in England, the team went on an international tour. First they visited France, where they were received like royalty. Next, in 1922, they toured Canada and the United States. Arriving in Quebec, the Canadian FA promptly passed a resolution endorsing the position of the English FA, and consequently the team was not able to find any opponents. In the United States, they found a different problem, namely the absence of any women soccer players. As a result, they persuaded the men of the American Soccer League (ASL) to play against them. The tour itself was commercially driven, and the matches proved a good draw, with attendance between 4,000 and 10,000 for the series of eight matches. Playing against America's top professional men, some of whom had played professionally in England and Scotland, they recorded three wins, three ties, and two defeats.[49]

Yet the alarm caused by the ASL in the United Kingdom had more to do with men than with women. Because the ASL refused to recognize the player transfer system, its teams were able to lure players by offering substantially more than the FL's maximum wage. In 1928 baseball's New York Giants (they had a soccer team in the ASL from 1923 onward) tried to hire Dixie Dean, following his record-breaking season, to play for the princely sum of $120 per week. While this was well below a baseball star's salary, it was three times what he was getting in England.[50] In the end, Dean did not move because it became clear that the ASL was running into problems. Unlike baseball, American soccer did not manage to achieve a unified structure until the 1990s, and leagues were constantly entering the market and then folding, a process that prevented fans from maintaining long-term attachments.

Another example of an outlaw league comes from the famous Colombian episode of the late 1940s and early 1950s. During this period, the owners of teams in the Colombian League, supported by the military junta, trawled South America and Europe to attract the best players.[51] In 1950 seven English stars left to play in Bogota, reputedly for sums as large as £5,000 per year, leaving behind the meager earnings of £1,000 under the maximum wage in gray and rainy England. Even more famously, the Milionarios club of Bogota recruited Alfredo di Stefano, one of the greatest players of all time, who was then a professional in Argentina. Altogether, 109 players left Argentina for Colombia, following a lengthy strike over wages. Again no transfer fees were paid, since the Colombian FA was at the time in dispute with the league, which was not officially recognized. Mexico, Peru, and Guatemala also created outlaw leagues during this period. Another outlaw league was spawned in 1957, when the New South Wales Federation of Soccer Clubs split from the Australian Soccer Football Association and therefore was temporarily separated from FIFA.[52] During this period several Austrian, Dutch, and Czech players were recruited on generous salaries without the payment of a transfer fee.

In practice, outlaw leagues seldom lasted for long and so did little to raise the earning potential of most professionals. Low incomes in soccer, as in baseball, created the conditions in which some players could be tempted into match fixing. Soccer has a long history of bribery and corruption scandals. One common motive has been to secure success in competition. We have already mentioned the accusation levied against the Argentines in the 1978 World Cup, but there are many other examples, mostly involving payments by clubs to ensure promotion or to avoid relegation. Player involvement with gambling is also widespread. In England, players have typically been paid a bonus for each match they win, and it was not uncommon for a player to take out insurance by betting on a defeat. In the 1960s a syndicate was uncovered involving dozens of players fixing the outcome of matches to win bets. In 1965 ten players were jailed for their offenses, but strikingly, only small sums of money were involved. The highest sum mentioned in court was £100 for a single game (about $180), yet one of the convicted players sacrificed a career that might have led to his playing on England's World Cup–winning team of 1966.

Toward the end of the 1950s, the international system started to come under pressure. First, while the FIFA family expanded rapidly as decolonization created new nations in Asia and Africa, the European clubs began to exert greater and greater power on the world stage. As economic growth in Europe increased the purchasing power of the top European clubs, they became more interested in international competition. The European Cup, a competition played between the national league champions of each country, was inaugurated in 1955. This rapidly came to be seen as the preeminent club competition in the world, just as the World Cup dominated international representative competition. The appeal of both competitions rested significantly on the new medium of television, which started to create a truly global perspective among the fans.

Second, star players became increasingly restless with the meager incomes they received, often aware of how much more they would have earned in a sport like baseball. In England, the players' union set out to challenge the maximum wage system. The Football League had enjoyed a huge boost in attendance after World War II, and club income had risen accordingly, but player salaries had barely kept up with inflation. Even the insular British had noticed how much could be earned overseas, where a maximum wage rule did not exist. The revival of the players' union also reflected the greater recognition of labor rights in the postwar period. Despite this, the maximum wage had risen to a mere £20 per week by 1960. Unprecedentedly, the players threatened to strike. At first the clubs blustered, but once they could see that the union was serious they caved, and the maximum wage was abolished at the beginning of 1961.

Another important development in England during this period was a legal challenge to the retain-and-transfer system. George Eastham was a player transferred to Newcastle in the north of England in the early 1960s, but he quickly decided he preferred life in London. Eastham asked to be transferred to Arsenal, which was willing to buy him. But Newcastle refused to release him, and Eastham took his case to the High Court. In a landmark judgment, Justice Wilberforce ruled the system illegal. This did not immediately lead to free agency, and even under the reformed system, clubs were able to demand transfer fees not only for players whose contracts had not expired, but even for players whose contracts had ended. Nonetheless, from 1965 a player had the right to insist on moving to another club at the end of his contract if he so wished. In France, the players' union won free agency in 1969, with no transfer fee payable on the termination of a contract. While the transfer system continued to thrive in the rest of the world for the time being, legal storm clouds began to gather.

By the 1960s, the amount of money a club could generate from selling a star player was substantial enough to make a difference to the financial future of a club. For example, it has been said of many players that their sale enabled a club to finance the construction of a stadium. Transfer fees could also be a good investment for the buying club. After Alfredo Di Stefano moved from Milionarios of Colombia to Real Madrid in Spain in 1953, he was largely responsible for creating that club's global reputation.

His transfer fee was 5.5 million pesetas (about $250,000). He had, in fact, already signed with Real's arch rivals Barcelona, but, with the full backing of the Franco regime and the captive Spanish Football Association, the original deal was overturned and Madrid had its man. With him, the team won eight Spanish league titles, and even more remarkably, five consecutive European Cup championships. Broadcast across Europe, the success of Real Madrid was widely credited with sustaining the Franco regime in Spain and cemented the image of Real as one of the greatest clubs in Europe. Certainly no club has since come close to emulating its record.

Transfer fees escalated rapidly in the 1960s as international competition for top players intensified and the big teams became more and more interested in succeeding in international competition. In 1960 the transfer fee record stood at $290,000;[53] by 1970 it had reached $590,000.[54] In 1973 the great Johan Cruyff was transferred from Ajax of the Netherlands to Barcelona of Spain for $1.3 million, and in 1982 the Argentine Diego Maradona was transferred from Barcelona to Napoli of Italy for around $6 million. Although the big-spending Italian clubs dominated the transfer market, the Spanish and the English were never far behind. In 1978 the English finally lifted their ban on foreign imports and started hiring stars from around the world.[55] Broadly speaking, the South Americans, especially the Brazilians and Argentines, continued to be highly prized in southern Europe, while in northern Europe imports from the Scandinavian countries and Eastern Europe, especially Yugoslavia, tended to be more favored. From the 1980s onward, African players also started to find their way into the European market.

Mobility within Europe was enhanced during this period by a new player in the transfer market, the European Union (EU). The Treaty of Rome, signed in 1957, which established the framework for the common market among the member states of the EU, was a time bomb waiting to explode in the face of football's administrators. Since the days of Kenesaw Mountain Landis, there has been a long tradition of lawyers becoming sports administrators in the United States, which is hardly surprising given the mountain of sports litigation the major leagues have created. In soccer, however, it would be fair to say that until the 1980s a book on the law governing professional soccer, if such a thing had existed, would scarcely have filled more than a couple of hundred pages. Few countries outside the United States possessed a developed competition law system under which the governance of the leagues and the national associations might be challenged; in many countries, soccer was controlled through informal networks, where political connections mattered more than a firm grasp of the letter of the law.[56]

A large fraction of soccer's commercial transactions took place in a convenient cloud of secrecy, convenient not least as a means of evading the tax authorities. Secrecy also enabled many of those party to transactions, such as the team managers, to accept bribes to smooth the process of a transfer. And even in countries where economic relations were more tightly regulated, such as the United Kingdom, the simple fact that the sums of money at stake were so small meant that there was little to litigate over. For example, even in 1988, the total revenue from English professional soccer was no more than £100 million per year (about $150 million). As a result, soccer administrators the world over complacently assumed that the competition laws did not apply to them.

The EU, however, had created a legal system enshrining principles that applied to all EU citizens. As the EU expanded from six member states in 1957 to twenty-five in 2004, these rules came to apply to all the major European soccer nations.[57] First among these rules, from the point of view of soccer, is the free movement of labor within the EU. According to the law, workers in all industries are free to move among member states, a rule that conflicted with the transfer restrictions imposed by soccer's national associations. By the early 1980s, most countries operated a rule stating that a team could field only a limited number of foreign players, typically two per team. In 1985 the European Commission insisted that players working legally in an EU member state be freed from any restrictions on playing anywhere inside the EU. This led to some prolonged negotiations and resulted in the "3+2" agreement in 1991, which permitted each team to field up to three non-nationals plus two more if the latter had played on the club youth team for at least three years. Still, this was not quite free movement of labor within the EU, and a further challenge was not long coming.

The catalyst for revolutionary change was sparked by the case of a minor player. Jean-Marc Bosman was a Belgian player who wished to transfer from RC Liege in Belgium to US Dunkerque in France. Under Belgian rules, Liege was allowed to fix a fee for the player without negotiation; as a result the transfer fell through because Dunkerque could not afford the fee. The case reached the European Court, and the clubs tried to argue, among other things, that soccer as a sport was not subject to normal commercial law. The Court ruled in December 1995 not only that soccer had a business dimension, which meant that laws relating to businesses had to be respected, but also that the transfer system restricted the freedom of movement of employees (footballers) in the European Union in contravention of article 48 of the Treaty of Rome. While the judgment referred specifically to players moving between member states, it carried the revolutionary implication that a transfer fee for any player out of contract would not be legally enforceable. In the immediate aftermath of the judgment, a number of players whose contracts were nearing an end received a windfall increase in salary as it became clear that their clubs were no longer entitled to a fee (for out-of-contract players), and so the players could market themselves as completely free agents.

Over the following five years, the European Commission negotiated with FIFA and UEFA (the association of the national soccer governing bodies of Europe) over what would be an acceptable transfer system. The final agreement in 2001 closely resembled the French system, enabling clubs to claim a transfer fee for players up until the age of 23, as a reflection of any investment in a player's development.[58] Beyond the age of 23, however, no transfer is payable once a player's contract ends, but transfer fees can still be paid if a player has time on his existing contract. Hence, despite the Bosman judgment, the transfer market has continued to operate for players within contract, and the transfer fee record has been broken several times since the

Bosman judgment. In 1992 the record stood at £13 million for a single player, but rose to £18 million in 1997 when the Brazilian Ronaldo moved from Barcelona to Inter Milan, £32 million in 1999 when the Italian Christian Vieri moved from Lazio to Inter Milan, £37 million in 2000 when the Portuguese Luis Figo moved from Barcelona to Real Madrid, and £46 million when the captain the of the World Cup–winning French team, Zinedine Zidane, moved from Juventus to Real Madrid in 2001.

At the same time, players, especially the stars, were receiving a far larger fraction of the total revenue that they generated. By the end of the 1990s, it was possible to argue that the contractual position of a star player in soccer was now actually better than that of a star baseball player. While transfer fees remained, international competition meant that potentially dozens of clubs competed to sign the top players when they came on the market, and contracts were typically shorter. Top-level clubs that spent 20 to 30 percent of their income on players' wages in the 1950s were spending over 50 percent by the 1980s,[59] and in the 1990s many clubs were spending more than 70 percent of their income on player wages.[60] With the advent of mega television contracts, soccer club revenue levels became comparable to those of Major League Baseball. Most of the players in the bigger European leagues were earning over $1 million by the end of the 1990s, and annual salaries in excess of $10 million were being paid to some of the superstars. Dixie Dean must have turned in his grave. But if the players could no longer consider themselves exploited, many were starting to question the financial viability of the league system.

CHAPTER FIVE

Fans, Franchises, and Financial Failure

Why Baseball Clubs Make Money and Soccer Clubs Don't

In April 2004 *Forbes* published a striking comparison between soccer and baseball. The television audience of 1.1 billion for the World Cup final in 2002 dwarfed viewership for the World Series. The English Premier League alone generated TV rights income of $670 million, almost equal to Major League Baseball's $700 million. Manchester United, with a stock market value of $1.2 billion and operating income of $92 million, is a bigger club than the New York Yankees, with an estimated value of only $832 million and reported operating losses of $26 million. According to *Forbes,* the top twenty European soccer clubs had an average franchise value of $443 million, revenues of $159 million, and operating income of $16 million, bigger on every count than the figures for Major League Baseball ($295 million, $129 million, and –$2 million respectively). By implication, the future of soccer looked bright and that of baseball looked bleak.

Yet in July 2004 *Business Week* published an article head-lined "Can Football Be Saved?" According to *Business Week*:

Many of the organizations at the core of the sport—the roughly 400 first-division teams from Ireland to Ukraine—

116

are in dismal financial shape. Clubs typically have a shot at turning a profit only if they qualify for the elite UEFA Champions League or the UEFA Cup, the two main postseason tournaments.

Even top teams in football-crazy countries lose money. Deloitte estimates that Italy's first-league clubs collectively lost $485 million in the 2002 season on sales of $1.4 billion—and probably lost at least $360 million last year. It all adds up to a crisis which, if left unchecked, could leave the whole game permanently weakened. Even in the much admired British Premier League, probably only five teams out of 20 made a pre-tax profit in the season just ended.[1]

Ten years ago, no one would have compared a baseball club with a soccer club in business terms. Baseball clubs have long been run on clear business principles and have produced significant revenue streams; soccer clubs have been largely social and political organizations that have generated a tiny cash flow and have set out to do little more than balance the books. The influx of new money, especially broadcasting income, has dramatically raised the profile of soccer clubs, but as the *Business Week* article suggests, the clubs still struggle to balance the books.

In this chapter we compare the financial organization of baseball and soccer clubs. Notwithstanding claims that they are losing money, we argue that all the evidence points to baseball clubs as significant creators of profit. This follows from the monopolistic nature of Major League Baseball, an aspect of the game that has given rise to concern over many years. In soccer, by contrast, we argue that the nature of the competitive structure of the game limits the ability of all but a small elite to generate profits.

Baseball

By and large, Major League Baseball franchises make money. Of course, some make more money than others, and occasionally some owners even find themselves out-of-pocket. But the general picture is one of financial good health. The fundamental reason that makes us confident of this conclusion is that baseball is a monopoly. Monopoly, being the absence of competition, is almost always profitable. Indeed, the fact that it is easy for a monopolist to make a profit means that monopolies are usually regulated by government in order to protect the interests of consumers (consider electric power supply and its regulation). But because baseball is not regulated, the monopolists are free to make as much money as they can. Of course, there will always be an argument about how much money, and in a later section we will show how baseball can often conceal its underlying profitability. But the important point we make here is that, on the whole, the baseball monopoly is profitable, and this contrasts sharply with the financial crises experienced in the soccer world.

Ownership Structure

By 1915, following the demise of the Federal League, Major League Baseball had become an unchallenged monopoly. Since 1922 MLB has benefited from a presumed exemption from the nation's antitrust laws. Thus baseball is not only the United States' national pastime; it is also a closed, legal, and unregulated monopoly.

Baseball clubs are not subject to potential competition from new teams, unlike clubs in the open, promotion/relegation soccer leagues in the rest of the world. Nor is baseball subject to state regulation and controls, as soccer is in France and other countries.

Without the normal competitive pressures of the marketplace and without sport-specific state intervention, baseball is left to be self-governed by its owners. Owners run their franchises according to their own goals, subject only to the constraints they impose on themselves via the national (commissioner's) office. Owners' objectives and the operation of the national office have changed over time.

In his book *Sports in America*, renowned author James Michener suggested that the profile of the typical team owner evolved in a particular pattern:

> In the early years of every professional sport, the owners were men of great dedication and expertise. . . . Their type was soon superseded, however, by the business tycoon who made his fortune in trade, then dabbled in sports ownership both as a means of advertising his product and finding community approval. The beer barons—Jacob Ruppert with his New York Yankees and Augie Busch with his St. Louis Cardinals—were prototypes; they became famous across America and the sales of their beer did not suffer in the process. It is interesting that when William Wrigley, the Chicago tycoon, wanted to buy into the

National League, he was strongly opposed by Colonel Ruppert, who feared such ownership might be used to commercialize chewing gum.

Then came a third echelon of ownership, the corporate manager who bought a club not only to publicize his business enterprises but also to take advantage of a curious development in federal tax laws.[2]

While Michener's taxonomy is broadly accurate, one could easily quibble with aspects of it. For instance, the American Association was launched in 1882 by brewmasters, rather than pure sportsmen, who were seeking promotion for their companies. And while corporate ownership has certainly been increasing in recent decades as franchise prices have skyrocketed from a few million to several hundred million dollars, it has done so in fits and starts, rather than in a linear progression. Further, Michener leaves out some of the more interesting nuances, such as the tendency for joint ownership of both media companies and baseball teams.

In 2004, baseball teams are owned both by corporations and by partnerships. The corporations are in media-related fields, such as newspapers, television, and radio. The partnerships are formed by individuals whose wealth comes from such disparate sectors as real estate, finance, media, restaurants, software, supermarkets, car sales, banking, law, and sports.

With such varied backgrounds, it is not surprising that team owners often profess different objectives for their franchises. Some owners claim that they bought the team to make a contribution to their community. Others state they got involved for love of the game and strive only to break even. Some openly acknowledge that they run their team as a business and seek to maximize profits. Many see their team as a vehicle to promote a broader portfolio of businesses.

Club Finances

Baseball franchises today are worth roughly between $150 million and $800 million. There are no more than a handful of people in the United States who could afford to make that kind of an investment playfully. Although owners seek different kinds of returns from their teams, it is safe to assume that they are all seeking a return on their investment.

And most get it. The most common return is direct profit. Until 2004, however, owners and commissioners had been fond of claiming financial losses. Most recently, Commissioner Bud Selig testified before the U.S.

House Judiciary Committee in December 2001 that in the aggregate Major League Baseball lost $232 million in 2001. As we shall see, public pleas of poverty or reported book losses have little to do with baseball's underlying financial reality.

One of the most common ways for team owners to hide their true gain is through related party transactions (RPTs). RPTs occur when the owner of a team also owns a company or companies that do business with the team. In these instances, the owner trades with himself and can do so at any prices he likes.

Consider an example from the Chicago Cubs. According to 2001 figures that MLB Commissioner Bud Selig delivered to the U.S. Congress, the Chicago White Sox income from local TV, radio, and cable was $30.1 million, and that of the Chicago Cubs was $23.6 million. Yet anyone who has heard of Sammy Sosa knows that the Cubs are the far more popular team in the Windy City. TV ratings bear this out: in 2001 the Cubs' average ratings were 6.8 on free-to-air broadcasting and 3.8 on cable; those of the White Sox were 3.6 and 1.9, respectively. And this doesn't take account of the fact that the Cubs games are shown on superstation WGN, which reaches 55 million-plus homes nationally.

So how can we understand Selig's figures? The Cubs are owned by the Tribune Corporation, which also owns WGN. The Tribune Corporation, by pricing the Cubs television rights well below their market value, is transferring revenue away from the Cubs and lowering the costs (raising the profits) of WGN. According to *Broadcasting & Cable*, the industry's authoritative source, the Cubs' local media earnings in 2001 were $59 million. If the Cubs reported this figure instead of $23.6 million, then their reported $1.8 million loss (in Selig's figures) would become a $33.6 million profit in 2001![3]

In 2002 the Tribune Corporation set up a new business (Wrigley Field Premium Tickets) to resell Cubs tickets at well above the retail price. Apparently, this brokerage company sold tickets to a Yankees–Cubs game with a face value of $45 for as much as $1,500. Since the Cubs offered a legal defense in a scalping violation lawsuit that it was not the Cubs but a different business that was selling the tickets, it seems fair to presume that the Cubs also did not report the additional gate revenue to MLB.

Why would the Cubs (and all other baseball teams) want to reduce their reported revenues? There are several possible reasons. First, since 1996 MLB has had a revenue-sharing system that levies a tax on a team's net local revenues. In 2001 this tax was at 20 percent (in 2004 the effective marginal tax rate is closer to 40 percent).[4] Thus for every dollar in local revenue not reported in 2001, the team saved just under 20 cents.[5] Since WGN pays no such tax to the broadcasting industry, it is preferable for the parent corporation, Tribune, to have the profits appear on WGN's books.

Second, baseball teams (and even the Cubs, who were seeking public permission to erect higher left-field stands in 2002) seek various kinds of public support for their facilities. The more impecunious they appear, they believe, the more likely it is that such support will be forthcoming.

Third, every few years the owners negotiate with the players over a new collective bargaining contract. The owners consistently seek new restrictions in the labor market to lower salaries. One of the justifications for these restrictions invariably is that the teams are losing money. Whether or not the Players Association is convinced by such arguments, it appears to be de rigueur in the collective bargaining ritual.

Fourth, MLB is the only professional sport in the United States that has a presumed antitrust exemption. Periodically, MLB is called before Congress to justify this special treatment. One of the arguments that MLB has repeatedly trotted out—most recently by Selig before the U.S. Congress in December 2001—is that the industry cannot possibly be abusing its market power because it is not profitable.

Fifth, ownership may believe that claims of poverty help to justify higher ticket or concessions prices to the fans.

What the Tribune Corporation does with the Cubs and WGN, George Steinbrenner does with the Yankees and the YES Network (their own regional sports network), John Henry does with the Red Sox and NESN, Time Warner does with TBS and the Braves, and so on. In each case, the team's true financial return is unlikely to be found on the bottom line, and it seems reasonable to conclude that the team's income statement will not tell the whole story.

The fact that baseball franchises may look less profitable than they really are when they are owned and managed within a portfolio of businesses raises an even more profound question. If the team is not managed as a profit center, but rather as a vehicle for promoting the owner's other investments, will this be in the long-term interests of the league as a whole? There are reasons to think it might not be.

For instance, George Steinbrenner used his New York Yankees to create the YES regional sports network in the nation's largest media market. In 2001 YES had a market value upward of $850 million. The dominance of the Yankees is clearly good for building up YES in the short term, but is it good for MLB? Rupert Murdoch admitted that his purchase of the Dodgers paid off because it enabled him to prevent Disney from creating a regional sports network in southern California.[6] In 1998 Disney had signed up its MLB Angels and NHL Mighty Ducks to a ten-year cable contract with Fox Sports Net West II for a seemingly well-under-market $12 million a year. It is not unlikely that Disney received other benefits from the News Corp. (such as carriage at an attractive price for Disney's many cable channels on the News Corp.'s worldwide satellite distribution systems.) Amid all this wheeling and dealing, was anybody really paying attention to the interests of the Dodgers or the development of baseball in California?

Tom Hicks hopes to use his ownership of the Texas Rangers to develop some 270 acres of commercial and residential real estate around the ballpark in Arlington and to grow his Southwest Sports Group, among other things. It's clear that the political leverage that can be derived from team ownership might help do the land deal, but how would the land deal help the baseball team? Dick Jacobs exploited his ownership of the Indians to promote the value of his downtown real estate.

And so on. When team owners view the success of their team in terms of the consequences for their entire business empire, the needs of the league itself are not likely to figure prominently in decisionmaking. For instance, most people agree that a degree of competitive balance is essential for the long-term health of the league. But the owner of a given franchise may perceive a significant short-term gain across his entire business portfolio by building a dominant team. Thus the short-term interests of the owner may conflict with the long-term interests of the sport itself.

Another important potential return lies in the tax shelter provided by sports team ownership. Anomalously, the IRS allows team owners to attribute half the purchase price of a franchise to the value of player contracts. It then allows the owner to amortize this value, usually over five years. Thus if the Yankees are purchased by Donald Trump for $800 million, Trump could claim that $400 million of that is attributable to the player contracts he obtained in buying the team. He could then write off $80 million in amortization costs each year for five years. So, if his Yankees had an "above the line" profit of, say, $30 million, Trump could deduct from that

$80 million in amortization "costs" and report a book loss of $50 million. Next, if Trump's individual income tax showed $50 million of taxable income, he could carry over his book loss from the team and end up with no taxable income. Assuming that Trump faces a marginal tax rate (including New York taxes) of 40 percent, owning the Yankees in this example would save him $20 million (40 percent of $50 million) in tax payments.[7]

Team owners also often pay themselves a salary or a consulting fee of several million dollars. These "salary" payments are, of course, entered on the income statement as a cost item and reduce the reported profit, but they constitute another economic return to ownership.

Some owners use team ownership for financial leverage. For example, an owner, rather than contributing, say, $100 million in equity capital toward his partnership's purchase of a team, can loan the partnership $100 million at 10 percent interest. In both cases the owner contributes $100 million in capital, but in one case it is equity capital and in the other it is debt capital. When it is debt capital, the team partnership has to pay $10 million in interest to one of its members, and this interest is registered as a "below the line" cost. The owner, in this case, takes his return in the form of interest, rather than in the form of profit.

Or, an owner can use his team asset as collateral in order to obtain financing on better terms for a loan to be used in another business. In this instance the return comes in the form of easier or cheaper access to capital.

With very few exceptions, owners also earn capital gains when they sell the team—and these are often substantial.[8] According to Rodney Fort's estimates, during the 1990s the average annual rates of franchise appreciation were 11.3 percent in MLB, 17.7 percent in the NBA, 10.7 percent in the NHL, and 12.7 percent in the NFL.[9] John Moag, using a different methodology and updating through mid-2002, estimated the annual rate of return to owning a baseball franchise to be 12.4 percent from 1960 to 2002, which would put it well above the return to common stock ownership for the same period (6.9 percent for the S&P 500 through June 30, 2002).[10]

A significant part of the investment return is indirect. For instance, team ownership makes an individual prominent in his community and thereby provides him with opportunities to develop new business relationships and to leverage political influence—potentially benefiting the owner's other investments as well as the sports team.

Other returns to ownership include the fun, perquisites, power, and ego gratification owners enjoy. Ownership, in part, is a consumption good. Thus it makes sense to think of owners as maximizing their total (consumption and investment) return, not just their financial profit.

In each of these instances—related party transactions, tax benefits, capital gains, business connections, political ties, and consumption benefits—the investment return will not show up on the income statement and is long term in nature. Indeed, it is precisely because of these hidden and indirect returns to ownership that the value of baseball franchises keeps rising. If negative or zero reported profits were the whole story, then it would defy all the laws of economics for the asset value of baseball franchises to increase over time.

In mocking the owners' claims of perennial penury, Don Fehr, the executive director of the players' association, has often said that there are two lasting truths about the baseball industry: no team ever has enough pitching, and no team ever makes any money. Fehr will need a new quip, because in early 2004 the commissioner's office decided to put a happy spin on baseball's finances.

The first indication of this about-face came from MLB's CFO Jonathan Mariner, who told the *Sports Business Journal* in late April 2004 that only five MLB teams are in danger of not meeting the league's pending debt restrictions. Since only teams with positive earnings can meet the new debt rule, baseball has decided to stop complaining.[11] Bud Selig now proudly proclaims that baseball has an economic system that works.

The real story about the owners' newly found contentment is that the 2002 collective bargaining agreement included a number of provisions that have depressed salaries. The provisions include effective revenue-sharing tax rates between 39 and 47 percent; luxury taxes on high payrolls; a new rule restricting the amount of team debt; a new requirement that all deferred salaries be fully funded within eighteen months; and a new provision that grants an extra top draft pick the next year if a team fails to sign its pick. Complementing these provisions, companies that insure teams for player injuries issued stricter new guidelines that significantly limit and make more expensive injury coverage.

Together these factors have put a significant drag on player salaries. Free-agent signings after the 2002 season saw the size of the average new contract decline by 16.5 percent, and by 26.6 percent after the 2003 season. Median player salaries fell from $750,000 in 2002 to $652,088 in 2003, or by almost

9 percent. Average salaries were $2.49 million in 2004, down 2.7 percent from 2003. That might not seem like much, but it is a big turnaround from the 11.5 percent annual growth rate in salaries from 1995 through 2003.

Oddly, while the 2002 CBA contained provisions to contain salary growth, it is also intended to promote competitive balance in the league—a subject we discuss at greater length in chapter 7. Here, it is important to note that the revenue-sharing system in MLB does not elicit appropriate incentives for promoting stronger performance from weak teams. Teams in the bottom half of the revenue distribution face a marginal tax rate of over 45 percent. That is, every time they spend an extra dollar on payroll and generate, say, an extra dollar in gross revenue, they get to keep only 55 cents (at most) of that dollar. The low-revenue teams scarcely have any financial inducement to invest their transfers. Thus, although the low-revenue teams received approximately $270 million in revenue transfers from the top-revenue teams in 2004, they are not required to spend it on improving their rosters, nor do they have any incentive to do so.

In general, both because of this tax/revenue-sharing system and the absence of a promotion/relegation mechanism in baseball, the relationship between improvements in team performance and increases in team revenue, while present, is weak.

In contrast, as we shall see, in Europe, with the promotion/relegation system and, to a lesser degree, the supranational Champions League and the less than full sharing of the national television contracts, team playing success and team revenues are much more closely related.[12] As a corollary, potential revenues are more closely correlated with city size in baseball and other closed U.S. leagues, whereas in open European leagues, city size is largely neutralized as a source of revenues, and team success is more fully a function of team management.[13]

Today, around 54 percent of reported team revenues goes to pay Major League Baseball players' salaries. The typical MLB team, however, also spends approximately 10 percent of revenues on its extensive player development system (which includes five or six minor league teams). The balance of revenue pays for team expenses (travel, coaches, trainers), front-office costs (administration, ticket sales and marketing, promotion, and public relations), stadium rent and maintenance, financing, and profits.

Team revenues in baseball come from several sources, the importance of which varies considerably from team to team. In 2004 the average baseball team generated around $130 million in revenues. Of this, approximately $30 million came from MLB's central fund (primarily national television and radio, Internet, international, sponsorship, and licensing revenues). This sum is distributed equally to all teams. Local revenues averaged roughly the following: gate, $48 million; concessions, merchandising, and parking, $10 million; luxury and club seat premiums, $10 million; signage and sponsorships, $10 million; and reported local television and radio, $22 million.

The spread in local revenues among teams, however, is very large. For instance, in 2004 the Yankees' local revenues were between $250 million and $300 million, whereas the Montreal Expos' local revenues were below $15 million. While the Expos received in excess of $30 million in revenue-sharing transfers, the Yankees paid revenue-sharing and luxury taxes in excess of $80 million. Other clubs lie between these extremes.

Overall the conclusion is clear. Though not without its distributional and idiosyncratic issues, baseball economics is working for the owners. Indeed, in 2004 it is working so well that even the commissioner's office no longer denies it.

Governing the Owners

The distributional issues among owners, together with their different objectives for team performance, distinct economic backgrounds, and disparate personalities, more often than not have created serious issues of league governance. Without market competition or government regulation, as exist to varying degrees in the open soccer leagues in Europe, baseball has depended on a strong leader to bring owner squabbling under control. Ironically, when such leadership was not forthcoming from the commissioner's office, it often appeared, as former commissioner Fay Vincent observed, that the owners depended on the players' union to save them from themselves.[14]

Historically, as much as baseball, with its heterogeneous array of owners, needed a cohesive guiding force, the commissioner's office was weak. The first commissioner in the modern baseball era (since 1903) was Kenesaw Mountain Landis. Following his appointment in January 1921, he set out to provide the game with strong leadership. After Landis's aggressive actions to curtail gambling in the 1920s, however, the owners began to resist his initiatives. The owners learned by dealing with Landis that whatever the public rhetoric might be about the commissioner's role, the commissioner was the owners' employee. If the commissioner crossed the owners, they could either clip his wings or dismiss him.

Peter Ueberroth, selected as commissioner in 1984, was well aware of this limitation. Before accepting the job, he sought and received various safeguards to ensure his ability to act independently.[15] Ueberroth's leadership, however firm, was errant. He, along with owners Bud Selig and Jerry Reinsdorf, orchestrated the collusion against the players during 1985–87. Each of three arbitration cases found the owners guilty of colluding to restrain competition in the players' market.[16] As a result, the owners were on the hook to pay $280 million in damages. Ueberroth also seemed to spend more of his time at his home in southern California and consulting for various corporations than working for baseball at his office in New York.

Bart Giamatti replaced Ueberroth in 1989, but suffered an untimely death after only five months in office. His successor, Fay Vincent, clashed with the owners almost from day one. His most serious transgression was pressing the owners to end their lockout and open spring training camps in 1990. From the owners' perspective, this action resulted in a less favorable collective bargaining agreement. The owners returned the favor and, after a nasty battle, forced Vincent to resign in 1992. Next time, the owners took no chances and decided to anoint one of their own.

Bud Selig, then principal owner of the Milwaukee Brewers, was selected as "temporary" commissioner in 1992. The argument that the owners had long used before the U.S. Congress—that baseball did not need either competition or outside regulation because it had an "independent" commissioner who looked after the game's and the fans' best interests—now lost whatever shred of credibility it ever held. After six years of his temporary status, during which time Selig had a temporary commissioner's office set up in Milwaukee, where he continued to receive an executive salary with the Brewers of roughly $500,000 a year in addition to his lofty commissioner's compensation, the owners, in 1998, decided it was time to make Selig's job permanent—though his field office in Milwaukee remains.

Selig's independence and impartiality among owners have been questioned on more than one occasion. Many believe that he should not have received a salary from the Brewers while serving as full-time commissioner of all clubs. Others believe that his plan to "contract" (eliminate) the Minnesota Twins after the 2001 season suggested a conflict of interest. He would contract a team from MLB's thirteenth largest media market and thereby expand the uncontested reach of the Brewers' (from MLB's smallest media market) market to its west by several hundred miles. Selig has also been criticized for the details of the 2002 revenue-sharing system that benefited his family's team more than any other in its net increase in revenue-sharing receipts (his daughter Wendy remained CEO of the Brewers until 2002 and continued as chair of the board through 2004, as his family continued to own a majority of the team). Cities have been critical of Selig's heavy hand in extorting large public subsidies for stadium construction under threat of team relocation or contraction.[17]

The list of alleged missteps goes on, but it is not our purpose here to indict the commissioner. To the contrary, it is to observe that, in one important sense, Selig has been successful where other commissioners have failed. Whatever his shortcomings, he has strong communication skills and seemingly boundless energy, even at 70 years of age in late 2004. Selig has been able to convince the owners to expand the powers of his office. With expanded powers to fine miscreant owners, to unilaterally introduce additional revenue-sharing measures, to distribute monies from his discretionary fund, to certify proper use of revenue transfers and compliance with new debt rules, as well as the use of more traditional powers to approve trades, adjudicate game disputes, select the host city for the All-Star Game, and decide on other matters, Selig has employed his leverage to bring rebel owners in tow. Because of Selig's statesmanlike leadership and powers of persuasion, owners today appear to behave with greater unity of purpose than ever before (possibly excepting their collusion in the mid-1980s when they were behaving illegally). This unity has also created some direction that has benefited the sport economically—not only in negotiations with the players' association, but also in starting new ventures, such as MLBAM (baseball's pioneering Internet wing), growing the game internationally and extending the game's commercial opportunities.

This financial success notwithstanding, a relevant question for the future is this: without competition and without effective outside oversight, what will happen to the interests of baseball's fans and its host cities?

Soccer

While baseball franchises have benefited from their status as part of an unregulated monopoly, soccer clubs have struggled to survive in a highly competitive economic environment. The root cause of this competitiveness is the open system of entry: anyone can set up a team, and any team can enter the leagues through the system of promotion and relegation. Since soccer clubs were not originally intended as vehicles for making money, and since originally there was very little money in the soccer business, this did not much matter. In recent years, though, sums of money comparable to the income streams of MLB have entered the game, leading to an environment of cutthroat competition and financial instability.

Structure of Ownership

In England and Scotland, in some ways, the top soccer clubs are business organizations recognizably similar to Major League Baseball clubs: they are incorporated, with boards of directors, and they produce annual financial records according to generally accepted accounting principles. In other ways, however, the ownership organization of British soccer clubs departs from that of MLB. First, British clubs are somewhat more transparent than baseball clubs since no U.K. clubs are subsidiaries of larger business enterprises, and they are all required as limited companies to file annual accounts open to public inspection. Second, British clubs frequently issue stock to the public, and shares are openly traded on the exchange. Although there have been a few instances in which MLB has allowed a team to sell stock to the public, these flotations have always involved a minority of shares and they have been very rare. In 2004 no MLB team had publicly traded equity.

Third, since 1999 most British clubs have Shareholder Trusts. These trusts buy shares of stock in clubs on behalf of individuals but hold the stock collectively. The trust then controls a larger block of stock that it can use to give its members (fans) more leverage at club board meetings where team policy is set. Although this movement is still young and the importance of these trusts varies considerably from team to team, it is a notable vehicle for fan participation and improved communication between team management and team fans.[18] Again, this is in distinct contrast to practices in MLB, where fan participation in ownership is not only discouraged but also generally prohibited, and there has never been a fan trust organization. Indeed, MLB has also outlawed municipal ownership of teams. In 1987 the owner of the San Diego Padres, Joan Kroc, attempted to give the team to the city, but MLB disallowed her gift.

Outside the United Kingdom, the ownership of soccer clubs is more complex. It is common for soccer teams in Germany, Spain, and elsewhere to be run by an athletic club. The club sponsors teams in other sports and operates fitness centers and athletic grounds for its members. Many of Europe's greatest clubs, such as Real Madrid and Bayern Munich, are sporting associations with membership numbers as high as 100,000. Each member pays an annual subscription and votes to elect a club chairman who is as much a politician as a businessman. Barcelona, the soccer club that symbolizes Catalan nationalism in Spain, illustrates this model. Its most famous president was Josep Sunyol, a lawyer and newspaper proprietor from a wealthy family who was elected club president in 1935. Before this, he had used his newspaper to articulate a vision of soccer as a political vehicle for Catalan nationalism, following the defeat of the Republicans in the Spanish Civil War. In 1936 he was shot by Franco's Falangists while attempting to meet a group of Republicans holding out in the mountains outside Madrid.

Since then the presidency of the club has become slightly less risky, but elections are still highly charged political events. Candidates typically compete for votes by promising to bring the top stars to the club. In the 2000 election, candidate Luis Bassat promised to bring Zinedine Zidane to the club if he won (Bassat lost the election and Zidane moved to Real Madrid), while in 2003 candidate Joan Laporta promised to bring David Beckham to the club (Laporta won the election, but Beckham went to Real Madrid).

In the United States, baseball teams can relocate (or threaten to do so), and an owner's loyalty to a host city is contingent on continuing goodwill (and subsidies) from local government. In Europe and South America, relocation is not an option. There is no rule that prohibits relocation, but the very idea is widely considered anathema. Perhaps more important, there is no demand from cities for teams to relocate to their district, since every city already has at least one team, and promotion and relegation ensures that any city of even moderate size can see its team promoted to the top division, if money can be found to hire players.

The bond between local government and club tends to be very close in Europe. Local governments have historically invested heavily in the success of the local team, but unlike in the United States, they have also retained some control over the management of their investments. Thus, although local governments in both the United States and Europe have funded stadium development, in the former, revenue streams have been assigned more or less unconditionally to the club, while in the latter local government has retained significant influence over decisionmaking. In Europe, this has constrained the ability of clubs to maximize revenues. For example, the local government may veto ticket price increases and prevent the installation of luxury boxes. In recent years, the accountants at Deloitte & Touche have highlighted the lack of control over stadiums as a key constraint on the growth of club incomes outside the United Kingdom, where the clubs have funded their own stadium redevelopment. For example, while Manchester United generates 1,500 euros per seat per year ($1,860), most Italian clubs generate little more than 500 euros ($620).[19]

European soccer clubs have attracted their fair share of colorful business personalities. Perhaps the most successful example of recent years has been Silvio Berlusconi, the Italian tycoon, who used his ownership of Italy's leading club, AC Milan, to promote the expansion of his media empire. In 1993 he entered politics, founded his own party, and was briefly prime minister in 1994. In 2001 he became prime minister again and, despite challenges by the courts over financial irregularities and accusations of corruption, has held office for longer than almost any other politician in postwar Italy. AC Milan fans have not had reason to complain either. The club has won seven domestic championships since he took over the club in 1986, and has made six appearances in the European Cup and Champions League finals, four as victor. Over an even longer period the Agnelli family has retained a close relationship with Juventus of Italy, while various other businessmen have dabbled in soccer finance and politics. In France, the business maverick Bernard Tapie used his investment in Olympique Marseille as a springboard to a political career. In England, a thirty-six-year-old Russian, Roman Abramovitch, who owns a large stake in Sibneft (a leading Russian oil company), Aeroflot, and significant parts of the Russian aluminum industry that give him an estimated net worth of $13.5 billion, bought the Chelsea Football Club in 2003 and rapidly set about putting together a dream team.[20]

Despite significant contributions from public funds, soccer club accounting has tended to be opaque, to say the least. In most countries, neither the clubs nor the governments have felt obliged to clarify their financial position, and this lack of transparency has ensured that clubs have plenty of room for maneuver. This might sound like an opportunity to cash in at the public expense, but most European experts believe that those who control soccer clubs have not been principally motivated by profits, but by the prestige associated with team success. In the jargon of economics, team owners are thought to be "utility" rather than "profit" maximizers. Of course, this then begs the question, what is meant by "utility"?

As we have already seen, owners in the United States often own a baseball team as part of a portfolio of businesses and are interested in maximizing the profit from that portfolio. Even if this means taking losses on a baseball club in order to raise profits elsewhere, we should still think of the owners as profit maximizers. Such instances may exist in Europe. For example, Berlusconi's control of AC Milan helped him to acquire and maintain a dominant position in Italian sports broadcasting. However, these circumstances are relatively rare, not least because media owners have not been prominent in the ownership of soccer clubs.[21]

But most owners of soccer clubs are thought to be principally interested in sporting success, either because they have been lifetime supporters of the team or because they see this as a way of building their personal prestige. Two good examples in the first category are Sir Elton John and Sir Jack Walker. Elton John has been a Watford fan since childhood and has intermittently invested in the team, bringing them the notable success of reaching the FA Cup final in 1984. Jack Walker made a fortune in steel and invested somewhere in the region of $100 million in his local team, the Blackburn Rovers (as a result, the club won the Premier League Championship in 1995). These cases clearly relate to childhood obsession. Other owners, like Roman Abramovitch of Chelsea, seem to fit more into the category of seeking personal prestige. In either case, the primary motivation does not seem to be financial returns.

On a more modest scale, most soccer club directors or committee members do not seem to see the generation of financial returns as their primary responsibility. Even where clubs are commercially organized, governing bodies like the FA have placed significant restraints on the pursuit of profits through measures such as the maximum dividend. Indeed, it was not until 1982 that the Football League withdrew its rule prohibiting the payment of a salary to club directors. By implication, anyone interested in running a soccer club should be doing it for the love of the game rather than the love of money. The commonly held view has been that those in charge of the finances should aim to balance the books, while freeing up maximum resources for spending on players to enhance the standing of the team.

Even if one accepts this interpretation at face value (and it is possible to find several examples of owners in soccer who have enriched themselves just as much as any "profit maximizer" might have been expected to), the distinction does not always translate into radically different conduct. For example, whether the gate money goes to pay dividends or to pay players, owners will tend to charge the highest ticket prices that the market will bear. And these ticket prices are often higher in Europe than they are in the United States. For example, most seats at Arsenal Football Club in London are now priced in the range of £30–£50 ($50–$90). Similarly, teams in Europe now do as much as they can to maximize broadcasting, merchandising, and sponsorship revenue. On the revenue side, there is little to choose between a profit maximizer and a utility maximizer.

The real difference lies in the attitude toward investment in the team. The market for soccer players has few of the constraints found in baseball. There is no limit on the number of players on a team's roster. There is no draft system to give weak teams preferential access to new players. There is no luxury tax to penalize teams that spend excessively, and there is no restraint on cash transactions in player trading. Player trading and cash transfer payments (which are limited in baseball at the commissioner's discretion) are an essential part of a league system with promotion and relegation. Teams that are promoted need some means to acquire talent that will enable them to compete at a higher level, while teams that are relegated need to be able to offload talent so that team expenditure will match the lower level of income that teams earn in lower divisions. Trading is also the mechanism by which developing stars can move from lower-ranked teams to higher-ranked teams, and by which aging stars play out the end of their careers. While most trading is between divisions in a given country, there is also a substantial amount of trading within divisions and, more recently, between countries.

Financial Performance

Unlike in the United States, where many fans still seem to dislike player mobility, which they view as an indicator of disloyalty to a team, there is no evidence of any distaste for player mobility in Europe or other soccer markets. To be sure, most fans would prefer that good players stay with their team, but there is little objection to trading in principle. A player who spends his entire career with the same team is viewed as something of an oddity. Admired for his loyalty, perhaps, such a player will always be subject to the suspicion that he would not have been able to adapt to a different environment. One factor explaining the European fans' embrace of player mobility may be that even if a star player is transferred from a local team, he will still be available to play on the national team in international competition. Local fans will thus have a regular opportunity to see the player competing.

Trading in soccer is also a relatively reliable means to improving team performance. In soccer, the relationship between team payroll and performance is very close. In most European soccer leagues it is possible to explain between 80 and 90 percent of the variation in team rankings simply by team payroll.[22] In contrast, in baseball since 1994, the variation in team payroll has explained between 20 and 50 percent of the year-to-year variation in team performance.[23] The tighter relationship in soccer indicates that the market for soccer players works quite efficiently, in the sense that players get paid what they are worth (at least in relative terms). This is also not surprising if players are regularly traded and there is an absence of restraints on team expenditures (such as luxury taxes or debt limits).

If player payroll is a good indicator of success, it is because wage payments closely track player performance. However, since a large fraction of players in soccer are acquired through the transfer system by payment of a transfer fee, this is no guarantee that total player expenditure—that is, payroll plus net transfer spending—is closely related to team performance. Transfer spending is an inherently risky activity, since a trade takes place on the basis of expected future performance, and frequently player performance does not match up to expectations. Statistically, there is a very poor correlation between transfer spending and team performance. This may appear paradoxical, but players who do not live up to expectations are soon dropped, and wages are contingent on maintaining a place on the team. Furthermore, most players will accept a trade, which means that they can continue to play soccer rather than sit out a contract on a high wage when they have no prospect of appearing for the team.

Player trading nowadays involves substantial payments in the form of transfer fees. For example, total expenditure on player transfers by the Premier League was £364 million in the season 2000–01 and £323 million in the season 2001–02. This amounted to 40 percent and 30 percent of total Premier League revenue in each season, respectively. Much of this money was spent by teams gambling on the possibility of avoiding relegation, achieving promotion, or gaining entry to lucrative competitions such as the

Champions League. These are high-risk gambles, and if they do not pay off they leave a large hole in the profit-and-loss account of a club. With such a large fraction of total income being gambled in the player market, it is not surprising to find that club finances are frequently unstable.

Evidence of a financial crisis is often not clear-cut at many soccer clubs, because so few accounting records are made public in most countries and crises tend to be managed behind closed doors. In England, however, where accounting data on clubs are publicly available, it is possible to trace many episodes of financial crisis. It is worthwhile to understand the causes of some of the past financial crises before returning to the current plight of the clubs.

Financial failure leading to bankruptcy has been relatively rare in the soccer world, but in a very small number of instances teams have been forced to leave the league. One of the earliest was in August 1893, when Accrington FC was forced to resign, after being blacklisted for failing to pay a debt of £7.35 (about $36). Upon resignation the team was replaced by Middlesbrough Ironopolis, but financial problems also forced that team to resign two seasons later. There have been other examples of teams resigning at the end of the season because of financial difficulty, but such events pose few problems for the league itself since it is always possible to elect a new team. More serious is the problem of a team forced into resignation during the season.

The first such team was Wigan Borough, which was elected to the League in 1920. Confronting strong competition from two Rugby League teams also located in the town, it struggled to attract support. Wigan Borough appears to have spent heavily in order to achieve some success.[24] In September 1931 it revealed to the League Management Committee that the team was £20,000 in debt (at a time when the English transfer fee record stood at £10,890) and appealed for a subsidy. The league demanded that the club produce a rescue plan within four days or face expulsion from the league. In the event, the club resigned and the games it had played up to that point in the season were declared null and void. Wigan was the most extreme example of financial failure during the depression of the 1930s. Another team, Orient, faced persistent financial problems in the 1930s and even received a donation of £3,450 from Arsenal in 1931. It came close to expulsion in the summer of 1933 after failing to pay all of its wages for the previous season. Given an ultimatum by the Football League to pay by June 22, the club managed to raise the money after receiving a number of donations, one from the Prince of Wales. A different example is provided by Thames FC, a team that played at West Ham Greyhound Stadium in east London and was already in debt when elected to the league in 1930. Faced with strong competition from established east London clubs, Thames failed to attract much support and decided to disband the club in May 1932. Other clubs on the financial edge during this period include Accrington Stanley, New Brighton, and Rochdale.

Following the Second World War, soccer in England enjoyed a boom, as attendance reached an all-time high. By the 1960s, however, the game was coming under pressure from alternative leisure activities, and weaker teams in particular lost support. Moreover, the decline of traditional British industries such as textiles affected the Lancashire-based clubs, which were disproportionately represented in the league. Accrington Stanley, a team that was elected to the league in 1921 but had struggled financially for many years, offered to resign in March 1962, faced with debts of £62,000. At the time, this event provoked great shock, since soccer was generally seen to be in a healthy state. The club continued to play in the lower-level Lancashire Combination League until 1966, but then folded. Another team that suffered at least in part because of the decline of the textile industry was Bradford Park Avenue. Having entered the league in 1908, it had played in the Second Division as recently as 1950, but slipped into debt by the 1960s. At the end of the 1960s, mismanagement made the situation even worse, and the club was voted out of the league in 1970. Following a few seasons in a semi-pro league, the club was closed down in 1974.

Another wave of financial crises hit the Football League in the early 1980s, triggered by a combination of declining attendance and increasing player salaries. In 1983 Charlton Athletic was sued by Leeds United for an outstanding transfer fee payment of £30,000. Other clubs said to be in financial trouble at the time included Bristol City, Hereford, Hull, Bradford City, Wolves, Derby, Swansea, Middlesbrough, Hartlepool, Southend, Tranmere, Halifax, Newport, and Rotherham. These were "smaller" clubs, the ones that had traditionally struggled to make ends meet, but now questions were raised about the indebtedness of "big" clubs such as Chelsea, Nottingham Forest, Manchester City, Leeds United, and Aston Villa. A report published in 1982 found that the total match receipts for that season for all ninety-two league clubs totaled a mere £35 million, generating a £6 million operating loss.[25]

During this period, some clubs in distress started to approach the players' union to negotiate wage cuts and, in many cases, direct subsidies. Other clubs solved the crisis by selling their grounds to the local authority. Clubs with attractive locations were able to sell land for redevelopment. Several clubs that did not own their grounds were forced to relocate when they were unable to pay the rent. Despite this, no club failed during this period.

The low point of the popularity of soccer in England came in the 1985–86 season. Beset by the seemingly universal blight of hooliganism, Football League attendance fell to 16.5 million, compared with the peak of 41.3 million in 1948–49. For no very obvious reason, after 1986 a recovery began. Somehow soccer became fashionable again, its appeal spreading from its traditional working-class roots to the middle classes. Soccer throughout Europe also benefited by the decision of the European Union to open the broadcasting market to privately owned pay TV companies, who provided competition in the market for rights to the established terrestrial broadcasters. In 1988 a satellite broadcaster first entered the bidding in England and prices started to soar (the story of soccer broadcasting is explained in more detail in the next chapter).

With growing attendance and mushrooming broadcast income, English club revenues exploded in the 1990s. In 1991–92, the season before the creation of the Premier League and the first satellite broadcast contract, the top division of twenty clubs generated a total revenue of £170 million. In little more than a decade, this figure increased to £1,132 million, a compound growth rate of almost 21 percent per year. Despite this, few clubs have succeeded in registering substantial profits. Although eleven clubs in the Premier League over the seasons 2001–02 and 2002–03 were quoted on the stock exchange, only Manchester United has paid out a significant dividend to shareholders. Accountants from Deloitte & Touche surveyed the operating profits of clubs in the Premier League during its first ten years of existence, and of the £644 million reported total profits, 36 percent was accounted for by Manchester United alone, and 87 percent by seven teams, out of thirty that had appeared in the Premier League.

Premier League teams, however, have been in a relatively comfortable position.[26] About 62 percent of total income is spent on player wages and salaries, a figure not dissimilar from the that in the major leagues in North America and probably sustainable in the long term.[27] The real crisis, however, has gripped the teams in the next division down, tier two of the English league system. (Tier two was renamed from Division I to FL Championship for the 2004–05 season).[28] Here teams on average devote 72 percent of their revenue to wages and salaries, and for one-quarter of the teams the figure was over 80 percent. Coventry City had total revenue of £16.5 million, yet spent a remarkable £18.3 million on player payroll.

The problem of the second-tier teams in a promotion-and-relegation system is not difficult to understand. In the 1990s, income increased more rapidly at the top level of soccer, where the broadcast rights are most valuable, than it did at the second, third, and lower levels. By 2002–03 the average Premier League club had an annual revenue of £60 million, five times larger than the average revenue of a tier two team. In tier three, average club revenue was only £4 million. While these revenue gaps may not be as large as those between major league, AAA, and AA baseball, no major league team is spending money to avoid being sent down to the minors, and no minor league team is spending in anticipation of promotion to the majors, and, in baseball, minor league player salaries are subject to strict controls.[29]

The economics are inexorable. The lowest TV payment to a Premier League team in 2001–02 was £10.9 million, more than the total revenue of over half the teams in Division I. Any promoted team can expect an immediate cash injection plus a virtual guarantee of selling out every game for the following season. Faced with this juicy carrot, the donkeys of the lower divisions strain every muscle to win the promotion race. But every season only three teams are promoted, leaving a lot of disappointed and exhausted competitors behind. Worse still, teams that are relegated from the Premier League face an immediate revenue collapse and must struggle to unload players, when everyone knows that they are desperate to sell. It is nearly impossible to realize substantial transfer income from player contracts in this situation. On occasion, a team may suffer relegation by two divisions within a period of two to three years, and in such cases financial catastrophe is almost inevitable.

In the United Kingdom, a team that becomes technically insolvent must enter a process known as "administration." More demanding than the Chapter 11 bankruptcy procedure in the United States, administration requires the appointment of an independent financial manager whose responsibility is to liquidate all debts as quickly as possible in a fire sale of assets and either find an investor to take over the business as a going concern or close it down completely. From 2000 to 2004, nineteen of the ninety-two professional teams in England entered this procedure; three of them twice.[30]

Of the teams entering administration, six were in tier two of the English league system, eight in tier three, and five in tier four. No Premier League team has yet entered administration. In five of the nineteen cases, however, the team in question had been relegated from the Premier League within the previous three seasons, and three were about to be relegated for the second time in three seasons.

It would be unfair to place the entire blame for the financial crisis on the promotion-and-relegation system. One of the most high-profile cases of recent years relates to Leeds United, a team that has moved up and down the divisions over the years but won the English League Championship as recently as 1991–92. It is a team that has always enjoyed a strong supporter base, but in the late 1990s the club fell under the control of a group of ambitious managers who borrowed heavily to attract top stars. In 2001 Professor Bill Gerrard of Leeds University Business School placed a "sell-on" value of £198 million on the team's squad, a valuation that was then reported in the club's annual accounts, despite the fact that the book value of the squad was a mere £64 million.[31] Confident of the value of its investment, the club's management borrowed heavily to finance their payroll. But everything went wrong for the club in that year. It had gambled on winning the European Champions League, but the team lost in the semifinal. This near miss cost it in the region of £10 million in lost broadcast fees, gate revenues, and merchandising. Moreover, the team also failed to qualify for participation in the Champions League in the following season, denying it access to future prize money. Once it became clear that the club could not balance the books, creditors started calling in their loans and the club was forced to sell players. The club's most famous player, defender Rio Ferdinand, whom it acquired for a fee of £18 million, was sold to Manchester United for £30 million. Soon after this, however, clubs began to realize that Leeds was a forced seller and the fees tumbled. By early 2004 almost all of the stars of 2001 had been sold, raising about £55 million (slightly less than the book value in 2001) and still leaving the club with large debts.[32] Without stars, the club's performance on the field deteriorated, and it became clear by March 2004 that the club would be relegated. By then, creditors had lost patience with the existing directors and the club was restructured under new ownership. Nevertheless, it was obvious to all that the real cause of the club's difficulties had been the over-ambitious plans of the late 1990s and the failure to win the Champions League in 2001.

If the crisis in England has been mostly restricted to second- and lower-tier clubs, the problems in Italy go all the way to the top. In February 2004 the Italian fraud squad raided the offices of all the clubs in Serie A, the top division, and of the league authority. The reason for this unprecedented step was the suspicion that assurances, provided by the clubs, that they were trading solvently were untrue. Certainly there is widespread recognition of the financial crisis in Italy, and in December 2002 the Italian parliament passed legislation that would enable clubs to restructure their debts.[33]

The financial figures are quite remarkable. Total reported operating losses for the eighteen clubs in Serie A have increased from €144 million in 1996–97 (€8 million per club) to €982 million in 2001–02 (€54 million per club). The current losses appear unsustainable when set against the total revenues of only €1,148 million in 2001–02 (excluding extraordinary items such as player trading).[34] As a result, total indebtedness in Serie A has increased to €1,742 million. In other words, club indebtedness is about 50 percent greater than club revenue on average. Since the clubs do not own the stadiums in which they play, they own almost no assets other than player contracts.

In 2002 Fiorentina, one of the leading Italian clubs of the 1990s, fell into bankruptcy. Or rather, one should say that the individual who owned the soccer club was bankrupt. Vittorio Cecchi Gori is a business and film producer (of, among others, *Life Is Beautiful*, which won three Oscars in 1998) who invested heavily in the soccer club. Following a divorce and the loss of his parliamentary seat, which gives immunity from prosecution, fraud investigations were started, and his business empire started to crumble. By 2002 Cecchi Gori could no longer pay the player salaries and the club was declared bankrupt. As one of the most well supported clubs in Italy, the soccer club itself was rescued from the financial wreckage under the new name of Florentia. The only problem for the fans was that the penalty for financial failure was relegation to a lower level of the Italian soccer pyramid. Florentia was obliged to reenter at the fourth tier of competition (Serie C2). Having played before average crowds of 30,000 in 2002, it was playing against teams with average attendance of as little as 1,000 in 2003.[35]

Fiorentina's collapse was a result of poor financial management. The case of Parma was something worse. Parma is a relatively small city with no great soccer history. From the 1980s onward, the club came under the control of Parmalat, a local dairy business that grew like topsy to become one of Europe's biggest food companies. The soccer club benefited from this, with star players and unprecedented success during the 1990s. At the end of the 1990s, Parmalat attracted the attention of the financial authorities. The investigation focused on assets that were significantly overvalued, and once they were written down to realistic values it became clear that the group was insolvent. Not surprisingly, investment in the soccer club dried up and star players were sold. Former Italian champion Napoli, already relegated to the second tier,[36] was further demoted in August 2004 to Serie C1 because its financial house was not in order.

Given the continuing level of indebtedness in Serie A, further collapses are to be expected. While AC Milan and Juventus can be reasonably confident that these losses will be absorbed by the conglomerate enterprises that support them (the Berlusconi empire and Fiat, respectively), few other clubs have reason to be optimistic that their debts can be serviced in the longer term.

Why have the top clubs in Italy struggled financially when most teams in the English Premier League have remained solvent? Italy has long been one of soccer's greatest strongholds, and by the late 1980s, Italian teams were dominant in European competition. Almost all of the world's best players were employed by Italian clubs. The ultimate standard of club soccer competition is the European Cup, which became the Champions League in 1993. In the decade from 1989 to 1998, an Italian team competed in the final nine times and won it four times. There was no question that Serie A was the best soccer league in the world. The finances of Italian clubs reflected this dominance. In 1991–92 total Serie A revenue was around 400 million euros, compared to the 255 million euros (£170 million) generated by England's top division. During the 1990s, the Premier League's revenue grew much faster than Serie A's, so that by the mid-1990s the position was reversed (as mentioned above, the principal reason was that match day revenues—gate and stadium revenue—rose much faster in England). During the 1990s, Premier League clubs increasingly competed to attract the top stars, but Italian clubs did not surrender their ambition to dominate European competition. Because their revenues were not rising as rapidly, Serie A payrolls as a share of revenue reached 75 percent by 2000–01, compared to only 60 percent in the Premier League. The only way that Serie A clubs could keep up with the Premier League was to borrow money. And, as we have seen, by 2004 this strategy was becoming increasingly untenable.

It is important to note here that the development of the Champions League has also contributed to this emerging financial instability. Before 1993 each of the winners of the European national leagues competed for the European Cup, a single-elimination tournament. This was seen as the most prestigious prize in European club soccer, but most teams played relatively few games in the competition (with about fifty members, a single-elimination competition requires no more than six rounds, and all but eight teams would appear in three rounds or fewer). However, UEFA (the European governing body of soccer) expanded the tournament in 1993 to give access to more teams, especially those from the dominant soccer nations such as Italy and England, and to enable these teams to play more games. With more television coverage, qualifying teams were capable of boosting their income substantially. As a result, the incentives to spend at the top end of the top division in each country increased enormously, while incentives to share income within the national divisions (already weak) were further undermined.

If the economics are this simple, why didn't the Serie A clubs simply cut their spending? Here one final piece of the jigsaw needs to be fitted into place. Italian clubs have suffered financial crises before, but have in the past always managed to weather the storm. Good political connections have meant that municipal governments have been willing to bail out clubs in one way or another. What has changed in recent years has been domestic pressure to control spending and external pressure to control public subsidies from the Commission of the European Union. Domestic pressure has arisen because of government budget cuts and new obligations such as the commitment to control public sector deficits imposed by membership in Europe's new currency, the euro. External pressure arises from enforcement of the Treaty of Rome, the fundamental law of the European Union. The treaty significantly restricts the ability of national or local governments to subsidize businesses because of the adverse effect this can have on other businesses inside the European Union. Thus the Italian government is not permitted to subsidize the hiring of players by football clubs in Italy since this would limit the ability of clubs in other EU states such as Germany, Spain, or England to hire these players.[37] So whereas in the past the Italian clubs would probably have been bailed out by government, this time such support has not been forthcoming.

This story helps to explain the pattern of financial crises across Europe. In Belgium, for example, five clubs have been forced to leave the league owing to bankruptcy in the past five years. Perhaps the most striking examples are from Spain. Spanish clubs have to a significant degree replaced Italian clubs as the dominant force in European competition. From 1998 to 2002, five Spanish teams competed in the Champions League final and won it three times. Real Madrid has reemerged as Europe's dominant team, and clubs such as Barcelona, Valencia, and Deportivo La Coruña have fielded star teams as well. These successes, however, were not yet fully reflected in the earnings of Spanish clubs. By 2001–02 the revenue of the top Spanish division had risen to around €1,369 million, 20 percent more than the revenue of Italian clubs, but nearly 30 percent less than the revenue of the Premier League.[38]

Views differ on whether the player expenditure of Spanish clubs is sustainable, but one thing that is clear is that Spanish clubs have not entered into financial crisis. In 2002 it was widely predicted that Real Madrid would disintegrate financially, having paid £37 million for Luis Figo in 2000 and £47 million for Zinedine Zidane in 2001, but in fact, the club was able to pull off soccer's greatest ever real estate deal. They sold their training ground, located in the heart of downtown Madrid, for an estimated $400 million to a local property developer. In part, the deal depended on the city government agreeing to redesignate the purposes for which the land could be used, and as a result, the European Commission conducted an investigation into whether the deal constituted a form of illegal state aid. The Commission found that nothing improper had happened, but few people doubt that clubs like Real Madrid enjoy almost unlimited support from their regional government. It is hard to imagine such a club ever being allowed to fail financially.

In some countries, there currently appears to be no financial crisis at all. France, as in so many things, represents the antithesis of the American system. All sport in France is licensed by the state, which in exchange subsidizes governing bodies charged with developing sport on behalf of the state. Thus the Fédération de Football Française (FFF) possesses a legally sanctioned monopoly over organizing soccer competitions in France. Appointment to this body is politically controlled, at both the local and the national level. The Ligue de Football Professionnel (LFP) and the owners of the football clubs, therefore, can do nothing without the consent of the politicians of the FFF. Not surprisingly, much of the history of French soccer concerns the struggle between team owners and the FFF. Owners, of course, cultivate friendships with politicians, and during the 1970s and 1980s, a group of powerful and autocratic owners emerged to dominate the soccer scene. Roger Rocher at St. Etienne, Claude Bez at Bordeaux, and Bernard Tapie at Marseilles were larger-than-life businessmen, closely connected to local politicians, who invested heavily in their teams and produced both domestic and European success. However, these figures also attracted powerful enemies, while the combination of public and private funds inevitably led to accusations of corruption. While the teams remained successful, these individuals were untouchable, but once crises appeared both on and off the field there was no escaping the final denouement. In the early 1990s, all three ended up in jail, Rocher for making illegal payments and fraud, Bez for fraud and tax evasion, Tapie for bribery (match fixing).

Faced with this crisis, which was also financial, the government set up by decree a new body, the Direction Nationale de Contrôle de Gestion (DNCG), to act as a financial regulator. The DNCG has the power to inspect the financial accounts of all clubs, can forbid financial transactions (including the acquisition of players) on prudential grounds, and can force teams that are not trading solvently to be relegated and even to be stripped of their professional status. The DNCG has shown itself willing to use these powers, as, for example, in the case of Toulouse in 2001, which was relegated by two divisions because it lacked financial guarantees. Some commentators have questioned the willingness of the DNCG to discipline the larger clubs,[39] but there is no question that financial controls are much stricter than in most of Europe, to the point where debt levels have been falling since the second half of the 1990s. Set against this financial stability, however, is the fact that French clubs have performed poorly in European competition. Although the French national team won the World Cup in 1998 and the European Championship in 2000, testifying to the high quality of players being produced in France, few of these players are employed by French clubs; most of them play for clubs in Spain, England, and Italy. Not surprisingly, attendance at club matches in France is lower than in these other countries.

The French system of regulation has attracted much attention in Europe, to the point where UEFA introduced a system of national club licensing in 2004. The idea is that each national association must annually license its professional clubs to participate in national competition. Licenses are granted to teams that credibly meet financial criteria. Teams refused a license will not be permitted to compete. In principle, this system could produce the same kind of financial stability as has been created in France, but the system will only work if national associations are willing to enforce it. Even in France, where the powers of the DNCG ultimately derive from the state, the credibility of the regulator has been challenged. In other countries, where either the involvement of the state in professional sport is less accepted or the state is less willing to impose financial discipline, the system may be ineffectual.

More generally, many question whether it is really appropriate for sport to be governed through regulation rather than competition. In the United States, sports leagues and clubs are responsible for their own finances. If clubs and leagues fail to control themselves financially they face the discipline of the market.[40] In theory, competition among businesses leads to efficiency and satisfaction of consumer interests. UEFA, however, monopolizes the organization of the game and in many cases prohibits competitive solutions. For example, if Italian soccer is bankrupt, it would be possible in theory for England's Premier League or Spain's Primera Liga to establish new teams in Italian cities and compete. More credibly, perhaps, the top teams from the Serie A could join with Spanish and English teams to form a European Major League. All of this is prohibited by the European governing body, however. Moreover, any teams that defied UEFA's authority would be likely to find themselves unable to recruit players. The affected players, in turn, might even be ruled ineligible to represent their national team.

Thus far, at least, soccer's governance structure has proved a huge success, judging by the international popularity of the game. Competitions organized by the international governing bodies, such as the World Cup and the European Champions League, have proved enormously successful and have complemented the powerful attraction of domestic soccer league competition. What has suffered are the commercial interests of the soccer clubs. Through regulation imposed by national and international governing bodies, clubs, especially the biggest clubs, have been prevented from establishing competitions and competitive structures that would maximize their profits. In the United States, by contrast, the absence of national and international governance structures has enabled established leagues to maximize profits while devoting insufficient resources to the wider development of the game. We will have more to say about these contrasting approaches in our final chapter.

CHAPTER SIX

Watching the Money

Baseball and Soccer Broadcasting

Robert Redford's 1994 movie *Quiz Show* deals with the scandal surrounding the revelations that a popular game show of the 1950s, *Twenty-One*, was being fixed. In the movie, based on a true story, a congressional researcher uncovers a plot to fix the show involving TV executives at NBC and the corporate sponsor, Geritol, and forces them to testify before Congress. The researcher challenges the owner of Geritol, played by Martin Scorsese, in private to deny that he had fixed the show. Scorsese replies nonchalantly that, of course, the show was fixed, but that it didn't matter. Even if the viewers knew, they wouldn't care, and even if he weren't allowed to fix it, he could produce the same effect simply by setting easier questions. Because, Scorsese explains, people were not watching because they cared about the questions; they just wanted to watch the money.

Watching the money is an integral part of broadcasting, whether it be movies or sports. Most of us struggle to imagine what it would be like to earn as much as movie stars or sports stars, but we enjoy trying. Many people are infuriated by the large sums that these individuals earn, although really it is the medium that has created these excesses, not the stars. Stars have talents that are well beyond the range of most of us; that is why they are stars. What they are paid depends on how big an audience they can reach. One reason that Cameron Diaz or Tom Cruise, or Alex Rodriguez or David Beckham, would not have made so much money a hundred years ago is that the media did not exist to give so many people the opportunity to see what it is that makes them so special.

From the point of view of sports, it is, above all, live broadcasting that counts. Sports offers the excitement of suspense. Without uncertainty of outcome, the attractiveness of watching sports is much diminished. In this chapter we explore how the broadcast media have developed in tandem with sports competition in baseball and soccer over the past century.

Baseball

Baseball cut its first media deal back in the 1890s. Western Union paid the National League for the right to relay game updates to saloons and poolrooms. Adumbrating concerns that would surface first with radio and then with television, some owners protested that providing such contemporaneous game information would diminish fans' incentive to come to the ballpark. Nonetheless, the practice spread, and by 1913 Western Union paid each team $17,000 annually over five years for telegraph rights.

Baseball's growing popularity also caught the attention of the motion picture industry, which in 1910 offered baseball $500 for the right to film and show the World Series. In 1911 this fee increased sevenfold to $3,500.

Deals with Hollywood produced little disagreement among the owners, but radio was another story. In early 1920 an executive from baseball's New York Giants argued that radio coverage of games was "impossible and absurd [because] it would cut into our attendance. . . . We want fans following games from the grandstand, not their homes."[1] Still a majority of owners and Commissioner Landis were willing to try audiocasting on a trial basis. On August 5, 1921, the first radio broadcast of a game, between the Pirates and Phillies at Forbes Field in Pittsburgh, was produced. Later that year the World Series between the Yankees and Giants was carried on radio via a relay: a sportswriter from Newark, New Jersey, reported the games from the Polo Grounds in Manhattan via telephone to WJZ, a Newark radio station, which then repeated the information over the air. The next year an estimated 5 million Americans listened to the live radio broadcast of the

World Series, as the Giants defeated the Yankees for the second straight year. Some owners began to see radio not only as a source of revenue, but also as an effective means of promoting interest in their teams. In 1925 Cubs owner William Wrigley was so convinced of this advertising potential that he invited any Chicago station to broadcast his team without payment of a rights fee. Though Cubs attendance did not suffer, many recalcitrant owners refused to allow radio broadcasting of their teams' games. It was not until 1939 that all MLB teams allowed their games to be carried live on radio. In that year, radio rights for the World Series sold for some $400,000.

It was also in 1939 that the first baseball game was televised, a battle between Columbia and Princeton Universities for fourth place in the Ivy League. Major league owners, however, were not ready yet for the television revolution. It was not until 1946 that the Yankees led the way in local television deals, signing MLB's first team contract for $75,000. Although novel in concept, the impact of the early TV deals was minimal. In 1948 there were only 190,000 television sets in use in the entire country.

In 1949 MLB inked its first deal for live television coverage of the World Series and All-Star Game. Commissioner Happy Chandler negotiated a six-year contract with Gillette for $1 million a year. Gillette, however, then sold the rights to NBC for $4 million a year, prompting Cardinals owner Fred Saigh to brand Chandler—a former senator from Kentucky—a "bluegrass jackass."

The use of television in the home began to explode. In 1950 an estimated 10.5 million sets were in use. By 1953 fifteen of baseball's sixteen teams had local television deals, and ABC introduced its national game-of-the-week format. The number of television households continued to grow throughout the 1950s, reaching 34.9 million in 1955 and 45.8 million (87 percent of U.S. households) in 1960.

As America embraced the television, advertisers took notice. The budding sitcoms of the 1950s attracted a predominantly female audience. In baseball and other sports programming, companies saw an opportunity to reach large numbers of men in their twenties and thirties. This is one of the most valuable target groups for advertisers because young men tend to have high levels of disposable income, but they also tend to have a limited interest in most other programming genres. Sports reels them in, and this became the basis for one of history's most successful marriages. Television companies needed the advertisers, and the advertisers needed baseball.

Baseball, in turn, looked to TV for both exposure and revenue. Despite its matrimonial tussles, the relationship remains strong to this day.

Together, radio and television contributed only 3 percent of baseball's revenues in 1946, but this share rose to 16.8 percent by 1956.[2] MLB's average annual television network revenues then rose from $1.195 million in 1956 to $3.25 million in 1960, $16.6 million in 1970, $47.5 million in 1980, and $365 million in 1990. Behind this growth is another important story.

In September 1961 the U.S. Congress passed the Sports Broadcasting Act. This act gave team sports leagues an antitrust exemption for over-the-air national television packages. That is, the separate teams in MLB, the NFL, the NBA, and the NHL could join together, form a cartel, and sign a single television package. Among other things, this not only meant that MLB could bargain with the networks as a monopolist and extract a higher rights fee; it also meant that the league had the option to distribute television revenues more equally.[3]

In fact, during 1962–64 baseball's television agreement provided that each team would be paid according to the number of appearances it made on the national broadcasts. The Yankees dynasty that began in the late 1940s was still playing itself out in the early 1960s, so the Yankees garnered the lion's share of TV appearances and revenue from the CBS contract. Then in 1964, CBS bought the Yankees, ensuring the team's continued television prominence. Accordingly, the Yankees received some two-thirds of baseball's national television money in 1964, or, stated differently, CBS paid itself two-thirds of MLB's rights fee.[4]

In 1965, provoked by the abuse of the national contract with CBS (and the Yankees), MLB decided to follow the lead of the NFL and distribute national television revenues equally to all teams. Thus, as the TV contract grew, so did the share of MLB revenues that were equally distributed. Together with the introduction of the reverse-order amateur draft in 1965, the end of the Yankees' special relationship with the Kansas City Athletics,[5] and the retirement of most of the stars from the Yankees teams of the early 1960s, baseball entered a period of increasing competitive balance.

This period—although punctuated by some mini-dynasties of medium-market teams—was to come to an end after the national television contract ended its four-decade-long winning streak in 1993. Following the 1990–93 contract with CBS, worth an annual average of $365 million, MLB signed a deal with NBC and ABC in 1994 known as the "baseball partnership." The basic idea was to present a regionalized game of the week and to share net revenues among the networks and MLB. The partnership lasted for two years, and MLB's annual television revenues fell by over 60 percent.

The drop in shared revenues coincided with the introduction of rich local cable contracts in certain big-city markets. The Yankees, for instance, had a twelve-year contract with the local cable sports channel MSG that brought the team an annual average of over $40 million. The rapid growth in local cable deals, together with the introduction of new stadiums in some cities, led to sharp increases in revenue inequality across the teams. The disparity between the top- and bottom-revenue teams grew from around $30 million in 1989 to over $270 million in 2004.[6] And along with this widening revenue differential, competitive imbalance, manifested most vividly in another Yankee dynasty, reappeared.

The Yankees' remarkable success with cablecasting in the New York market eventually led other teams to seek to emulate them. The 1990s, in consequence, witnessed a sharp turn toward cable and pay television, away from free-to-air television.

The cable sports boom began with the creation of ESPN in 1979 and was extended during the 1980s and 1990s as a growing share (today around 85 percent) of America's television homes became hooked up to cable or satellite transmission. ESPN's national cable model was soon followed by superstations (local free-to-air stations whose signal was uplinked to satellite and then distributed around the country via cable or satellite systems) such as TBS or WGN and then by regional sports networks (RSNs). From the perspective of baseball teams, cable provided the advantage of being able to create two revenue streams: one from advertising, just like free over-the-air television, and the other from subscription payments from interested households.

Teams that control their own cable outlet, as do the Yankees, Red Sox, Braves, Phillies, Twins, Blue Jays, Orioles, Astros, and Royals (with more on the way), also have the ability to shelter income from MLB's increasingly costly revenue-sharing system. This provides yet another impetus toward cable-ization.

With the technology available and the viewing culture adapting, cable came to dominate local baseball broadcasting. Whereas in 1987 there were an average of 80.7 baseball games per team broadcast on free TV and only 35.1 games on cable, by 2003 these numbers had practically reversed, with

41.3 games on free TV and 90.1 games on cable. Higher local media revenues for MLB teams have accompanied this migration to cable. Together these local media revenues grew from $116.9 million in 1985 to $342.1 million in 1990, and to approximately $655 million in 2002—and these are only reported revenues.[7] Teams that own their cable or broadcast television station can shuffle revenues away from the team. Within this local media revenue total, cable has played a larger and larger role. Team revenues from local cable deals grew from roughly $200 million in 1999 to $275 million in 2000, and to $350 million 2002—an annual growth rate of 20.5 percent over the period.[8]

For baseball fans, cable migration is bad news not only because it costs them more money to watch their favorite team on television; in addition, disputes between teams and cable distributors have resulted in some teams' games not being carried at all.[9]

Part of the dispute between cable distributors and teams had to do with whether the teams' games would be placed on basic cable (with the general service delivered to most households for a set monthly fee) or be part of a premium cable selection with an additional charge of several dollars per household per month. Teams want to be included on the basic service and to be paid the monthly fee per number of households subscribing to this service, resulting both in more subscription and more advertising revenue. Many cable distributors, however, resist putting teams' games on a general service because only a minority of their subscribers watch baseball. Charging these non-fan subscribers to watch baseball means either that the cable companies charge lower prices for the rest of their service or that they lose customers. Meanwhile, non-baseball-watching consumers feel cheated when they are charged for a service that they don't use.

One issue for the teams is that in many markets there is only one RSN to bid for the cable rights to their games. Without competition, the RSN is able to pay a below-market price. In other markets, such as New York, in the late 1990s there were two RSNs, but they were both run by the same company, Cablevision. Cablevision, in turn, is partly owned by the NewsCorp, which until early 2004 owned the Dodgers, a competitor of the Yankees and Mets. Under these circumstances, the Yankees believed that they could not get a fair market price for their games and decided, in a joint venture with the NBA's New Jersey Nets, to form their own local RSN. Thus the YES Network was born in 2000. In 2004 the subscription and advertising revenue of YES approaches $250 million. Of this, perhaps $30 million is used for operating costs, and another $20 million is spent to purchase programming other than the Yankees. Although the Yankees' net revenues from YES border on $200 million annually, in 2004 the team was reporting cable revenues of around $55 million to baseball's revenue-sharing system. The Yankees were not the only team using this tax-evasion tactic.

For instance, the Boston Red Sox own 80 percent of the New England Sports Network (NESN). During the 2001 season, NESN went from being a premium channel in most of New England to an expanded basic channel, and revenues rose sharply from roughly $39 million in 2000 to above an estimated $50 million in 2001. With some $15 million in costs, NESN probably cleared $35 million before paying rights fees to the Red Sox.

In the data that Commissioner Selig presented to Congress in December 2001, the Red Sox reported $33 million of total local media revenue for 2001. Approximately $10 million of this came from the local Fox channel WFXT for the rights to broadcast sixty-seven Sox games on over-the-air television and another $5 million from WEEI for radio rights. This suggests that the Sox only reported $18 million of NESN income to MLB for revenue-sharing purposes.

Other teams, in order to generate a competitive bid for their cable rights, or to emulate the financial bonanza and tax sheltering created by the YES Network, have attempted to form their own RSN. Some have succeeded. Some have not. In the meantime, the development of local cable markets has sharply increased the revenue inequalities across teams.

Baseball has also had modest success since 1995 in growing its central television revenue. During 1996–99 MLB signed contracts with FOX, ESPN, and NBC that averaged $425 million annually. In the period 2000–2005 MLB signed contracts with FOX and ESPN, yielding an average of approximately $560 million annually.

Supplementing significantly the national TV contracts has been the growth of foreign, Internet, and satellite revenues. Foreign television revenues were around $40 million in 2002, but with the new six-year deal in Japan for $275 million (which allows for some 300 MLB games to be televised each year) and new pacts in Canada and elsewhere, these revenues now reportedly exceed $100 million annually.

Baseball's new Internet business, MLBAM, founded in 2001, has had remarkable success. MLBAM provides online merchandising, news, live audio, and video streaming of virtually all games, packages of video high-lights, among other services, and in 2004 was projected to have gross rev-enues approaching $140 million. These revenues have been growing at over 40 percent per year. There even has been talk of taking a minority portion of MLBAM public, based on a valuation of over $2 billion.

Revenue from satellite distribution, such as DirecTV, has been more modest. After expenses, revenues from all of these sources (foreign, Internet, and satellite) amount to nearly $5 million per team in 2004.[10]

As a result of the growth of central revenues and baseball's new revenue-sharing system, the revenue differential among teams has been narrowing, and will likely continue to do so. Nevertheless, the growing disparity in local media revenues and perverse incentives in baseball's revenue-sharing sys-tem are working to frustrate hopes for the fans of many small-city teams. In the next chapter, we look at how MLB has tried to deal with the competitive balance issue.

Soccer

In the United States, broadcasting is a private enterprise licensed by federal regulatory authorities. For most of the twentieth century, broadcasting in Europe and the rest of the world was a public service produced and distrib-uted by government agencies. This made for some fundamental differences in the nature of sports broadcasting between the United States and the world outside. First, government influence made sports broadcasting a more politically sensitive issue, particularly in countries where the political regime was not settled but might change from liberal democracy to military junta to socialist republic. Second, state broadcasters were typically monop-olists, a fact that significantly affected the terms of any deal with a sports league. Third, government control usually meant that listeners were required to pay a license fee out of which broadcast services were funded, while funding through advertising was strictly limited.

In the United Kingdom, for example, the BBC was created in 1922 as a joint venture among radio set manufacturers, including Marconi, Western Electric, General Electric, and Metropolitan-Vickers. In order to avoid the perceived "chaos" that had marked the inauguration of radio broadcasting in the United States, it was agreed that the BBC should monopolize broad-casting, while paying a license fee for the right to broadcast to the General

Post Office (the public body that claimed jurisdiction over the airwaves).[11] The BBC itself made no money, its investors being content with the increase in sales of radio sets that they manufactured. In 1926, following the recommendation of a government report, the company was turned into a corporation whose governors are appointed by the government and whose privileges and responsibilities are defined by a parliamentary charter (essentially its present constitution).

Given its public service remit, the BBC focused heavily on educational (usually high-brow) material in its early years, and only slowly developed an interest in sports. When it did so, it found that the soccer authorities, the Football League in particular, were less than enthusiastic. The first live soccer broadcast in the United Kingdom was a league match between Arsenal and Sheffield United on January 22, 1927. However, most of the early broadcasts were commentaries on excerpts of FA Cup and international matches, access to which was controlled by the gentlemanly and public-spirited FA. The FA Cup final, then the showcase of the English season, was first broadcast on radio in 1928. In 1929 the FA went so far as to demand a fee and the BBC refused, so only match excerpts were broadcast. In 1930 the FA asked for £100 for the right to broadcast the Cup final ($486 in 1930, or about $5,500 in today's money), which the BBC was willing to pay only on the condition that it could decide how the money was spent. In the end a compromise was reached, thanks to the timely intervention of the bishop of Buckingham, in which the money was paid to charity and the broadcast went ahead.[12]

The businessmen of the Football League were less inclined to compromise, and from the beginning most saw radio broadcasting as a threat to attendance at their matches, much as the barons of baseball did. Some of the larger clubs, such as Arsenal in London, welcomed the broadcasters, but in a league constituted of ninety-two clubs, the voices of the smaller clubs prevailed.[13] When the FA Cup or international matches were broadcast, they claimed, they lost fans at league matches. The deepening depression seemed to strengthen their case, and in 1931 the Football League banned all radio broadcasting of its matches in the United Kingdom (although, as a concession, broadcasts to the empire were to be permitted).[14]

Little changed with the introduction of television. The FA Cup final was broadcast for television by the BBC in 1937, but this was largely experimental given that, by this date, fewer than 2,000 television sets had been sold in the United Kingdom. Nonetheless, the Football League clubs refused to have anything to do with it, and in 1948 voted that no league matches could be televised (by which date there were around 25,000 televisions and broadcasting was limited to a forty-mile radius around London).

By the 1960s matters had changed. Competition in TV broadcasting was introduced in 1955 by the creation of a privately owned channel, ITV, funded by advertising.[15] TV penetration in the United Kingdom had reached 55 percent of households in 1960, and ITV was willing to pay to expand its audiences. The management committee of the Football League yielded to financial temptation and in that year reached a draft agreement with ITV to broadcast twenty-six live matches for £150,000 (around $2.6 million in today's money). However, most of the First Division clubs refused access to the cameras, and so only relatively poor matches were shown. The transmission was a failure and the plans for live broadcasting were shelved.[16] The views of club chairmen were summarized by Bob Lord, the opinionated, if not very well informed, chairman of Burnley, the team that won the league championship in 1960: "Television is not for professional football. It will damage and undermine attendances, as it did to baseball in America."[17]

Finally, in 1964, the league agreed to a one-year deal with the BBC to allow broadcast of highlights for £20,000 a year (around $336,000 in 2004 prices), and in 1965 two ITV broadcasters paid £3,000 to show thirty minutes of recorded highlights on a Sunday afternoon. This was the only form of broadcasting permitted by the clubs until 1983, by which time the league was generating a mere £500,000 a year (equivalent to about $1.3 million today). The bargaining position of the league was not helped by the fact that the broadcasters were permitted to negotiate jointly; and when ITV attempted to offer a substantially larger fee if they could obtain exclusive rights, the antitrust authority obliged them to return to joint negotiation.[18]

Nonetheless, by then soccer on TV had become an important feature of British sporting culture, thanks to the growth of the game internationally. The first World Cup matches to be broadcast on television were the 1954 finals held in Switzerland, the rights having been given away for free by the Fédération Internationale de Football Association (FIFA). Television turned the World Cup from a sideshow into the world's most popular sporting event. By 1966, when the finals were held in England, over 400 million people watched the game worldwide. Twenty-six million watched in the United Kingdom alone (48 percent of the population).[19]

While growing audiences demonstrated soccer's commercial potential on TV, FIFA was still led by an old-fashioned Englishman, Sir Stanley Rous, who solemnly warned of the threat that commercialism posed to the game. In 1974 he was unseated by Dr. João Havelange, a Brazilian who adopted a more entrepreneurial approach to the game. Havelange won the job by promising to expand the income from FIFA competitions and to give the lion's share to developing nations, who were now in the majority within FIFA. Throughout his twenty-four-year tenure, Havelange was also consistently accused of using FIFA income to buy support. Commercial innovation was rapid. From the 1970s, FIFA built a partnership with Adidas, the sporting goods company, and from 1978 with the Coca-Cola Corporation, which was keen to associate itself with the world game. Together the growth of TV exposure and sponsorship expanded FIFA's income in the same way that media exposure had enriched major league baseball in the United States. In 1982 the TV rights for the World Cup generated 100 million deutsche mark ($80 million at today's prices).[20] The total revenue of the 1986 World Cup in Mexico was estimated at nearly $100 million ($170 million in today's money), with one-third of the revenues from TV rights and one-third from sponsorship.[21] This amounted to revenues of nearly $2 million per game played.

By this time, the connection between televised soccer and large sums of money started to impinge on the thought processes of the directors of the larger Football League clubs in England, as well as club directors elsewhere in Europe. Soccer on TV had expanded slowly at first in other European countries because the spread of television itself was quite slow. In 1960 only 21 percent of German households, 13 percent of Italian households, 12 percent of French households, and 2 percent of Spanish households possessed a television. The "swinging sixties," however, brought significant income growth among European consumers, and by 1970 the figures were 69, 54, 59, and 28 percent, respectively. By 1980 the saturation point had been reached.

In Germany, matters were complicated by the fact that a national professional league was not created until 1963, and opposition to commercial development was even stronger than in the United Kingdom. Although the public service broadcaster, ARD, showed delayed highlights of Bundesliga matches, broadcast of live matches was prevented by the league. At the same time, Germany's remarkable World Cup exploits (winners in 1954, 1974, and 1990, runners-up in 1966, 1982, and 1986) could all be watched live and in full on TV. In Italy, 28 million watched the nation's defeat in the 1970 World Cup final, while 37 million (65 percent of the population) are said to have witnessed its victory in 1982.[22] Nonetheless, the teams of Serie A refused to allow live broadcasting of league games by the public broadcasting channels, and fans were offered only a highlights program, typically shown on Sunday evenings after the matches had been played. Only in Spain did broadcasting of league matches become a regular feature before the 1990s, largely thanks to the use of television as a political tool by the Franco regime.

The role of television in soccer has long been a matter of controversy in Spain,[23] but there is little doubt that live soccer was frequently shown at politically sensitive moments. For example, May Day rallies were a regular focus for left-wing opposition to the fascist regime, and so the state television company would reschedule and broadcast popular matches on this date. Between 1960 and 1976, Spanish television typically broadcast one league match live every week during the season. Special compensation agreements were entered into to account for lost gate revenue, and it is estimated that Spanish TV paid in the region of 600 million pesetas (about $50 million in today's money) for these rights[24]—not a large sum by today's standards, but considerably more than was being paid by national broadcast companies in most other countries. A similar situation existed among the South American military dictatorships.

One factor that was leading the larger clubs to change their attitude to live broadcasting was the advent of pan-European club football. From the late 1950s, three parallel European club competitions were organized by UEFA, the European governing body. This meant that in any year as many as five teams per country might be involved in European competition, and these matches could generate significant numbers of armchair fans who identified with the clubs that carried the nation's flag. TV revenues for these games could also be a significant boost for an individual club. In some countries, such as Germany, the national league continued to control the broadcast rights and shared the money from European broadcast rights with all league members, but most teams playing in Europe kept the money for themselves.

The decisive factor in the explosion of live soccer in Europe was the deregulation of broadcasting that occurred during the 1980s, partly due to the wave of privatization and deregulation that swept the world in the 1980s, and partly at the behest of the European Union. In Italy, private companies, notably the Fininvest conglomerate controlled by Silvio Berlusconi, had successfully lobbied for the removal of the public service monopoly and were able to offer their own private channels by 1980. In Germany, private sector broadcasting was permitted in 1983. In France, Canal+ became the country's first commercial broadcaster in 1984. Post-Franco Spain finally licensed commercial TV in 1988. In 1989 the European Union Directive "Television without Frontiers" required all member states to give broadcasters access to their national market, effectively increasing the potential for competition. The purpose of this directive was to create a single European market in broadcasting, particularly with the development of new technologies such as direct-to-home satellite broadcasting.[25]

Thus, by the end of the 1980s, there existed a significant number of new competitors offering pay TV services: Berlusconi's Fininvest in Italy, Canal+ in France, Kirch and Bertelsmann in Germany, Antena 3 in Spain, and BSkyB, a joint venture 40 percent owned by Rupert Murdoch's News International, in the United Kingdom. Each had made large investments in new and expensive delivery systems, each was hungry for viewers, and none of them had any significant programming to show. All of them realized that there were two main drivers that would attract subscriptions: Hollywood movies and premium sports. Signing long-term contracts with the studios was easy enough, but premium sport was more difficult. Unlike the United States, where there are competing major league sports, Europe is a sporting monoculture: only soccer consistently delivers viewers. Traditional broadcast soccer events, like the World Cup, were attractive, but were likely to be politically protected and were in any case too irregular to form the basis of a subscription service. The only option was domestic league soccer.

In England, the Football League had already bitten the bullet in 1983 and signed a contract with the BBC and ITV to broadcast ten games (out of 462 played in the First Division) for the sum of £2.6 million (about $7 million in today's money) to be divided equally among its ninety-two clubs (about $77,000 each). This concession was born of desperation from the financial crisis of the early 1980s (discussed in chapter 5) and was of little avail in the absence of competition between the BBC and ITV.

The first bombshell came in the form of a bid from the first U.K. satellite broadcaster in 1988 (BSB, which later merged to become BSkyB). Although

BSB didn't win the contract, ITV broke ranks with the BBC and paid £44 million for a four-year contract beginning in 1988 to show eighteen matches per season, still not much by contemporary American standards, but clearly pointing the way to a revolution in broadcasting.

Moreover, once the big clubs realized how much money could be made, they started to flex their muscles. In 1985 the five biggest clubs (Manchester United, Liverpool, Arsenal, Tottenham Hotspur, and Everton) were agitating for more power and a larger share of TV money. Perhaps their resolve was strengthened by FIFA's announcement in 1987 that it had sold the rights to the next three World Cups for $522 million. The Big Five were threatening that if their demands were not met they would consider breaking away from the Football League. Several deals were made, not least the 1988 TV contract, which temporarily kept the big clubs happy. By the end of the 1980s, however, it was becoming clear that BSkyB was desperate to gain access to the rights.

The resolution, when it came, was mediated by the Football League's old rival for the governance of soccer in England, the Football Association. In 1991 the FA issued a "Blueprint for the Future of Football," which proposed the establishment of a Premier League, made up of the clubs of the old Football League First Division. Everything about the Premier League was to be the same as the First Division, the only real difference being that the Premier League clubs would keep all the broadcast money they were paid, rather than sharing it with the three remaining divisions of the Football League.[26] To the FA, this represented ultimate victory in a battle of wills that had gone on for over a century. More important, it left the big clubs free to negotiate a deal that offered more games for broadcast at a higher price. Almost the first act of the FA Premier League was to announce a deal with BSkyB paying £192 million ($386 million in today's money) over five seasons to show sixty live matches per year plus a highlights package reserved for the BBC. Ironically, ITV was willing to bid more or less the same amount to keep soccer on free-to-air TV, but BSkyB had an important insider connection. In 1991 Alan Sugar, a market trader who had moved into manufacturing satellite dishes, bought Tottenham Hotspur, despite having no apparent interest either in soccer generally or Tottenham in particular. At the meeting where the twenty Premier League chairmen voted on which deal to accept, Sugar strongly advocated the BSkyB bid and was reputed to be in telephone contact with the bidder during the closed meeting. So, within ten years of live league soccer coming to English viewers, it had migrated to premium pay TV subscription channels.

Throughout the 1990s, the value of Premier League broadcasting rights boomed. In 1996 BSkyB agreed to pay £670 million ($1.246 billion) to show sixty-six games per season over four years, and in 2001 renewed its contract over three years for £720 million ($1.339 billion). Much the same story developed in the rest of Europe. In France the clubs of Ligue 1, the top division of French soccer, obtained 65 percent of their income from ticket sales and 1 percent from the sale of TV rights in 1980–81. By 1990–91 the shares had shifted to 35 percent and 23 percent, respectively,[27] and by 2001–02 only 15 percent came from ticket revenue against 52 percent from the sale of TV rights.[28] Canal+, the pay TV broadcaster, and TF1, the terrestrial channel privatized in 1988, competed aggressively for live rights. While TF1 covered international competitions, Canal+ held the exclusive rights to live domestic club soccer from 1984 to 1999, generating as much as 30 percent of its subscriptions from this source,[29] and in 1996–97 it created a pay-per-view system that would allow viewers to watch any or all league matches for a fee ranging from 50 francs ($7.68) for a single game to 950 francs ($147) for a season.[30] By 1998–99 Canal+ was paying $114 million per year to the French Football League, but in this season it was forced to surrender its exclusive rights and bid in competition with TPS, a digital satellite service partly controlled by TF1. The result was that Canal+ agreed to pay an average of €294 million over the next five seasons, while TPS paid an average of €54 million. In 2002 Canal+ agreed to pay €480 million per season from 2004 onward (currently $595 million) to regain exclusive rights.[31]

Live domestic league matches and pay TV came to Italy in 1993–94, when the Lega Calcio was paid €93 million to be distributed between the teams of Serie A and B. In 1996–97 all games were made available by the league on pay-per-view,[32] and revenue jumped again, to €199 million. By 2000 the annual revenue of €596 million represented more than 50 percent of club revenues in the top division.[33] In Germany, where competition for soccer broadcast rights started in 1988, pay TV broadcasting of live matches started in the 1991–92 season, and the Bundesliga's annual TV revenue increased from DM50 million to DM140 million. In 2000 Kirch agreed to pay DM750 million ($361 million) per season for the exclusive right to broadcast all Bundesliga games live on pay-per-view.[34]

Thus the European soccer leagues had moved from a situation where almost no live soccer was shown on TV and almost no revenue was generated from the sale of TV rights in 1990, to a situation, in 2000, where the largest leagues were collectively generating about $2 billion per season from the sale of live rights. These rights were entirely broadcast on pay TV, mostly on pay-per-view. Unquestionably, this was a revolution in European and world soccer. We have already seen how transfer spending and salaries of players escalated during this period, a process that Alan Sugar of Tottenham memorably described as "the prune juice effect."

The fans were dazed. Many were outraged by the conversion of what they saw as not-for-profit providers of community services into pure businesses. In many cases, the conversion was explicit. Sixteen English soccer clubs floated stock on the London exchange in the period 1995–97, following the amazingly successful public offering of Manchester United in 1991. Only a small number of clubs outside England followed suit, but they included some famous names: Ajax of the Netherlands, Juventus and Lazio of Italy, and Porto of Portugal. Numerous sociological studies appeared bemoaning the changes, and the Culture Department of the European Commission felt obliged to define a "European model of sport," in contrast to the "American model," of course.[35] To many Europeans, the "American model" was simply sport as business, with no respect for culture and tradition. The meaning of a "European model," to the European Commission and to many others, was a hierarchical system in which all sport was governed by regional, national, and international governing bodies, together with sporting associations (clubs) committed to social policy goals as well as business objectives, and leagues functioning under the promotion and relegation system. Such a structure, according to its proponents, ensured that a democratic voice was given to all interests in a sport, not just those with money.

This juxtaposition might seem a simplistic caricature, but events during the 1990s seemed to bear out many of the traditionalists' worst fears. There is no doubt that commercial pressures became more evident. Along with increased broadcast coverage came increasing revenue from sponsorship and advertising. Company names and logos on player shirts became universal, something that most American fans (outside of NASCAR and golf perhaps) would deem unacceptable. Clubs also had to make scheduling concessions to meet the demands of broadcasters, shifting kick-off times from the traditional Saturday and Sunday afternoon slots to nighttime, midweek, and even Saturday morning. Monday-night soccer, for example, was explicitly copied from the American broadcasting experience. Cash-hungry clubs also increased ticket prices significantly. During the 1990s, ticket prices for the English Premier League increased by around 20 percent annually. Soccer went through a process of gentrification when the traditional working-class fans could no longer afford regular attendance and middle-class yuppies were attracted to the game.

Worse still for the traditionalists, there was increasing talk of restructuring the game in ways that would preferentially enhance the income of the larger clubs. As international competitions, such as the World Cup, taught the clubs the potential of television, the larger clubs became more and more focused on their own international club competitions. Since its creation in 1956, the European Cup, a single-elimination competition among the champions of each of Europe's domestic leagues, had come to be seen as the most prestigious club competition in the world. But while it could draw huge TV audiences in, say, Italy or England, this was only when an Italian or English club was competing. Given that each country had only one entrant, the number of attractive matches each season was relatively small.

Broadcasters saw the potential for expanding the scale of European club competition, and they proposed a European Superleague as early as the 1980s. In essence, such a system would create a major league for European soccer, which might end up looking very similar to the American majors. Most clubs were not prepared to be so radical, but were willing to float the idea in order to extract concessions from UEFA. In 1992 UEFA inaugurated the Champions League to replace the European Cup. This permitted the larger countries (Italy, Spain, Germany, and England) to enter as many as four teams into the competition, which began with a group (all play all) stage, thus dramatically increasing the number of games played, television audiences, and therefore TV revenue.

In 1998 Media Partners, a Milan-based marketing company close to Silvio Berlusconi, suggested a thirty-two-team European Football League consisting of two divisions of sixteen. Throughout that summer rumors abounded that the larger European clubs were interested in joining this breakaway. In the end, the opposition of UEFA and the national associations caused the clubs to back down, but in 2000, fourteen of the largest clubs created the G-14. This association negotiates collectively on behalf of its members with UEFA and FIFA and has a number of revolutionary ideas on its agenda. In 2004, G-14 started proceedings in the Swiss courts against FIFA, with a view to the clubs receiving compensation for the release of players to compete in international tournaments like the World Cup (currently, the clubs that employ the players receive no share of any revenue generated by these competitions). Many believe that the G-14 is a European Superleague in embryo, and that they might start their own competition as early as 2006–07.[36] Rupert Murdoch, who already created the Rugby League in Australia to suit his television programming needs, supports this project, which would provide an excellent platform for strengthening his growing satellite television network in Europe.

Though fans may have been unsettled, they still kept paying to watch live soccer, and in increasing quantities. From an economic perspective, demand for soccer seemed to be insensitive to the price being charged for it, so that increasing prices led to rapidly increasing revenue for the clubs and expenditure for the fans. This situation attracted the attention of both politicians and the European antitrust authorities. Politicians were concerned that the siphoning of live rights toward pay TV would extend to those international representative games that had traditionally been shown on free-to-air TV, especially the major tournaments such as the World Cup. Fearful that angry TV viewers would vent their frustration at the polls, governments were quick to act. In 1990 the United Kingdom adopted the idea of an anti-siphoning law and created a register of "listed events" that would not be permitted to be shown on pay TV. These included showcase events such as Wimbledon Tennis, the Epsom Derby, the Olympic Games, the World Cup, and the FA Cup final, as well as important cricket and rugby matches.[37] Legislators in other European countries quickly followed, and event listing was incorporated into the revision of the EU "Television without Frontiers" directive in 1997.

While the domestic leagues and the Champions League have so far escaped listing (since, logically, most of the matches in these competitions had not been shown on free-to-air TV before the advent of pay TV systems), the rising tide of revenue has attracted the attention of the European competition authorities. By 1990 the United States had already amassed substantial experience in the application of antitrust laws to sport. At the risk of oversimplifying, and notwithstanding some maverick opinions, the received wisdom among competition law practitioners in the United States was that

—sports leagues are cartels whose members are the clubs;

—major leagues possess monopolistic powers given that there are few potential substitutes in the eyes of a fan for the highest level of competition; and

—antitrust treatment of sports cartels should be more tolerant than in all other industries since in a sports league no team has an interest in the failure of its sporting competitors.

In other words, while industrial cartels limit economic competition to the detriment of the consumer, sporting cartels can benefit the consumer to the extent that they help to maintain a league of commercially viable teams. From a legal perspective, each agreement among members of a league that restricts economic competition has to be assessed on its own merits (the so-called rule of reason). Sometimes legislation, such as the Sports Broadcasting Act, empowered the clubs to take specific actions (the collective sale of broadcast rights) without any risk of antitrust scrutiny.

Until 1990 competition law issues had not surfaced in Europe, for the simple reason that there were not significant sums of money in soccer. Once leagues and their clubs started to generate substantial incomes, the competition authorities had to develop their own theory of how these activities should be treated. Their first decision was that clubs were indeed businesses and hence were subject to the commercial laws of the European Union, at least to the extent that they engaged in commercial activities. This meant that European rules relating to the free movement of labor applied, as was demonstrated by the Bosman case, but also that clubs could not hide behind their avowed not-for-profit objectives to evade antitrust scrutiny.

The most important legal issue of the 1990s in European sport after the Bosman judgment was the collective selling of broadcast rights. The issue first arose in Spain, largely because of its long tradition of broadcasting live league matches on free-to-air TV. Spanish soccer underwent a major restructuring at the end of the 1980s that culminated in the 1990 Ley del Deporte, which reorganized the finances and legal standing of clubs. The law gave considerable powers to the national league, which then negotiated an eight-year deal for TV broadcasting.[38] The deal was then challenged in the courts by TV companies that had been excluded, and in a 1993 decision the Spanish competition court declared collective selling to be illegal, freeing the clubs to sell their rights individually from the 1993–94 season onward.[39] This outcome has clearly benefited Spain's two giant clubs, Real

Madrid and Barcelona. During the 1990s a patchwork of agreements emerged, with some matches moving to pay-per-view and some remaining on regional free-to-air channels.[40]

In Germany, the Bundesliga decided in 1989 to take over the marketing of broadcast rights for matches played by its member teams in European competitions such as the European Cup and the UEFA Cup. The money generated by the sale of these rights was then divided equally among the Bundesliga teams. In 1994 the German Cartel Office decided that, in fact, individual teams owned the rights and that therefore the Bundesliga was not entitled to control these rights. The Bundesliga appealed over the heads of the competition authority to the government to grant them an antitrust exemption, citing the U.S. experience, and this was duly granted.[41] In 1996 a Dutch court considered the question of who owns the broadcast rights to matches, following the objection of Feyenoord, a leading club, to the collective sale of domestic rights by the league. Since the broadcaster, Sport 7, collapsed before the judgment was announced, its relevance in this case was moot, but the court did express the view that rights belonged to the home team. In England, the largest ever competition law case to be tried in court was brought by the competition authority against the Premier League and the collective sale of its rights to BSkyB. In 1999 the court decided that collective selling was justified in the public interest. In the same year, the Italian competition authority concluded that the sale of television rights for Serie A and Serie B matches by the league was a violation of competition law and required the league to permit clubs to sell their rights individually.[42] In 2001 the European Commission expressed reservations about the legality of UEFA's collective sale of Champions League broadcast rights and agreed to permit collective selling only after extended negotiations that led to significant restructuring of the deal in 2003.[43] Also in 2001, the EC started investigating the collective selling of Premier League rights, reaching agreement in 2004 on a restructuring that would ensure from 2007 that no single broadcaster would be able to have exclusive access to Premier League rights.[44]

The reason that collective selling has triggered so much legal activity in Europe is the precarious nature of competition in European broadcast markets. Although the potential for soccer leagues to exploit consumers through collective selling raises antitrust concerns throughout the world, in a market such as the United States there is at least significant competition among broadcasters. In particular, the free-to-air networks in the United States have hitherto offered a significant quantity of live broadcast events. In Europe, most collective deals have been struck on the basis of exclusivity, and since there are no other sports rights that can drive subscriptions in the way that soccer does, the danger has been that each national territory in Europe would succumb to a pay TV monopoly. The fear of the competition authorities is that if pay TV broadcasters can monopolize soccer they will then be able to monopolize the entire pay TV market. In other words, collective sale puts together the most valuable rights in a single package, which then fall into the hands of a single broadcaster. The authorities seem to have hoped that if the rights could be kept divided, by prohibiting collective selling, this would in turn foster competition in broadcasting.[45]

Of course, one might also ask why, in the United States, free-to-air broadcasters have been able to win major league broadcast rights at auction, while Europe's terrestrial broadcasters have not. Here the answer may be the smaller national markets of Europe, combined with restrictions on the ability to advertise imposed by TV regulators (for example, the U.S. networks show around twenty minutes of advertising per hour, whereas in the United Kingdom only seven minutes per hour on average is permitted on commercial channels, and the BBC carries none). European networks simply don't have the financial muscle to compete with pay TV, and governments are unlikely to permit an increase in the number of advertising minutes per hour on the grounds of social policy.

In specific cases the major concern has been the excessive restriction of output entailed in collective selling. As part of the settlement with UEFA, the European Commission ensured that all matches that were not sold within the collective deal could be marketed by the individual clubs, so that fans will always have an opportunity to watch games if the demand is there. In the case of the Premier League, however, because only one-third of all matches played in a season are currently made available for live broadcast, many fans are denied access to games that they would be willing to pay to watch. The league and clubs have claimed that this is required to protect gate attendance, as they have always done. However, there is now a good deal of research into the question of how many fans are lost when a game is shown on TV, and almost all of the evidence shows that the number is tiny, and that the gate revenue that would be lost in most instances is well below the amount that would be gained from selling extra matches for television coverage.[46]

In the eyes of many fans, the attempt of the antitrust authorities to challenge collective selling has been wrongheaded. It was striking that in the U.K. Premier League all the supporter groups that testified supported the league. The reason for this is that many soccer fans see collective selling as the only way to redistribute income from rich clubs to poor clubs. These fans see the growing disparities in soccer income as undermining the ability of the smaller clubs to compete, which they see as the loss of a valuable tradition. Ironically, this issue often arises in disputes over the application of competition law in Europe and the United States. Most people agree that the purpose of competition law is to promote healthy competition in the market to the benefit of consumers, not to protect companies from competition. But U.S. observers often criticize European antitrust agencies for being too eager to use the law to protect specific competitors. For example, the purpose of using antitrust law to challenge the conduct of Microsoft was not to protect Netscape, but to ensure that no supplier in the Internet browser market is illegally prevented from competing. Applying this perspective to sport, the challenge to collective selling could not legitimately be used to preserve small clubs from the competition of their larger rivals, but simply to ensure that both clubs and broadcasters are able to compete to supply services to consumers. To the extent that a successful sports league depends on a degree of parity among its teams, of course, it may still be argued that protecting the revenue of small clubs enhances overall competition. A similar argument can be made for teams' financial stability.

In Europe today, only four domestic leagues do not sell live television rights collectively (Greece, Italy, Portugal, and Spain), while at least eleven domestic leagues do (including, Austria, Belgium, Denmark, England, France, Germany, Holland, Norway, Scotland, Sweden, Switzerland, and Turkey). As mentioned earlier, however, not all leagues with collective selling distribute the resulting television revenues equally among their teams. In England, for instance, 50 percent of collectively sold rights is distributed in equal shares, 25 percent according to a club's performance and 25 percent according to the number of television appearances by a club. In France, 73 percent is distributed equally. In Germany, slightly more than 50 percent is distributed equally. To be sure, the tendency is toward more equal distribution of collectively sold rights, but arrangements still depart markedly from the norm in U.S. sports leagues, where 100 percent of collectively sold rights are distributed equally to all teams.[47]

While broadcasting has been the driving force behind the dramatic revenue growth of recent years, it has also contributed to financial inequality. Even if collective selling produces some redistribution in the top divisions of Europe, the gap between the top divisions of clubs in small TV markets (for example, Scotland, the Netherlands, and Portugal) and the large TV markets (England, Italy, Germany, and Spain) has grown, as has the gap between the first and second divisions within countries. Under a system of promotion and relegation this has also helped to promote financial instability as teams have struggled to gain promotion and the riches that it promises. The large financial rewards associated with participation in the Champions League has added to the growing inequality and instability.

After the dot.com bubble burst in 2001, the broadcasters contributed to the sense of crisis in a different way. In 2002 two broadcasters that had invested heavily in sports rights fell off the edge.

In the United Kingdom, ITV Digital, a company set up to broadcast subscription services digitally using a terrestrial broadcast signal (rather than satellite or cable) had agreed to pay £315 million (nearly $600 million) over three years to show Football League First Division (that is, second-tier) soccer matches, starting with virtually no subscriber base. At the time, most observers correctly predicted this was not a viable business model, and by 2002 ITV Digital had to file for bankruptcy. With payments of £179 million outstanding, this should not have been of great concern to the teams of the Football League, since they believed that the contract with ITV Digital had been guaranteed by its two shareholders, Carlton and Granada, large media businesses with the capacity to pick up the bill. However, it turned out that the legal department of the Football League had failed to get the contract countersigned by the parent companies. Carlton and Granada refused to pay for something they had not signed for, but most of the Football League clubs had already made spending commitments in the form of player wage contracts that they had signed. As a result, several clubs were forced into administration, but none have yet disappeared entirely.

In Germany, Leo Kirch was an altogether much larger fish in the broadcasting ocean. His company, Kirch, was a film producer that started out in the 1950s and had amassed a large library of film content by the 1980s, when the legalization of pay TV services in Germany placed it in a strong position. In the 1990s, Kirch had competed aggressively to acquire sports content, not just in soccer but also in motor racing and other sports popular in Germany. In 2001 Kirch spent over $2 billion to acquire the rights to the 2002 and 2006 World Cups, and another $2 billion for a majority stake in Formula One, the most popular motor racing competition in the world. However, these deals relied on Kirch's being able to resell the rights it acquired, and once it became clear in 2002 that broadcasters around the world would not pay the required sums, Kirch was forced to declare itself insolvent. The German Bundesliga, whose broadcast rights Kirch held, was able to extract a financial guarantee from the German government if scheduled payments could not be made.

More generally, there is now a wide perception that the soccer TV bubble has burst. In Italy in 2002, the government was forced to allow the two main pay TV operators to merge, despite a 1999 law prohibiting any one company from holding more than 60 percent of TV rights in Serie A. Sky Italia, controlled by Murdoch's News International, now has a virtual monopoly of Serie A on TV. In France, the future of Canal+, part of the failing Vivendi business empire, remains in question, at least in part because of the perceived overpayment for French domestic league rights. In England, when BSkyB renewed its contract with the Premier League in 2003, it paid £1,024 million ($1.9 billion) for a three-year deal. This was about 15 percent less than it paid on the previous deal.

Despite all the gloom, there is still reason to think that rights values will continue to grow once European broadcast markets recover. Although it seems clear in hindsight that broadcasters were overpaying for rights at the end of the 1990s, they did not necessarily overpay by that much. Throughout the 1990s, cynics said that the media businesses would collapse, when in fact their strategy of buying premium rights and charging premium prices mostly paid off. Moreover, the advent of new media opportunities offered by broadband Internet and third-generation cell phones means that there are plenty of new sources of revenue to chase. Certainly if one looks at the United States as a model, a company can see the potential to increase revenue by adding more services and, as personal incomes start to rise again, by charging more. The only question marks, as ever, are (1) the willingness and ability of European clubs to take advantage of new opportunities and (2) as media revenues resume their ascent, whether the leagues will find a way to distribute their riches in a manner that preserves sufficient competitive balance and financial stability.

CHAPTER SEVEN

Uncertain Prospects

Creating Competitive Balance

What would it be like for a baseball fan to spend the summer watching reruns of the 2003 baseball season? Or for a soccer fan to rewatch the entire 2002 World Cup? Well, some might argue that reviewing the baseball season would be more interesting than the soccer competition, since that particular World Cup was not graced with many great games, while the 2003 baseball season was pretty exciting. But in either case, the word *excitement* would not feature heavily. For purists, there would be some interest in seeing great plays and appreciating the performances of some stars, but for most of us it would be plain boring. Even if you had not seen the game the first time around, watching almost any game is of limited interest if you know the result already.[1] What we value in sports more than anything else is the excitement of the competition and the uncertainty of the outcome.

Every match in a sports competition is uncertain, but some are more uncertain than others. Most of us like the idea of a competition in which David beats Goliath, but in truth, such outcomes are rare; the big guy usually wins. And if we regularly watch competition between unevenly matched competitors, we are soon likely to conclude that the results are predictable. We may even lose interest in watching altogether. This rather trivial observation is also of utmost importance when it comes to understanding the sports business.

If a league in which the results are predictable is a boring one, then it is in the long-term interest of the members of that league to ensure that in every season the championship is competitive. But at the same time, every team wants to win. There is no conflict of objectives here for the weak teams—anything that makes them more competitive will also help to balance the league. But for strong teams there is a conflict of interest. They want to win, but in the interest of the greater good, they may want to lose (or at least not win so often). Whether you are the owner of the New York Yankees or the manager of a leading Brazilian soccer team, making such commitments is not easy.

In this chapter we look at the issues surrounding measures to make championships more competitive—the "competitive balance" question. We discuss how the competitive balance issue came to be recognized by the leagues themselves. We also look at what the leagues have done to manage competitive balance and how they have used the issue to their advantage when dealing with governments and the antitrust authorities. Finally, we look at just how much competitive balance there is and whether, given the current state of play, more is needed.

Baseball

The competitive balance problem struck organized baseball early on. The first pro league, the National Association of Professional Base Ball Players (NA) of 1871–75, was plagued by many difficulties, but chief among them was strong dominance by the eastern clubs and clubs run as stock companies (as opposed to cooperatives).[2] In 1872, for instance, the Boston Red Stockings led the league with an .830 win percentage, while a co-operative club, the Washington Nationals, occupied the cellar with an uninspiring .000 percentage. And it didn't get much better. In the NA's last year, 1875, the Red Stockings' win percentage was .899, while the bottom team managed to win only two games out of forty-four.

As he set about organizing the National League in 1876, William Hulbert was mindful of the need to create more balanced competition along with ownership control. Thus some of the NL's new structures were to be justified on the grounds that they would promote more balance and stability. Many questioned Hulbert's commitment to balance, however, as he used his power to raid some of the best players from the Boston and Cincinnati NL clubs in the NL's first two years. Hulbert's own Chicago club dominated the league with a record of fifty-six wins and fourteen losses in 1876.

Clearly, if one team wins close to all of the games, the outcome is too predictable and the league lacks balance. [3] We need to be a little more precise, however. There are really two types of competitive balance that fans might care about: "within-season" and "between-season." Within-season competitive balance might matter if fans of weak teams that are far behind in the pennant race lose interest and cease going to the ballpark. It might even matter for the strong teams if their fans decide that the result is a foregone conclusion and therefore don't bother to turn out and support their team. Too much within-season imbalance seems likely to reduce fan interest. Between-season balance means that the same teams are either perpetually dominant or perpetually weak. This kind of imbalance is likely to have even more dire consequences for fan interest, as supporters of weak teams give up hope of ever winning anything and supporters of strong teams become complacent.[4]

If leagues were composed of only two teams, competitive balance, in either sense, would be easy to measure (although the league itself would be pretty dull). With two teams, competitive balance can be measured as the difference in the number of wins (matches or championships) between the two. With three teams it becomes more difficult, since there are three different gaps, each of which may be important. If team 1 and team 2 are neck and neck, while team 3 is way behind, is this more or less balanced than a league in which there exists a smaller but nonetheless distinct gap between team 1 and team 2, as well as between team 2 and team 3? The answer is, it depends on what the fans care about, and this is not easy to establish, especially when we start to consider leagues of as many as twenty teams.

Before dismissing this discussion as a sterile piece of academic theorizing, consider the claim that Major League Baseball has a competitive balance problem, advanced by Commissioner Selig and others in the late 1990s. How do we know this is true? It's true that the Yankees dominated the World Series—but is this the only gap that counts? Some people would say that dynasties can be good for the league, if they are associated with glamorous stars who capture the public's imagination. Clearly, to make good the claim that there is a competitive balance problem, some objective measure is required that can be shown to be associated with a declining interest on the part of the fans.

The measure most commonly used by economists over the years has been something called the "standard deviation of winning percentages," which is basically a way of adding up how far away each team ended up from a .500 winning record (if each team had a .500 winning record then the league would be perfectly balanced). This is, of course, a measure of within-season balance. According to this measure, the American League became slightly more unbalanced in the late 1990s, but little changed in the National League. In the American League, the average of these yearly measures was 0.061 in the first half of the 1990s and 0.073 in the second half, while for the National League the figures were 0.069 and 0.068. Statistically, these figures suggest very little change.

One way to measure between-season competitive balance is to consider the variation in a given team's performance over a period of years. If the variation is large, this suggests that the team enjoys rapidly fluctuating fortunes, and we can say there is a degree of between-season competitive balance. The between-season balance measure thus works in the opposite direction from within-season balance: the larger the number, the greater the degree of competitive balance. By this measure, there is slightly more evidence of increasing imbalance during the 1990s. In the first half, the between-season balance measure was 0.053 in the American League, and it fell to 0.047 in the second half, while in the National League the measure fell from 0.065 to 0.051.[5]

Coinciding with baseball's growing imbalance, attendance during the late 1990s was lower than it had been at the beginning of the decade. It was in this context that Commissioner Selig appointed his Blue Ribbon Panel on baseball economics. The panel produced its report in July 2000. The panel's participants—George Will, George Mitchell, Paul Volcker, and Richard Levin—did not pull any punches. They argued that the game's chief problems derived from the imbalance that had materialized since the mid-1990s. The implication of the panel's report is that it was the imbalance that caused the decline in attendance. Perhaps. Yet it is also true that millions of fans foreswore baseball after the work stoppage that disrupted the 1994 season in early August. That year, for the first time in ninety years, there was no World Series. Many fans had had enough of the bickering between the millionaire players and millionaire or billionaire owners. They walked away from the game. The relationship between competitive balance and attendance, as in the past and in other sports, was muddied as other factors interceded.

While the intuition on the relationship between competitive balance and attendance (or other forms of fan support) is strong, the empirical relationship is much more difficult to pin down. It is, of course, possible using statistical techniques to attempt to control for other influences and to isolate the impact of balance on consumer demand. But balance is not easy to define with a single or even several measures.

While economists define competitive balance by applying statistical terms such as standard deviation, idealized standard deviation, range, and decile ratios of win percentages,[6] it is not clear that fans are really affected by the changes that these statistics measure. Perhaps fans really care about whether their team is in contention or close to being in contention for the postseason when September rolls around. Perhaps fans want there to be some rotation at the top, so most teams have a chance of winning from time to time. Or perhaps fans want to see the skill of an organization rather than its financial resources determine which teams are successful. Indeed, fans may care about all of these things. They may also enjoy the prospect of having one team that tends to dominate—a team they can scapegoat and despise.[7]

We raise these problems because, while we believe that competitive balance is important, we also believe that the mechanism by which it asserts its importance is complex. In fact, there has not been a great deal of research that attempts to pin down the empirical relationship between competitive balance and demand, either in baseball or in any other sport. The work that is out there tends to support the hypothesis that more balance leads to more attendance (demand), but this conclusion is not uniform across all studies, and often the results are weak rather than robust.[8]

All this tells us that we should be careful when talking about competitive balance. As we shall see below, Commissioner Selig was worried about some other aspects of the competitive balance problem, and some problems that have nothing to do with competitive balance at all. Before delving into these issues, we consider the evolution of balance in baseball since its early years.

The 1870s were not a good decade for competitive balance in baseball. According to Bill James's "index of competitive balance," on a scale from 0 to 1, with 1 designating perfect equality, the 1870s scored a 21 percent, the lowest decade in baseball history.[9]

In 1879, of course, the NL introduced the reserve clause. Eleven years before the passage of the Sherman Antitrust Act, the NL's justification for the reserve clause openly admitted a restraint of trade. In its public statement of September 29, 1879, the NL stated: "The financial results of this past season prove that salaries must come down. . . . In view of these facts, measures have been taken by this League to remedy the evil to some extent for 1880."[10]

It was not long before the players began to protest, forming the Brotherhood of Professional Base Ball Players in 1885 and then the Players' National League of Base Ball Clubs (the Players' League) in 1890. In November 1889 the Brotherhood issued a manifesto condemning the reserve clause and the NL responded: "Finally, as a check upon competition, the weaker clubs in the League demanded the privilege of reserving five players who would form the nucleus of a team for the ensuing season. This was the origin of the reserve rule and from its adoption may be dated the development of better financial results." Here we find the NL conflating two possible justifications for restricting the labor market: preserving the competitive strength of weaker teams and improving financial performance for the league as a whole.

With the Players' League in 1890, groups of players attempted to leave the NL and play in the new league. The NL, in turn, sought injunctions in several cases to prevent players from jumping leagues. The NL claimed that the renewal provision in the reserve clause gave its teams the right to hold on to the players. In one such case, a federal district court judge, William P. Wallace, quoted from *Spalding's Baseball Guide* on the alleged necessity for baseball's reserve clause:

To this [reserve] rule more than any other thing does base-ball, as a business, owe its present substantial standing. By preserving intact the strength of the team from year to year, it places the business of baseball on a permanent basis, and this offers security to the investment of capital. The reserve rule itself is a usurpation of the players' rights, but it is, perhaps, made necessary by the peculiar nature of the ball business, and the player is indirectly compensated by the improved standing of the game. The reserve rule takes a manager by the throat and compels him to keep his hands off his neighbor's enterprise.[11]

Spalding here is arguing that baseball is a special business that requires cooperation among teams to produce its games and to avoid ruinous competition among teams for player talent. This argument is often heard today in sports league antitrust cases in the United States, where the league claims that one market restriction or another is necessary in order to maintain the cooperation and balance that is a precondition for a successful league. They maintain that even though there is a restrictive practice involved, this practice creates a more robust league, which in turn generates competition among more leagues in the broader sports industry. That is, the restriction is justified by a larger gain in competition (the so-called rule-of-reason defense.)

Since the granting of baseball's presumed antitrust exemption in 1922, baseball has not had to make recourse as frequently as other sports to justifications for its restrictive practices. Yet baseball used this argument in the *Federal Baseball* case that led to its presumed exemption, and has used it since when the exemption has been challenged.

The court of appeals decision in *Federal Baseball* of December 1920 cites an argument made by the AL and NL owners, as follows:

> If the reserve clause did not exist, the highly skillful players would be absorbed by the more wealthy clubs, and thus some clubs in the league would so far outstrip others in playing ability that the contests between the superior and inferior clubs would be uninteresting, and the public would refuse to patronize them. By means of the reserve clause and provisions in the rules and regulations, said one witness, the clubs in the National and American Leagues are more evenly balanced, the contests between them are made attractive to the patrons of the game, and the success of the clubs more certain.

In 1951 U.S. Representative Immanuel Celler of New York held hearings before the House Judiciary Committee on the possible abuse of its monopoly power by organized baseball. Ford Frick, National League president at the time, and soon to be MLB commissioner, testified at these hearings that

> In brief, the reserve clause simply reflects the facts that the ballplayer offers a unique and unusual service and that each individual club must be able to depend upon the availability of qualified personnel from season to season so that the competitive balance essential to the survival of organized baseball may be maintained.[12]

The testimony of Frick and others at the hearings seemed to have convinced Mr. Celler and his colleagues, who wrote in their conclusion to the hearings:

> Baseball's history allows that chaotic conditions prevailed when there was no reserve clause. Experience points to no feasible substitute to protect the integrity of the game or to guarantee a comparatively even competitive struggle. The evidence adduced at the hearings would clearly not justify the enactment of legislation flatly condemning the reserve clause.[13]

Just because the owners made the argument that the reserve clause was necessary to preserve the game's balance and the U.S. Supreme Court and the House Judiciary Committee believed them, however, does not make it so. Beginning with Simon Rottenberg's 1956 article in the *Journal of Political Economy,* economists have made a different argument: the reserve clause did not prevent small-market players from moving to big-market teams; it only prevented them from receiving competitive bids for the value of their services.[14] Under the reserve clause, players regularly moved to big-market teams (witness Babe Ruth's trade to the Yankees) as a result of a transaction that exchanged cash between owners. Players who have a greater value in a larger market generally find their way there with or without the reserve clause. Under reserve, the player does not receive the value he produces; the owner does. Under free agency, the player receives the value as owners bid against each other for his services.

The advent of free agency after the 1976 season provides a clear natural experiment of the owners' reserve clause claim. Were the claim correct, competitive balance in baseball should have deteriorated after 1976. It did not.

Indeed, according to a variety of studies and measures, competitive balance has actually improved over the past thirty years.[15] Of course, many other things in baseball have also changed during this period, so it is not reasonable to attribute this improvement to the demise of the reserve clause alone. Still, some have argued that free agency has made it both more expensive and more difficult to hold together a winning team and easier for a losing team to change its fortunes. If true, this would lead to a reduced tendency toward team dynasties. Such a tendency seemed to prevail until the early 1990s. Since then, however, both the Yankees and Braves have tended to dominate.

Competitive balance results also varied significantly under the reserve clause. After the imbalance of the 1870s (when the James index was 21 percent), balance improved steadily in each decade until the index reached 36 percent in the 1910s. For the next five decades, baseball's competitive balance drifted upward and downward only modestly, with the index settling at 40 percent in the 1960s.[16]

After 1965 balance by most measures improved. In 1965 baseball introduced its reverse-order amateur draft. The draft had the effects of (1) giving poorly performing clubs earlier draft picks and (2) eliminating the competition over draftees, and thus reducing signing bonuses. Also, fortuitously in 1965, baseball began to share national television revenues equally across its teams and the Yankees dynasty of the previous fifteen years came to an end. This was the result of the retirement or diminishing productivity of several of the team's aging star players and the closing of the pipeline of players from Kansas City once the Yankees were sold by Del Webb and Dan Topping to CBS in 1964.

According to James's index, competitive balance improved from 40 percent in the 1960s to 45 percent in the 1970s, 56 percent in the 1980s, and 57 percent in the 1990s. However, other indexes measuring the concentration of championships or other performance outcomes suggest that the improvement in balance ended after the 1980s. Indicators that divide the 1990s into halves agree that competitive balance worsened after 1995, if not earlier. The post-1995 increase in imbalance followed a sharp increase in revenue inequality across teams. The spread between top- and bottom-team revenues grew from around $30 million in 1989 to over $150 million by 1999. The growing revenue imbalance, in turn, was the direct result of three principal factors: (1) the explosion of some teams' local media contracts in the early 1990s, (2) the sharp decrease in national television revenue after 1993, and (3) the introduction of new, high-revenue-generating stadiums in several cities.

In an updated version of the Blue Ribbon Panel study completed after the 2001 season, the panel reported that during the seven years from 1995 through 2001 only four teams from the bottom half of team payrolls reached the postseason. And those four teams did not do very well once they got there. Of the 224 postseason games played over this stretch, teams from the bottom half of payrolls won only five games. Viewed differently, teams from the top half of payrolls had a postseason win percentage of .978! None of the four bottom-payroll teams went beyond the first round of playoffs.

Thus the concern of the panel seems to have been not so much that increasing imbalance was causing a dramatic decline in attendance (it wasn't), but that the growth of revenue imbalances was leading to competitive imbalance, which if not dealt with immediately would soon cause such a decline. This leads us into new territory. It is one thing to say that imbalance reduces fan interest, but quite another to suggest that a given imbalance can be quickly redressed by a specific redistribution of income. As ever with Major League Baseball, it is important to keep both eyes firmly fixed on the shells as the pea moves around.

The panel's recommendations included significant increases in the amount of revenue shared between the top and bottom teams; a luxury tax on high team payrolls; and the internationalization of baseball's amateur draft, among other measures.

Significantly, the panel recommended that in order to qualify to receive revenue-sharing transfers, low-revenue teams needed to have at least a $40 million payroll. This recommendation was not incorporated into the 2002 collective bargaining agreement (CBA).

The 2002 CBA did, however, follow other aspects of the panel's recommendations. It extended revenue sharing so that each team contributed 34 percent of net local revenue to a sharing pool.[17] Once collected from all teams, this money would then be redistributed equally to all teams. This sharing is supplemented by a distribution from the central fund about one-third as large that goes only to teams in the bottom half of revenues. Altogether in 2004, approximately $270 million was redistributed from the top to bottom half of teams.

Because when teams increase their local revenue, they not only pay 34 percent on the increase but also may reduce the amount of transfers they receive, the effective marginal tax rate on teams is above 34 percent. Moreover, because of the redistribution system employed, the bottom-half teams face a higher marginal tax rate (around 47 percent) than the top-half teams (around 39 percent). That is, if the Kansas City Royals hire a free agent for $8 million and the player ends up increasing team revenues by $9 million, the Royals keep only $4.77 million net and take a net loss of $3.77 million on the signing—hardly an incentive for the Royals to hire the player. (If all teams faced the same tax rate, other things equal, we would expect no change in relative payroll spending across teams. Since the bottom-half teams in the present system perversely face a higher effective tax rate, we would expect the distribution of payrolls to become more unequal. In fact, this is what has happened since 2002.)[18]

Notice, however, that a side effect of the system is that the free agent's value to the Royals is now diminished. Before the tax he is worth $9 million (his incremental contribution to team revenues), but after the tax he is worth only $4.77 million. The team logically would make this and any other free agent a lower salary offer. And indeed, this is precisely what happened after the 2002 CBA was signed. During the 2002–03 off-season, the average salary of newly signed free agents declined 16.5 percent. During the 2003–04 off-season, this number went down 26.6 percent. Average players' salaries in 2004 were $2.49 million, down 2.7 percent from 2003. That might not seem like much, but it is a big turnaround from the 11.5 percent annual growth rate in average salaries from 1995 through 2003.

MLB proclaimed the purpose of their new revenue sharing was to improve competitive balance, not to reduce salaries. At first glance, it may have indeed appeared as though the new system was improving balance. After all, on September 1, 2003, there were fifteen teams within four games of making it to the postseason playoffs, the highest number since 1995. And again in 2004, at the halfway point in the season, there were twenty teams within five games. Fans in a majority of cities again had a team they could root for and could do so with some reason. To be sure, Bud Selig was quick to take credit and attribute this apparent balance to the new revenue-sharing system: "Just look at how many of the 30 teams are in contention. That's a manifestation of how well the [revenue] sharing system is working. . . . I don't want to toot my own horn, but everything I have tried to do in the last 11 years worked wonders this year."[19]

The facts told a different story. If the new revenue-sharing system was to be credited with achieving greater balance, then it must be because the revenues transferred to the bottom teams were being spent on increasing payroll.[20] Yet despite the recommendations of the Blue Ribbon Panel, there was no payroll rule for teams receiving transfers, and the incentives of the system discouraged payroll increases—even more so for low-revenue teams. The only policy in place to have transfers spent on payrolls was an exhortation in the CBA that was to be enforced by Bud Selig: "Accordingly, each Club shall use its revenue sharing receipts . . . in an effort to improve its performance on the field. The Commissioner shall enforce this obligation.[21]

But Selig's family owned the Brewers, a low-revenue team. The Brewers benefited more than any other team from the 2002 CBA. Their transfers increased from $1.5 million in 2001 to $8.5 in 2002 and to $16.6 million in 2003. At the same time, the Brewers' payroll decreased from $52.7 million in 2002 to $40.6 million in 2003, and to $27.5 million on opening day in 2004.[22] Was Selig likely to enforce the exhortation?

Likely or not, he did not. By any of the common measurements of inequality—standard deviation, coefficient of variation, spread between top and bottom—team payrolls have grown more unequal since 2002. The standard deviation of payrolls increased from $2.47 million in 2002 to $2.73 million in 2003, and to $3.26 million at the beginning of 2004. The spread between the top and bottom team payrolls grew from $91.5 million in 2002 to $130.1 million in 2003, and to $155 million in 2004.[23]

The CBA's incentives are backwards. The present system penalizes success. Why should the Red Sox, in the sixth largest media market, pay almost $40 million in revenue-sharing taxes (the second highest amount in 2003), while the Phillies in the fourth largest market have been revenue recipients? The Sox are being penalized for succeeding, and the Phillies are being rewarded for failing.

Why, then, did the number of contending teams increase in 2003 and 2004? Although this outcome was much ballyhooed by the commissioner's office, the number of teams within four games of making the playoffs on September 1 of the season in question fell from fifteen in 2003 to fourteen in 2004. Further, the number of contending teams in 1995 was eighteen—greater than in 2003 even though there was no revenue-sharing system in place in 1995 and there were two fewer teams in the major leagues. Another factor behind the increased number of teams in contention is the fact that baseball added a wild card team to an expanded system of divisional play-offs in 1995, doubling the number of teams making it to the postseason.

The 2002 CBA contained other provisions that also served to blunt salary growth, including a new rule limiting team debt; a rule requiring teams to fully finance deferred salaries within eighteen months; and the reintroduction of the luxury tax. Even though baseball's luxury tax had a high threshold (only payrolls over $120 million in 2004 were taxed) and relatively low tax rates (between 17 and 40 percent, whereas the NBA had an effective luxury tax rate of over 300 percent), it seemed to have symbolic value as forbidden territory for many teams. In 2004 only the Yankees and Red Sox were above the threshold.

Nevertheless, even if the 2002 CBA did little to level payrolls and promote greater balance on the playing field, it seems to have served another important—perhaps more important—function by reducing revenue disparities among teams and holding down salaries. The magnitude of related party transactions and business synergies has grown enormously over the past twenty years. Now, in addition to the inequalities engendered by differential city sizes and stadium situations, the presence of related entities such as the YES Network and the New England Sports Network (NESN) (entities that can be worth as much as the ball club) can yield tens or hundreds of millions of additional dollars to a team owner. Such an owner sees a player's value in terms of what he produces not only for the team but also for the related entity. A player's value may double in the owner's eyes. An owner without such related party interests is now faced with even more extraordinary competing offers for the players he seeks. An owner who attempts to match these salary offers may soon face troublesome levels of indebtedness or other financial pressures. The league's financial stability may be threatened in the process. In this sense, the revenue-sharing system, by buttressing the resources of the financially weaker teams and blunting player salary growth, provides an important cushion for MLB.

Nonetheless, the issue of payroll disparity remains. Unlike soccer, MLB cannot rely on the race to avoid relegation or on auxiliary competitions such as the FA Cup to sustain interest in poorly performing teams. As long as baseball's revenue-sharing system contains perverse incentives, it is unlikely to contribute significantly to a leveling of the playing field. Within- and between-season imbalance will likely persist, and one day some MLB teams may wake to nearly empty ballparks.

Soccer

The Portuguese soccer season of 2000–01 was one to cherish. In that season Boavista became only the fifth team ever to win the league championship since its inception in 1938. By the end of 2004 still only five teams had ever won the championship—Benfica twenty-seven times, FC Porto nineteen times, Sporting Lisbon eighteen times, Boavista once, and Os Belenenses once (way back in 1946). In the same period only seven teams have ever finished as runners-up, and the big three account for fifty-nine out of the sixty-six of these second places. So, in total, out of 132 first- and second-place finishes in the Portuguese league since its founding, 123 have been taken by only three teams.[24] When it was founded, the first division contained only eight teams, but by the 1980s there were four divisions of eighteen teams each in the promotion- and-relegation system, giving the opportunity for any one of these seventy-two to win the league one day.[25]

Portuguese soccer is extremely unbalanced when it comes to winning the title race, but this is not all that unusual in soccer. In the 108 championships of the Scottish Football League played between 1891 and 2004, 50 were won by Rangers, 39 by Celtic, and the remaining 19 championships by a mere nine teams, despite the fact that the Scottish League contains forty teams joined together by promotion and relegation. In Norway, Rosenborg BK won the title twelve times in a row between 1991 and 2003,[26] while in the Ukraine, Dynamo Kiev failed to win the title only once in the same period.[27] In Greece and Turkey, only teams from the largest cities (Athens and Istanbul) have enjoyed more than fleeting success. Olympiakos, AEK Athens, and Panathinaikos have won the Greek championship in every season but two since the national league started in 1960,[28] while Galatasaray, Besiktas, and Fenerbahce, all from Istanbul, have won the Turkish title in every season but six since the league began in 1959.[29] In all of these countries, the leagues consist of sixteen to twenty teams and are connected to lower divisions via promotion and relegation.

The larger European leagues are also dominated by a small number of teams. In Italy, there have been twelve different winners of Serie A, but three teams alone (AC Milan, Juventus, and Inter) account for forty-two of these victories.[30] In principle, thanks to promotion and relegation, there are more than one hundred teams that could have won Italy's championship. In Spain, there have been seventy-three championships since the league was founded in 1928, and of these either Real Madrid or Barcelona has won forty-five, with only eight other teams accounting for the remaining victories.[31] In England, Manchester United has won eight out of the twelve championships since the FA Premier League began in 1992; and between 1976 and 1990, Liverpool won ten out of the fifteen Football League Championship titles.[32]

Most soccer leagues in the world do not have postseason playoffs for the championship,[33] but if they did, few teams in each of the top divisions could meet the balance standard set by Selig's Blue Ribbon Panel, that well-managed teams have a "regularly recurring reasonable hope of reaching postseason play." Most soccer clubs that start the season in the top division do not expect to win the league or even to come close; nor do their fans expect that their team will ever win the national championship.

Competitive imbalance is a fact of life at every level of world soccer. Consider the World Cup. Of the seventeen World Cup championships played before 2002, five were won by Brazil, three each by Germany and Italy, and two each by Argentina and Uruguay. Together with England and France, that makes only seven victorious teams. Only four other teams have ever appeared in a World Cup final (Czechoslovakia, Hungary, Sweden, and the Netherlands). So from FIFA's world of 204 nations, only eleven teams have been among the thirty-four finalists of the World Cup. The European Championship (played for nations, not individual teams) has been spread a bit more evenly, with nine different winners of the twelve titles. Yet of the forty-one championships of the Copa America, played mainly among the soccer nations of South America, Brazil, Argentina, and Uruguay together have won thirty-five times. There have been thirteen different winners of the African Nations Cup since it started in 1957, with three teams (Cameroon, Egypt, and Ghana) winning half of the total of twenty-four titles.

Measuring between-season competitive balance is difficult in a league system with promotion and relegation, since the identity of the participants is always changing, but it is not difficult to see that there is little between-season balance in soccer.[34] Most leagues and competitions in soccer are dominated by only a small number of teams. Because of the promotion-and-relegation system, however, within-season balance is significantly greater in soccer leagues than in the North American major leagues.[35] Because of relegation, teams only give up when they have no hope of surviving in the division, not when they are merely out of contention for the championship title.

Apart from the national league championships, the other important club competition is the UEFA Champions League, which started in 1993. The issue of dominance in the Champions League has been controversial. On the face of it, the tournament seems quite balanced when compared to the national leagues. For example, since the introduction of semifinals in 1994, there have been twenty teams competing at this stage out of a maximum of forty-four. Since the introduction of quarterfinals in 1995, thirty-five different teams have competed at this stage (the maximum would have been eighty). Twelve different teams have competed in the final over twelve years, and nine different teams have won. In other words, nearly as many different teams have won the UEFA Champions League since it was inaugurated in 1993 as have ever won the Italian or Spanish championships since they began in 1928–29. But in another sense, which we consider next, it is quite unbalanced.

The Causes of Imbalance in Soccer

The reasons that certain clubs and countries dominate competition are not hard to find. At the international level, countries normally do well at particular sports because of population, wealth, and history. For example, the United States dominates the Olympic track and field competition because it is one of the world's most populous nations, giving it a large pool of natural talent from which to draw; because it is one of the world's wealthiest nations, giving it the means to train and develop its talent; and because it was one of the first nations to take up modern track and field in the nineteenth century and benefits from that accumulated experience.

In the soccer world, the dominance of Brazil is in part attributable to the nation's great size and long-standing experience in the game. Italy and Germany also have long experience and, as we have seen in earlier chapters, have been willing to devote substantial resources to winning. However, it must also be said that many national teams, perhaps happily for interest in the game, repeatedly under- or over-perform. One example is England, with only one World Cup victory and a fairly modest international record over recent decades, despite its status as inventor of the game and its wealthy national league. Spain is another under-performer that has never won the World Cup, despite a long tradition of soccer and a very powerful national league.[36] The over-performing category must include Argentina and Germany, the former because of its modest population size (37 million) and Germany because of its remarkable persistence. In the thirteen World Cups between 1954 and 2002, Germany appeared in the final seven times, won three times, and reached the quarterfinal stage of every World Cup since being permitted to reenter the tournament in 1954.[37]

Some smaller nations have also pulled off significant surprises. Denmark shocked the whole of Europe when it won the 1992 European Championship. After having failed to qualify for the finals, it was only admitted to the tournament at the last minute as a replacement for Yugoslavia, because of the latter's descent into civil war. In 2004 Greece was ranked as an 80-to-1 long shot to win the European Championship, but won despite having to play the host Portuguese team in the final.[38]

The domination of national leagues by particular clubs is quite easy to understand. Competitive dominance in league sports in the long run is almost always attributable to superior economic resources. In soccer as in baseball, teams that can hire better players and coaches win more often.

Among the smaller soccer nations, the teams that dominate are usually located in the largest cities. The Greek and Turkish examples have already been mentioned. In Russia and the Ukraine, teams from Moscow and Kiev dominate. In the Netherlands, Ajax of Amsterdam is the most famous team. In Scotland, Celtic and Rangers, both from Glasgow, dwarf their competition. In Austria, FK Austria Wien and Rapid Vienna have been the dominant teams; and in Portugal, Sporting and Benfica from Lisbon have vied with Porto, the second city, for dominance of the national championship.

Among the larger countries, the causes of dominance are slightly less clear-cut. Spain has been dominated by Real Madrid, from the largest city, and by Barcelona, from the second largest city, but this dominance also reflects important political tensions. Italy has been dominated by two teams from the second city, AC Milan and Inter, and a team from the smaller but industrially significant city of Turin (Juventus), while the two teams of the largest city, Roma and Lazio, have struggled. In Germany, the decentralization of power after World War II worked against the emergence of dominant teams, and the country's largest industrial agglomeration, Essen, does not have a major team. Nevertheless, Bayern Munich has succeeded in dominating the Bundesliga to a degree, reflecting both the city's size and its economic power. In England, London teams have failed to dominate persistently, despite the fact that London is more dominant relative to its national economy than almost any other capital city in the world. Instead, it has been the teams of medium-sized industrial cities, Liverpool and Manchester, that have dominated the English leagues in the postwar era. This success may be related to the fact that the origins of professional soccer lie in the Lancashire region where the two strongest teams are based. But it is also important to note that the small size of the territories covered by the national leagues in most European countries means that geographic loyalties may be relatively weak. Wherever you live in the Netherlands, it would be easy to travel to Amsterdam to watch Ajax at the team's home ground. Likewise, it is sometimes said that most of Manchester United's supporters live in London and travel up for the weekend to watch a match. Moreover, in open promotion/relegation leagues (as opposed to closed leagues with territorial monopolies) it is not such an advantage to be a team from a major city. In 2004–05, London had six teams in the Premier League and has had as many as nine (out of twenty teams in the league.)

Like baseball in the United States, the expansion of TV coverage has come to be seen as a major contributor to competitive imbalance in European soccer. Initially, TV's impact was muted because rights were collectively sold to state monopolies for very low prices. However, the advent of competition and new technologies in broadcasting has changed that. For example, in a number of European countries, pay-per-view is now the only way to see live league football, notably in Germany, France, and Italy. In the first two countries, the rights are still sold collectively and the income shared, but in Italy the rights are sold individually, with most of the money accruing to the dominant teams.

The relationship between TV income and the UEFA Champions League has also given rise to concerns in recent years. As we saw, the Champions League has been, if anything, much more balanced, measured by the turnover in teams that compete at the final stages, than any national league in Europe. The concern, however, is not club dominance but national dominance. The UEFA Champions League generates most of its revenue from the sale of TV rights, estimated to be worth 420 million euros (around $500 million). The competition is open to teams from all of UEFA's fifty-two member countries, but the number of places in the competition is skewed toward the largest soccer nations, which also tend to be the largest broadcast markets. The distribution of broadcast revenue is also heavily skewed toward teams in the last stages of the competition, which tends to be dominated by teams from the larger nations. For example, the four semifinalists have received about one-quarter of all the money distributed to teams since 1994, and 84 percent of the semifinalists have come from the large markets of Italy, Spain, Germany, England, and France. Spain and Italy have dominated the final, producing half of all the winners and two-thirds of all runners-up. Many have concluded from this that (a) the large-market teams get most of the money, (b) in a post-Bosman world the wealthy teams can hire all the best players, and (c) fans will be attracted to the leagues fielding the best players and may lose their allegiance to the smaller national leagues in the longer term. Thus it is feared that the UEFA Champions League is increasing the dominance of leagues from large markets and undermining the long-term viability of leagues from the smaller markets. And as already noted, within national leagues the extra revenue from the Champions League reinforces the dominance of leading teams.

The Absence of Redistributive Measures in Soccer

If William McGregor, the founder of the English Football League, had had his way, soccer leagues would have developed very differently. At the league's foundation he proposed that the gate money for each match be divided equally between the two teams. Since this was the only source of revenue for the clubs back in 1888 and therefore teams would have had equal resources, it is conceivable that the Football League would have emerged as a perfectly balanced league, and that such a system would have spread throughout the world. However, his proposal was voted down by ten of the twelve teams in the new league. In its first season, the imbalance of the league was so great that Preston North End won the championship easily and completed the season unbeaten in twenty-two matches (a feat not repeated until 2003–04, when Arsenal went undefeated in thirty-eight matches).

One objection raised by some of the teams to McGregor's proposal was that not all teams were equally responsible for generating the income of the league. Therefore, to reward all teams equally for an unequal contribution would not only be unfair; it might also undermine the incentive to compete at all. This argument contains more than a grain of truth, in that the competitiveness of any league depends on the incentive to compete and to achieve success. A frequent criticism by U.S. economists of the redistribution systems in the U.S. sports leagues is that they undermine the incentives of the weaker teams to compete. For instance, when first-round draft selections are at stake in the NBA, there is some evidence that teams try to lose in order to secure an earlier pick.[39] Even more critically, if a team is based in a small city with limited potential to generate income from success, the owner will be tempted to pocket any revenues that are redistributed by the league rather than devote them to enhancing the quality of the team.

However, there are two features of the soccer world that might mitigate against these tendencies. First, as discussed in chapter 5, the consensus among analysts of European leagues is that the European clubs generally are not conventional profit maximizers, but win maximizers instead. Whereas a profit maximizer will think twice about spending more than is strictly necessary on the team, a win maximizer will spend everything he can lay his hands on. In that sense, redistribution will work more effectively in a league of win maximizers.[40] Second, there is promotion and relegation. Teams at the bottom of a soccer league do not have the luxury of resting up and preparing for the next season that they do in the U.S. major leagues. Any team that gives up in soccer faces the near certainty of relegation, ensuring that all teams, even if they are profit maximizers, have an incentive to spend their resources on improving team quality.

There is some irony, therefore, in the fact that soccer leagues lack the redistribution mechanisms that might enable the weak to compete with the strong, while in U.S. leagues such mechanisms are commonplace, despite the fact that that they are less likely to work. In Europe, there are almost no gate-sharing arrangements. There are no arrangements for the sharing of income from merchandizing such as exist in the United States; and while collective selling of media rights exists in most European leagues, the distribution formulas tend to favor the stronger teams. Within the labor market, there is no roster limit to restrain the hoarding of players by large teams and no draft system that can be manipulated to favor the weaker teams. There are no salary caps or luxury taxes that might, at least in theory, restrict dominance. In short, none of the panoply of restraints that help to promote competitive balance exist in European soccer.

Historically speaking, perhaps the most important reason that U.S.-style restraints did not develop in European soccer is that until quite recently money didn't matter that much. In most countries, dominant teams relied on strong political connections. Even for teams where business connections mattered (notably Juventus and Fiat), these connections also had a significant political dimension. With such backing for the strong teams, complaints about competitive imbalance were seldom heard. The economic revolution in soccer since the 1980s has changed that. First, the growing importance of European-level competition meant that traditional political ties were less effective, particularly for dominant teams in the smaller European countries. Second, the degree of financial inequality has increased.

Increasing revenue inequality in soccer has, in fact, been a steady trend since the 1950s. Because of promotion and relegation, soccer fans tend to worry about the inequalities both between each level of competition and within each level. (It is as if baseball fans worried about the disparity between Major League Baseball and Triple A, and between Triple A and Double A, and Double A and Single A.) At every level, revenues have grown rapidly, with the most dramatic increases since the early 1990s, but the growth in revenue has tended to be fastest at the highest levels.

Inequality has certainly grown within each level of competition. To take the example of England, the revenue gap between the highest and lowest earner in the top division increased steadily from about 2:1 in 1950 to about 8:1 in 2000. Fans of big and mid-sized teams might care about this gap. But fans of mid-sized teams are likely also to care about the gap between the lowest and highest revenue of the second-level division, and this ratio has increased from just over 2:1 to nearly 6:1. Because teams can move up and down the divisions quickly, fans care about the gap between the divisions as well.

The gap between teams in the relegation zones of the top level and second level has also grown, from near equality in 1960 to a ratio of over 5:1 by 2000. The gap between the top of the second level and the bottom of the third level has also increased from around 4:1 to 13:1. In other words, as the total soccer revenue has grown, the inequality in the distribution of that income has grown, at every level of competition. This means not only that teams in lower divisions are likely to find it difficult to match the player spending of dominant teams, but also that teams that suffer a run of bad results are threatened with a precipitous fall in income.

Thus it does not seem surprising that, by the 1990s, clubs, especially the smaller clubs, and administrators started talking about the need to import some American-style restrictions. At different times, there has been talk of salary caps, roster limits, draft systems, and gate revenue sharing. Thus far, however, all of these ideas have foundered on the issue of practicality. Take a salary cap, for instance. In theory, at least, this might make some sense in a closed American league, where all teams play the same number of games against the same level of opposition. In Europe, by contrast, some teams compete at more than one level—for example, the Champions League and the national championship. Consider the case of Porto, the winner of the Champions League in 2004. Inside Portugal, a salary cap that would help to promote opportunities for all of the small Portuguese teams would have to be quite low, since most Portuguese teams have crowds of no more than

5,000 per game and have TV rights of limited value. To defend their Champions League title, however, Porto needs to compete with Real Madrid and Manchester United, both of which can pack in more than 70,000 per game and possess some of the most valuable TV and media rights in the sports world. There is no salary cap that could realistically enable Porto to compete in Europe while giving the other teams in the Portuguese league a fair shot at the title.[41]

Even without the Champions League, the promotion-and-relegation system allows teams with very limited capacity to compete to reach the highest level on occasion, creating levels of imbalance that American-style restrictions could not handle. For example, in Italy in 1996, Castel di Sangro, a team from a village of 5,500 inhabitants, got itself promoted to Serie B (the second-tier league). This meant that in 1997 this team competed against soccer giants such as Torino and Genoa, both of whom have won the Italian Championships in their history and can fill large stadiums. The story of Castel di Sangro is an exciting one,[42] and a good example of the opportunities created by the promotion-and-relegation system; but by the same token, it illustrates that no practical redistribution scheme could have equalized competition among these teams and, arguably, such equalization in these extreme cases would have been counterproductive. Taking resources from teams like Torino and giving them to Castel di Sangro could not have increased the latter's attendance (as it was, almost the entire village went to watch the home games), while the measure would have been likely to decrease the former's attendance figures. Overall, redistribution would probably have reduced league income.

Does It Really Matter That European Soccer Is Unbalanced?

As we have seen, most of the national leagues in soccer are highly unbalanced in the sense that only a small number of clubs have a realistic chance of winning the league championship. In any given season, it can be predicted with a fairly high degree of certainty who the top two or three contenders will be, and from year to year the identity of these contenders does not usually change. Is there any evidence that this imbalance has done anything to undermine interest in soccer in Europe or elsewhere?

Arguably not. Soccer has been unbalanced throughout its history, yet it has managed to become the world's most popular sport, and in most countries where it is played it dominates sporting culture more than, say, baseball does in the United States. This is because soccer has so many other attractive attributes: the national interest, local club loyalty, local rivalry, the different levels of competition (national league, Cup and international club competition), and the excitement of promotion and relegation. Take the example of Tottenham Hotspur, which for most of the past decade has been a mid-table Premier League team with no realistic hope of winning the championship. Of the nineteen home games played in a season most will be sellouts. Each game has its own special attraction. First, the game played against Arsenal, Tottenham's traditional London rival, is probably the most important game of the season. Then there are matches against the leading teams, Manchester United, Chelsea, Liverpool, which give the fans a chance to watch famous national and international stars. Then there is the prospect of qualifying for a European competition. While only the top four qualify for the Champions League in the following season, teams ranked up to sixth can qualify for the UEFA Cup, another pan-European competition that is attractive to the clubs.[43] If, in any season, Tottenham does not have a realistic chance of finishing in the top six, then it is almost certainly in danger of finishing as low as eighteenth, in which case the team is threatened with relegation. Sometimes both possibilities remain realistic until the end of the season. For example, in 2002–03 Tottenham finished tenth, four wins behind the team that came in sixth, and only three wins ahead of West Ham, which was relegated. Despite the fact that Tottenham's season was undistinguished, to say the least, its fans had plenty of excitement. Statistically, the gap between the winning teams and the losing teams in any season is much smaller in the soccer world than in the baseball world because of the relegation threat. Relegation is like a championship within a championship, in which the winner's prize is survival. With all of these different dimensions of competition in which Tottenham is involved, competitive balance, in the sense of having a realistic chance of winning the league title, does not seem to matter that much. Of course, one factor that distinguishes soccer from baseball in this regard is that the teams in England's Premier League play only nineteen regular season home games per year, while those in MLB play eighty-one home games. Other things equal, it is easier to sustain interest with a shorter schedule.

Growing imbalances between divisions are particularly troublesome. As we have seen, the revenue gap between the first and second level, and the second and the third, has widened dramatically in the past half-century.

This fact appears to have seriously damaged the oldest surviving team sports competition in the world, the English FA Cup. Started in 1870, the FA Cup is a single-elimination competition open to all FA members, and its final in May has been the traditional showcase of the English season. The competition's later stages involve primarily the teams of the four divisions, and traditionally any FA Cup match played between two teams would attract far higher attendance than the equivalent league game.[44] However, in more recent years the superior revenue of teams in the top division has rendered competition with the lower divisions so unequal that the outcome is scarcely in doubt. As a result, the top division teams have paid less attention to the competition and the fans have lost interest. Nowadays, a match between two Premier League teams, or between two Football League First Division teams, will attract a much higher attendance if it is a league game than if it is an FA Cup game.[45] In this particular instance, therefore, it appears that the lack of competitive balance may have caused at least a relative decline in attendance. However, it remains true that most of the important games in the soccer world are league games, and for these attendance has risen significantly over the past decade in England and in many other countries, reflecting increasing interest in soccer.

Yet competitive balance in soccer does matter, just not for the reasons usually advanced. Throughout their legal battles in the 1990s (such as Bosman, collective selling), the leagues have advanced the view that they need to maintain competitive balance to maintain fan interest, but the evidence to support this view, as we have seen, seems rather limited. The problem with Europe's imbalances is mostly financial rather than emotional, and has to do with the management of clubs rather than the preferences of the fans.

The imbalances in the revenue-generating potential of the different levels of competition in Europe have created a system where teams have incentives to spend more than they can afford in order to reach the next level or avoid being sent down a level. Prudence would suggest that club directors should not respond as sensitively to these incentives as they do, but prudence and club management is a marriage that is seldom consummated. Because so many teams are now engaged in overspending, the financial viability of entire leagues is being called into question. Clearly, if half the teams in a league are bankrupted, then there is a danger that the league competition itself may collapse.

Teams in a sports league are interdependent: if one fails, all are threatened. This raises a difficult problem for the European authorities. The source of the instability, it appears, is the system whereby teams can compete in several levels of competition at once and can be moved up and down the leagues. Much of the excess spending appears where clubs are on the verge of jumping up or falling down from one level to the next. It is, in a sense, the size of the leap or the fall that causes teams to adopt such precarious strategies. The Champions League, with it huge paydays for the top national teams, has created an extra precipice for clubs to negotiate. These characteristics, the thrills and spills caused by the rising and falling, are cherished by soccer fans. Since promotion and relegation is so much a part of the fabric of the world soccer system, most soccer fans would be horrified at the suggestion that it be abandoned. Getting rid of it would be a revolutionary change, which few people want to see and which might even drive fans away from the game. In the next and final chapter, we suggest an alternative for soccer that preserves a modified promotion/relegation system and adopts elements of the closed system of U.S. sports leagues.

CHAPTER EIGHT

Crossing Cultures
and Learning Lessons

What Americans Need to Know about
World Soccer and the World Needs to
Know about American Baseball

One observation that must be obvious to the reader by now is that baseball and soccer have very different institutions and histories. The early development of soccer was fashioned by the attitudes of mid-Victorian English gentlemen, while baseball reflected the ideas and attitudes of contemporary Americans driven by a more commercial spirit. The British "noblesse oblige" required that all be permitted entry into the world of soccer, but that everyone should know their place. American businessmen, by contrast, set out to create an exclusive monopoly. As it expanded, soccer was first molded by the ideas of other European nations, then of South Americans, and ultimately of the world. Notwithstanding its adoption south of the border and in Japan, baseball has remained a distinctly American cultural phenomenon.

Despite this separate development, we have shown in this book how administrators in each sport were often conscious of developments in other sports, perhaps most notably in the adoption of the league format in England in 1888, which several contemporary commentators described as an explicit copy of baseball's National League. It also seems likely that the British retain-and-transfer system was patterned after baseball's reserve clause. Since those days, the organizational structures of each sport have developed to the point where it would be no simple matter for one sport to imitate the practices of the other. At present it seems unlikely that the Europeans would adopt the U.S. closed sports league model or that the U.S. leagues would decide to open their monopoly leagues by assimilating the promotion/relegation system. Yet it would equally be folly to think that the two sports have nothing to learn from each other. Indeed, the fledgling commercial tie-up between the Yankees and Manchester United shows that some of the biggest organizations in each sport believe they can learn and benefit from each other. Moreover, the emergence of powerful businessmen, such as Rupert Murdoch and Malcolm Glazer, who have investments both in European soccer and American baseball, seems to ensure that some cross-fertilization in the future is inevitable.

Soccer and baseball are each beset by their own problems. We believe that these problems can be better understood by seeing how the other sport has dealt with them. While the organization of these sports has evolved over time and been conditioned by societal forces, in significant measure the sports' initial structures developed out of historical accidents. There is no necessity that a sport must continue to be run in a particular way, or for that matter that a given sport must continue to be popular.

For soccer, the immediate problem is the financial crisis among the major European clubs, and we will discuss what lessons the organizational structure of baseball has for European soccer clubs. Baseball, by contrast, does not currently face a crisis that is nearly so pressing.[1] Nonetheless, many of baseball's followers are concerned that the game is stagnating, threatened by rival sports in the race to attract both participants and fans, not least by soccer, which is making significant inroads into the United States.

Soccer's Crisis

Despite being the world's most popular game, there is a near universal financial crisis in soccer, most notably among those clubs in Europe that have been the mainstay of competition and the principal suppliers of talent to the world game.[2] Moreover, since the European clubs are largely responsible both for talent scouting and training, the financial crisis threatens the very foundations of the professional game.

While many Europeans set out in the 1990s to define a distinctly European model of sport, explicitly in contrast to the overt commercialism of the "American model," most of the causes of the current financial crisis stem from institutions that are deemed to be of European origin. These are:

—a hierarchy of governance built upon regional, national, and supranational governing bodies;

—a hierarchy of league competition connected through the medium of promotion and relegation;

—the operation of clubs as not-for-profit associations; and

—reliance on regional and national political support for investment and financial bailouts.

These organizing principles, it should be said, served the sport well for more than one hundred years. It can be argued that nationalism has been the greatest single promoter of soccer. Without the national associations it would have been difficult, probably impossible, to channel nationalistic urges into the promotion of the game, even if this was not a strategy openly contemplated by most of soccer's administrators. Promotion and relegation as a competitive device has ensured that even if national championships were dominated by only a small number of teams, fans of lesser teams had reason to stay interested in the league throughout the season, and of course fans of small teams everywhere had reason to hope that they might one day see their team compete at the highest level. The not-for-profit status or conduct of most clubs meant that they were prepared to engage in developmental activities that might bring limited direct returns, such as international tours to developing soccer nations. This was especially true of the early years of the game's development when English and Scottish clubs toured the world, but to the present day the tradition of the soccer tour, whether for the major clubs or for the village team, has remained a recognized feature of the game. Last, it can be argued that political support was essential to establishing many of the most popular clubs in the world, and that this support enabled these clubs to build stadiums that would otherwise have been beyond the means of the club's finances, and to ride financial crises when they have arisen from time to time.

Whatever the rights and wrongs of these arguments, it is hard to believe that soccer could have become any more popular than it is. In England, soccer long ago supplanted cricket, the erstwhile national game, as the most widely followed sport. In most other countries where soccer is played it is by far the dominant sport. There is an argument that says that soccer's success is due to its very simplicity. Compared to American football and ice hockey, where much expensive equipment is required, soccer no doubt has some advantages. But many other sports need little equipment (including baseball), and it is not entirely true that soccer requires nothing more than a ball (for example, two goals are also required). Furthermore, as American football demonstrates, it is not true that sport needs to be simple or inexpensive to play in order to become a successful spectator sport. It seems reasonable, therefore, to believe that soccer's administrative structure contributed, at least in part, to its remarkable expansion in the twentieth century.

But in the 1990s the soccer world system collided with the European common market and the revolution in broadcasting technologies. Soccer became the vehicle by which new companies offering satellite pay TV systems could attract subscribers, and these companies were prepared to pay sums of money that transformed soccer clubs from something like a mom & pop store to something more like a baseball franchise. When Manchester United was floated on the stock exchange in 1991, the business was valued at $86 million (£46 million), yet by 1998 the broadcaster BSkyB had launched a bid to acquire the club for over $1 billion (£623 million). In the 1990s everyone could see opportunities in soccer, witnessed by the launching of no fewer than twenty British soccer clubs on the stock market in a heady period between 1995 and 1997. But by the end of the 1990s the problems were becoming clear for everyone to see, and even before the dot.com bubble burst, soccer shares were trading well below their original offer price.

One important reason for people's disenchantment with soccer as a financial investment was that even when clubs wanted to become profitable, they proved themselves unable to realize this ambition. In some cases, the failure could be attributed to poor management, but most professional investors decided that soccer clubs (except for Manchester United) were a poor investment, regardless of the management team.

The obstacles to making a profit from soccer are the same ones that had contributed to the development of the game. First, soccer's governing bodies restricted the opportunities for teams to develop new competitions. They have insisted on the rigid observance of the segregation of national leagues. In the United Kingdom, Celtic and Rangers of Scotland have frequently expressed an interest in joining the English Premier League, and several Premier League teams would welcome them, but the Football Association (FA), as the governing body, refuses to permit this. They have imposed conditions on the expansion of the Champions League. In 2002 the Union of European Football Associations (UEFA) announced that the number of games played in the competition would be reduced, arguing that this would increase TV audiences; the clubs were not consulted, however, and many felt that this slight was a direct challenge to their power. The governing bodies have also threatened to expand international representative competition at the expense of club competition. In 1999 Sepp Blatter, the president of the Fédération Internationale de Football Association (FIFA), announced that he would like the World Cup to be played in alternate years rather than every four years, further expanding the international representative calendar.

Second, promotion and relegation threatens the financial stability even of well-run teams. In Europe, every top division contains from sixteen to twenty teams, each team plays every other team home and away, a tie gets a team one point and a win three points, and the bottom (usually) three teams are relegated. Consider a season of thirty-four games, where maybe twenty wins and ten ties are enough to win the championship. A well-run team might decide that the cost of the players to achieve this feat would be too high, and that a mid-table position, with twelve wins and ten ties, would generate enough revenue to cover costs. In most years, it turns out that a team can be relegated despite winning as many as thirty-four points, equivalent to ten ties and eight wins. In other words, the gap between mid-table safety and relegation, involving a dramatic loss of income, is as small as four defeats, a losing streak that hits even the best-run teams. Faced with these pressures, financially prudent teams still spend all they can on players, not to win, but in order to maximize their probability of avoiding the drop.

Third, teams might have a better chance of avoiding ruinous financial competition if their rivals were mostly driven by common commercial ends. In practice, however, there are usually so many teams run by owners interested in the glory of winning trophies and prepared to spend what it takes, or controlled by local politicians seeking electoral glory, that the financially prudent find themselves falling behind in the league competition. At this point, investors realize that there is no hope and bail out—and are soon replaced by yet another glory seeker.

Fourth, if politicians find ways to support failing teams, once again the financially prudent are penalized. In 1995, for example, both Celta Vigo and Sevilla were relegated from the top division in Spain for failing to present their financial accounts to the soccer federation, but were later reinstated on the back of intense political lobbying, including death threats and a hunger strike.

To many European soccer fans, the withdrawal of professional investors from soccer is something to be celebrated, since most do not like the intrusion of commercial objectives into the "beautiful game." Many people reason that soccer thrived for nearly one hundred years without such attention, and that a return to the traditional values and mores of the game is desirable. However, this view neglects several developments in soccer that either cannot or will not be reversed.

On the positive side, soccer's income is unlikely to collapse to levels of the 1980s or before. In those days, when incomes were tiny, any wealthy local figure could step in and rescue a club in financial difficulty. In the 1980s the equivalent of $1 million would be enough to acquire almost any team and pay off its debts, and Europe has plenty of millionaires. Today, a major team in financial difficulty might require an injection of capital of anything up to $50 million, with perhaps another $50 million to invest in players. There are some people with this much wealth in Europe, but they are scarce, and many of them are not even interested in soccer. Without the likelihood of receiving financial support in the event of a crisis, the big teams need to achieve a greater degree of certainty about their financial position, rather than face the risks inherent in the existing system.

On the negative side, the enforcement of competition laws and rules against the provision of state aid within the European Union have further restricted traditional sources of capital in the event of a financial crisis. The 1995 Bosman judgment of the European Court of Justice ensured that all players would have free movement inside the European Union, stimulating the creation of a truly international market in players. The court's decision also established a form of free agency, which limited the ability of teams to generate cash from player trading that had been a well-established route to salvation for financially troubled clubs. While transfer fees continued to be paid in the aftermath of the Bosman case, there have been signs in the past few years that the value of trades is falling. Real Madrid has set the benchmark for player trades in recent years, spending more on acquiring talent than any other team. The transfer fees for Luis Figo in 2000 ($63 million) and Zinedine Zidane in 2001 ($77 million) set world records, but the club paid only $41 million in 2003 to acquire David Beckham, and in August 2004 Michael Owen, one of the world's top strikers, was acquired for a mere $15 million. This emerging trend may indicate that a trading system more akin to that of baseball, where relatively small sums of money change hands, will become the norm in the future.

If the Bosman judgment had implications for the ability of teams to cash in on their assets, rules against provision of state aid have implications for the ability of local or national government to bail out clubs in crisis. The strict rules of the European Union prohibiting public subsidies to private businesses were created in order to stop governments from distorting the operation of a European market in major industries such as steel, chemicals, and car manufacturing. In recent years, the authorities have assiduously used these rules to examine schemes that might involve concealed subsidies to soccer teams, such as provisions for the training of players (France), the accounting rules for clubs (Italy), and the use of the public planning system for construction projects (Spain). Added to the almost continuous investigation of collectively negotiated broadcast agreements, it is perhaps not surprising that soccer's administrators have felt themselves to be the focus of a concerted effort by government agencies to expose the game to unlimited economic competition. However, the attention of these bodies has been drawn by the fact that soccer has acquired a characteristic shared by all other activities that face similar scrutiny, namely that large sums of money are being exchanged for the provision of goods and services. If soccer is a business, then the rules of business apply. Soccer's governing bodies have at times lobbied the governments of the EU to grant them a special exemption from the competition laws through an amendment to the Treaty of Rome, the legal document that sets out the framework for European law. Indeed, they have even cited baseball's presumed antitrust exemption as a precedent, but there is little chance that an exemption will be granted.[3]

Thus it appears that while soccer's financial boom has left it in a position where it can no longer avoid being treated as a business, it currently lacks almost any means by which to insure itself against business failure, and is governed by rules that make the risk of failure very high indeed. In most industries, financial failure, while a tragedy for those personally involved, is not viewed as a disaster for the wider economy, and is even seen as evidence that the economic system is functioning properly. One company may fail financially because it does not attract enough customers (people no longer want to buy what it sells) or because it cannot serve its customers at a price they are willing to pay (it cannot control its costs), but such a failure benefits all of its rivals. One reason is that they can acquire some of the customers given up by the failing business; a more subtle reason is that fewer firms typically means a less competitive environment, so that each of the remaining firms can raise its prices a little without losing customers.

In the sports business, however, the financial failure of one team in a league is not a benefit but a threat to the survival of all of the other teams in the league. Each club relies on the other teams to produce the home matches that generate both gate and TV income. If one club cannot complete its games because it is bankrupt, then the other clubs will lose income. If enough clubs fail, then the viability of the league as a whole is threatened (a situation that was not uncommon in the early years of baseball). From a business perspective, teams in a league are more akin to banks than anything else—the failure of one threatens the financial stability of all.

One way to create greater financial stability within the soccer system is to introduce tighter regulation of team finances. Financial stability has been greater in recent years in countries like France and Germany, where independent commissions have had the right to investigate club accounts and either veto risky financial transactions or penalize financially imprudent clubs through relegation. In 2002 UEFA took a step toward creating such a system across all of Europe through the adoption of a club licensing system, which obliges every national association to certify that each club is financially viable at the start of the season. Properly enforced, this system could ensure the financial stability of soccer, but there are reasons to doubt that it will be properly enforced. First, big clubs still carry a lot of political power and can avoid sanctions through effective lobbying. Second, national associations are likely to differ in their standards of enforcement, and it is much more likely that the standard will be set by the softest rather than the toughest regime (if only because financial laxity will give the greatest chance of success in competitions like the Champions League), so that regulation will be weak.

In any case, financial regulation will not deal with many of the problems that beset club soccer. These include the growing concentration of power in the hands of big clubs from big countries, the marginalization of big clubs from small countries, the yawning gulf between clubs in the top divisions and those in the lower divisions, and the sudden and dramatic loss of income associated with relegation.

Nor would it do much to meet the agenda of the big clubs that employ the top players. These clubs see the potential to generate much more income by playing more games against each other. For example, Real Madrid, Manchester United, AC Milan, and Bayern Munich could generate a sell-out crowd and a large TV audience if they played each other home and away each season. Over a five-year period this would generate sixty premium matches; but in the five seasons from 1999 to 2004 these clubs played a total of only twenty-two competitive games against each other. Big clubs are also committed to obtaining a share of the income generated by international competitions in which their employees participate (such as the World Cup).

During the 1990s the clubs in Europe started to discuss the adoption of mechanisms such as those found in baseball and other American sports. In particular, their interest was focused on mechanisms that would restrain the growth of player payrolls. But restraints such as salary caps, luxury taxes, roster limits, and draft rules all turn out to be incompatible with the current system of competition in soccer. The greatest obstacle to their implementation is the dual structure of national domestic leagues and the Champions League: any restraint that would benefit one competition could destabilize the other, or at least bring no benefit. For example, a roster limit of thirty players would probably help balance competition in the domestic leagues but would make it almost impossible for Champions League participants to complete their longer schedule of matches; and a luxury tax that penalized teams that overspent in the Champions League would be unlikely to have any impact at all on the dramatically unequal domestic leagues. Similarly, effective salary caps in domestic leagues would make it highly improbable that any local team could be successful in pan-European competition.

Some in Europe would go further still and create a closed European major league, which would operate in a way similar to Major League Baseball. This idea is seen as anathema by most European soccer fans. Not only would it destroy the traditions of the national league championships, but the fans of medium-sized clubs would never get the opportunity to see their teams play against the big domestic clubs. This latter effect could be mitigated, however, if the European major league consisted of a large enough number of teams.

American experience shows that it is possible to design major leagues that combine the preservation of important local rivalries while expanding competition so that the biggest teams can meet each other in regular competition. The key to designing such a league is to develop a divisional structure that is regional, where teams in each division play each other but the number of interdivisional matches is limited. For example, it would be possible to design a European major league consisting of six divisions, each of ten teams. Teams would play each team in their own division home and away (eighteen games), and then would play three teams from each of the other divisions home and away (thirty games). The appeal of this system is that it would ensure that the most important domestic rivalries were preserved, while giving clubs more international exposure and thus boosting audiences. For example, the six divisions might be defined as:

North West: England and Scotland

South West: Spain and Portugal

West Central: France, Belgium, and the Netherlands

South: Italy, Greece and the Balkans

East Central: Germany, Switzerland, Austria

North East: Scandinavia and the eastern European states.

At once, by cutting out the weak teams from each of the national leagues, a more balanced competition would be created. Moreover, since these teams would now only be competing in a single championship, it would in turn be possible to adopt balance-enhancing restraints, such as roster limits, luxury taxes, or salary caps, which would also tend to promote financial stability. This system can also be designed to make for balanced competition in other ways. The pairing of teams from rival divisions could be decided on the basis of historic winning records. A team such as Real Madrid, for example, would get to play regularly against the likes of Manchester United, Bayern Munich, Juventus, and AC Milan, while a team such as Athletic Bilbao might, for example, play Aston Villa, Southampton, Genoa, and Hertha Berlin. Because winners would get the same number of points regardless of the quality of the opposition, weaker teams would have a slight advantage over their stronger rivals. It would be natural within this system to complete the season with a series of playoffs. For example, each divisional winner plus two wild card teams (such as the two best runners-up) might contest quarterfinals, leading to an overall European champion.[4]

Although such a system would be capable of increasing the quality of

European soccer played at the highest level, teams that currently compete at the lower levels of the larger national leagues, and all but the top one or two teams in most of the smaller leagues, would be deprived of competition from their larger rivals. However, such a restructuring might benefit the excluded teams in the longer run. For example, the majority of teams in Scotland and Portugal have limited support because they can never win their national championship. Cut loose from their overbearing rivals, they would have a better chance of competing in their national championship and could generate genuine excitement about the outcome of their leagues. Furthermore, there is no need to go as far as the Americans and create a closed league. Promotion and relegation might still work in such a system, but in a less destabilizing fashion. For instance, the worst-performing team (rather than the bottom three) in each division of the major league could be relegated each season, to be replaced by a team from their region. The competition for promotion could be determined by the outcome of a regional playoff involving the top teams from each of the national divisions in the region. This would ensure that all teams continued to have the opportunity to reach the highest level, while limiting the number of cases where teams suffered huge revenue fluctuations.

This, of course, is just one of many possible solutions that might be adopted to deal with Europe's current financial crisis. Its allure, in our view, is that the structure would expand the number of attractive games played while preserving the best match-ups within the current system. It would also enable the adoption of some of the restraints on economic competition to be found in the U.S. major leagues, without dispensing entirely with competition-enhancing features such as promotion and relegation. European soccer can learn from the American experience without becoming American.

Baseball's Dilemma

Notwithstanding the challenge of establishing an effective anti-doping policy, baseball faces no imminent crisis in 2005. To the contrary, most signs are rosy. Labor relations are basically restful—for the moment anyway. When the owners and players agreed to a new collective bargaining agreement in August 2002, they averted a work stoppage for the first time since the early 1970s. Television ratings have more or less stabilized. Attendance at the ballpark in 2004, aided by the introduction of new stadiums in San Diego and Philadelphia, was up smartly. On September 1, 2004, for the second year in a row, fourteen or more teams were within four games of making the postseason playoffs. Average salaries are drifting downward, and Commissioner Selig, rather than bemoaning baseball's economic fate, is pronouncing that the sport finally has a financial model that works.

End of story? Not quite. Baseball confronts several issues. Most significantly, it has a nagging, enduring, and major problem lurking just beneath the surface: the maintenance and development of its fan base, a problem that has both international and domestic dimensions. Moreover, if the industry's short-term cyclical upswing leads to too much complacency, then the long-term problem will only worsen.

Baseball's leadership has always focused on the United States. The introduction of a standard business model in the 1870s entailed the complete separation of the amateur from the professional game, the search for profits, the effort to control player salaries via the reserve system, and the challenge to knock off rival leagues. The introduction of the player reserve system in 1879 led naturally to disgruntlement among the players, which led, in turn, to other leagues essaying to capitalize on the players' unease. Between gaining control over the players and either making alliances with or defeating rival leagues, along with mitigating the excesses of gambling and alcoholism, the National League had its hands full.

Had it developed as soccer did in nineteenth-century England, the story might have been different. In England, there was never a complete separation of the professional and amateur games, and to the extent that professionalism did appear, its commercial elements were tightly reined in. Rather, the overarching Football Association set the rules for youth, amateur, and professional soccer. As the governing body, the FA was able to control part of the financial surplus from competitions and used some of these resources to promote the game.[5] The early promotional efforts of the FA, combined with the far-reaching trade and investment ties of the British Empire, helped to develop soccer internationally in its early years.

The United States had only an incipient political empire from the spoils of the so-called Spanish-American War of 1898 and only scant foreign investment until after World War I. There was no infrastructure into which baseball's international dissemination could feed. Furthermore, baseball was obsessed with its internal business affairs and gaining monopoly control of the industry. The one baseball man who expressed a broader vision was Albert G. Spalding. Spalding, a former player and owner of the Chicago NL team, was also a baseball entrepreneur who started a sporting goods company as well as a publishing venture. It was in Spalding's personal business interest to expand the baseball market worldwide, but he could not do it alone. He was able to organize a baseball tour after the 1889 season. The tour was originally only to go to Hawaii and Australia, but once in Australia, Spalding decided it would be just as easy to return home via Egypt and Europe as via the Pacific. The tour made short stops in several countries, and Spalding was particularly delighted with its reception in England. But in the end, the tour barely covered its expenses, and it was clear that, with soccer and cricket already rooted, developing baseball in foreign lands would not be a simple matter. Spalding turned his attention to promoting baseball as the authentic American game.

Serendipity planted baseball's seed in Japan, and there it sprouted. Outside of the United States and the Caribbean, Japan now stands alone as a country that has embraced baseball as its national sport.[6] Belatedly, in the 1990s, seeing the incipient international success of American football, basketball, and hockey, baseball began to make some half-hearted efforts to market its game outside the United States. While these efforts have picked up a bit since 2000, they are still too weak and disorganized to reap much success, at least so far.[7] The vast market of China seems to have been won over by soccer and, secondarily, basketball.

After exploring methods to involve major league players on the U.S. Olympic baseball team, MLB concluded that it was not worth interrupting the regular season. Accordingly, and not without irony, the U.S. team lost in the 2004 trials and never made it to Athens. Without the Olympics to showcase its talent, MLB is now trying to jump on the World Cup bandwagon to promote its diffusion. Here too there is irony, because the soccer World Cup did not commence until 1930, well after the sport had been adopted as the national game in dozens of countries around the world.

After reaching an accord with the Players Association, MLB planned to begin baseball World Cup competition with major leaguers in March 2005. But Japanese baseball demurred. The Japanese League objected to MLB's design to control the organization of the Cup, to play the medal round entirely in the United States, and to pocket the lion's share of the net proceeds.[8] MLB now hopes to begin the Cup competition in 2006, but at this writing Japanese baseball has yet to sign on. The new baseball World Cup project seems to exemplify MLB's long-standing marketing malady: it wants to receive immediate rewards for its investment and effort.

Domestically, baseball's situation is equally problematic. Although average game attendance was up in 2004, it was still below its level ten years earlier. Television ratings stabilized in 2002–04, but their longer-term trend is downward. For instance, between 1975 and 1988, the World Series ratings were over 23 every year.[9] Between 1989 and 1997, they were over 16 every year. Between 1998 and 2003, the ratings have been 14.1, 16.0, 12.4, 15.7, 11.9 and 12.8, respectively.

The problem with baseball's falling ratings goes beyond the simple explanation that there has been a multiplication of viewing options. Baseball's popularity is still strong in the over-50 crowd, but it is waning in younger cohorts, the audience of the future. This pattern is manifested in differential TV ratings. For example, the ratings of the 2003 All-Star Game were 11.7 for the over-50 male cohort and 7.7 for the 25–54 male cohort, yet they were only 5.6 for the 18–34 cohort. The ratings for the 1998 All Star Game for the 18–34 cohort were 9.0, a drop of 38 percent over the five-year period. Even more significant, the ratings for the 2003 World Series were 15.0 for the over-50 male cohort and only 3.9 for the 12–17 male demographic. The latter rating had fallen from 7.2 in 1999, a drop of 46 percent over the four years.

Another indication of the problem is declining participation in Little League Baseball. The number of participants worldwide peaked in 1997 at 2.59 million. Steady declines thereafter left the number at 2.32 million (a decrease of 10.5 percent) in 2003. In the United States alone, total participants came to 1.75 million in 2003. Youth participation in baseball is particularly troubling when the numbers are compared with those for soccer. According to the Soccer Industry Council of America, 3.6 million Americans under the age of 19 play soccer. Among U.S. youth aged 12 to 17, soccer participation rose 20 percent between 1987 and 1999, while baseball participation fell 7 percent. Of course, a soccer fan culture will not materialize overnight. Today's parents did not participate widely in soccer when they were young, but high participation rates over the past twenty years are creating a solid basis for next-generation soccer fandom in the United States. Baseball may be not only losing the marketing battle to soccer in China; it may also be gradually losing the battle in the United States.

The European soccer model for youth development is very different. The historical marriage of the professional and amateur game has meant that teams have their own player development squads that extend all the way down to youth soccer. For example, the English FA sanctions youth competitions for children from the age of 7, provides training courses for coaches, and makes financial grants for the purchase of equipment by registered clubs. Professional clubs offer a wide range of support for the development of youth teams, not from altruism alone, but from a desire to take a first option on emerging talent. Most teams in the Premier League now run their own youth academy, which offers training, support, and competitive soccer for gifted teenagers.

Another troubling development is the falling participation of African Americans in baseball. The share of major leaguers who are African American fell from 27 percent in 1975 to 17 percent in 1992, and to 10 percent in 2004.[10] Many factors lie behind this drop: the lack of space in urban areas for ballfields, the greater expense of equipment relative to sports like basketball, the smaller number of college scholarships available in baseball, among others. Yet these conditions have been present for decades. So why does the black participation rate in baseball keep falling? One factor is that baseball has not been embraced by pop culture. It isn't perceived to be as cool today as basketball and football.[11]

To disrupt this trend, baseball needs to make a major commitment. To its credit, MLB has begun to make some efforts. Since 1991 it has supported the Reviving Baseball in the Inner Cities (RBI) program. RBI was started independent of MLB in 1989 in Los Angeles. Since 1991 MLB has contributed around $1 million a year to support RBI's efforts. But RBI itself only serves kids over 11, and black participation in its ranks is falling, being supplanted by Latinos. Not many 12-year-olds are willing to pick up a bat for the first time.

Baseball has begun to engage in some other youth initiatives as well. Salutary as these individual efforts are, they are insufficient. For instance, on August 9, 2004, MLB announced a program that would allow fans to buy seats at certain games between mid-August and early September for as little as a $1 donation to the Boys and Girls Clubs of America.[12] This program, though billed as a charitable effort, will probably generate revenue for the participating teams, who will sell additional parking and concessions to fans who otherwise would not have come to the ballpark. Contrast the timidity of this initiative with one suggested to the authors by the director of an RBI program: give away 1,000 unsold seats for all weekend games in August and September to inner-city kids, along with a free hot dog and drink.

As African American participation has fallen, Latin American participation has soared. In 2004 Latin Americans constitute 28 percent of major league players and approximately 45 percent of minor leaguers. One important explanation for the growth in Latino participation is the investment MLB has made in baseball academies in the Caribbean. According to one estimate, MLB spends approximately $14 million yearly to run more than thirty academies in the Dominican Republic alone.[13] These investments reap large immediate dividends for MLB. Teams sign medium to top prospects on the cheap, rather than having to spend millions of dollars for the top U.S. amateur draft picks or for Japanese players on the bidding system.

Former players, politicians, and others have criticized MLB for setting up dozens of academies in the Caribbean, but none in urban areas in the United States. In 2004 MLB finally responded by inaugurating an academy in southern California.

MLB's investment in RBI and related programs came largely from the Baseball Tomorrow Fund, which, according to a provision in the 1996 collective bargaining agreement, was funded together with the Players Association in 1997 and 1998. It is not clear to what extent new resources have been devoted to these efforts since then.

It is also discouraging that MLB has not connected one major corporate sponsor to RBI. It is hard to imagine that corporations would not find it attractive to be associated with an inner-city/youth/MLB initiative. The problem seems to be that MLB views an RBI sponsor as a lost sponsor to MLB.

Reversing the existing momentum requires a major and sustained commitment. Timid programs with positive PR spin will accomplish little. Baseball still seems to be stuck in its historical pattern of seeking easy short-term gain.

Baseball's fixation on short-term results is plainly visible to all who care to look. Baseball decided in the 1980s to shift all World Series games to evening prime-time events. Why? Because the networks told MLB that doing so would boost its ratings and allow a higher rights fee. Baseball opted for the short-term gain even though it meant its future customers would not be able to stay up to watch the game's premier contests.[14]

In 2001, following the most scintillating World Series in recent memory, when the Arizona Diamondbacks came from behind in the bottom of the ninth inning of game seven to beat the New York Yankees, Bud Selig announced that baseball would contract by two to four teams before the 2002 season. The proposed timing of the contraction was as ludicrous as the idea. MLB's revenues had been growing at 15 percent annually during the previous six years, yet the commissioner was threatening to reduce output. The owners believed that the way to reduce the disparity between the top and the bottom teams was by lopping off the bottom. The side benefit would be that the rich teams would have to share less revenue with the poor teams. Rather than investing in growing the game in response to rapid revenue growth, the owners sought a misguided short-term solution. Not only did this provoke scorn from politicians in Washington and arouse the hostility of the Players Association, it also sent a signal to the youth of America that MLB had no interest in bringing baseball to emerging new markets. There may be no better way to invigorate interest in Little League in cities like Washington, D.C.; Portland, Oregon; Norfolk, Virginia; and Sacramento, California, than to give youngsters an opportunity to root for a local major league team and see superstars like Barry Bonds, David Ortiz, Albert Pujols, and Pedro Martinez play in person.

In 2003, in the face of falling ratings for the All-Star Game and pressure from its network, baseball decided that it would try to increase viewer interest in this traditional exhibition by making the game "count." The plan, which the Players Association accepted skeptically on a trial basis, gives the winning league the home field advantage in the World Series. Any fan over the age of 10 realized that this was an illogical scheme. Are players on the Red Sox supposed to try harder at the All-Star Game because a victory for the American League would give the Yankees home field advantage in the World Series? Or are the Red Sox supposed to root harder for the American League All-Star team? Why not simply give home field advantage to the team with the best regular season record? This was one gambit that didn't even pay off in the short run. All-Star Game ratings were flat in 2003, and they fell in 2004.

Early in the 2004 season MLB announced that it had reached a promotion deal to put logos from the *Spiderman II* movie on its bases. The deal would be worth several million dollars to baseball, but it would also sacrifice a long-standing tradition to keep advertising off the field and off the players' uniforms. Again the instinct seemed to be to grab an opportunity for short-term gain. In this instance, however, more sensible heads prevailed after baseball was excoriated in the national media for crass commercialism.

Baseball has had a long-standing problem with player drug abuse. Various sources suggest that, in the 1960s and 1970s, stimulants were not strangers in major league clubhouses. Marvin Miller, the former director of the Players Association, once observed that uppers and downers were laid out like "jelly beans" by team employees.[15] In 1983 four players went to prison on cocaine convictions. In 1985 then-commissioner Peter Ueberroth called for a drug testing policy, but the players and owners could not agree on a mutually acceptable plan. Meanwhile, drug use by professional athletes shifted from recreational to performance enhancing. Steroids enabled some players to gain a competitive advantage over others, in addition to being harmful to users. The NFL, at least, was quick to react, introducing a steroid testing program in 1987. The NBA began its testing program in 1999. But MLB still had no policy in 2002, when former MVP Ken Caminiti asserted to *Sports Illustrated* that half of major league players took steroids.

In 1998 Mark McGwire broke Roger Maris's home-run record while using a steroid analog, androstenedione. Steroids create power, and power makes baseball more interesting. Without a major scandal, owners were not in the mood to pull the plug on the power supply, and the leadership of the Players Association resisted the privacy invasion of a testing program.

Growing public pressure impelled MLB and the Players Association to incorporate a steroid program in its August 2002 collective bargaining agreement. The program was roundly criticized, however. Even after testing was triggered, tests would be conducted only twice a year (and never in the off-season) and there would be no suspension or fine for the first offense. The second violation brought a suspension of only fifteen days. With new, less detectable supplement compounds being introduced almost weekly and new methods of assimilating the substances into the body shortening the time the chemicals remained in the bloodstream to a few days or, in some cases, a few hours, it is not surprising that many players were not deterred from steroid use.

The result was that after the 2004 season baseball's greatest home run hitter Barry Bonds and slugger Jason Giambi were revealed to have used steroids.[16] Baseball fans thrive on records, especially home run records. If baseball's records are tainted, the sport is diminished. As we write, MLB seems finally ready to move toward a more serious testing and penalty program. There remain questions, though, about whether the drug policy they finally adopt will adequately confront the scientific conundrums of user identification and contain sufficient sanctions to inhibit indulgence.[17] Matters will only get more difficult in a few years, when performance-enhancing gene therapy will become a reality. As in other areas, baseball has mostly concentrated on putting out the short-run drug scandal fires, rather than on developing a solid, satisfactory, long-term policy.[18]

Part of MLB's myopia comes from its presumed antitrust exemption. Put simply, the industry has not faced competition from a rival league since 1915, and its restrictive practices have been protected. Baseball was even unchallenged on the national scene by other sports until at least the late 1950s. The result of decades of supremacy inevitably was the emergence of an arrogant, lax, and inefficient business culture. Long-term investing was simply unnecessary with short-term gain readily available.

Part of baseball's fixation on short-term results comes from the absence of strong and coherent leadership. Baseball today has thirty teams and thirty different owners. These owners have fundamentally different economic experiences in the game. Before revenue sharing, the top team earns more than $300 million in revenue and the bottom team earns less than $50 million. Some teams are in big cities, some in small. Some have new stadiums, some old. Some owners own related entities (television stations, concessions companies, real estate, ballparks, etc.), some don't. Owners are also divided by politics and personalities. In its modern era since 1903, baseball has had a weak commissioner.[19] The game's direction has been determined by a collection of argumentative and self-interested owners.[20] Without competitive pressures, baseball's lack of cohesive leadership and direction did not prevent it from being economically successful.

Baseball did not have a Football Association to see the big picture. Whatever faults might be laid at the feet of soccer's governing bodies, first the FA, then FIFA and UEFA, there can be no question that they have consciously and explicitly argued that the long-term interests of the game, its players, and its supporters should be at the forefront of policymaking.

Nor did baseball have a powerful commissioner like Pete Rozelle in the NFL or David Stern in the NBA. Rozelle benefited from a league that had extensive revenue sharing from its inception and hence functioned with considerable coherence among its owners. Stern ironically benefited from a league-wide financial crisis when he came into office that required firm action. After gaining a salary cap, Stern engaged his acute promotional instincts and undertook bold initiatives.

Baseball, however, had weak leadership and an assortment of disparate owners who could agree only on least-common-denominator policies. In collective bargaining, the lowest common denominator was that all owners were in favor of a salary cap. Owners' repeated insistence on a cap after 1976 and their inability to put a program of balanced restraints on the bargaining table help to account for the sport's tumultuous labor relations. In other areas, the owners have been concerned with troubleshooting and unable to formulate long-term development plans for the game.

For all of their management issues and problems, the governing bodies of world soccer are capable of articulating a vision for the sport as a whole. From its birth, soccer administration has taken place above the league level. National and international governing bodies have attempted to marshal resources to promote and expand their sport. Government oversight has provided another level of support. Though soccer's governing bodies sometimes lacked the foresight and ingenuity to respond to changing conditions and have often descended into conflict and backstabbing, there have always been visionaries who have taken the long view rather than a blinkered pursuit of near-term financial profit.

It is an irony, perhaps, that baseball, with a presumed antitrust exemption, has had the legal ability to make centralized decisions. The problem is that the central authority has been under the control of dozens of heterogeneous and small-minded owners, not subject either to the normal forces of competition or to government regulation.

In the end, what is good for baseball is what is good for baseball's fans. Those who run Major League Baseball have a responsibility to these fans to manage the game of which they are, temporarily, the trustees, in such a way as to ensure its long-term survival and prosperity. Should the contentment of the fans also create some prosperity for the owners, then perhaps few would begrudge them that.

Much the same can be said of soccer. Soccer at least possesses a governmental structure that enables the long-term interest of the fans to be articulated and supported. Defending these interests, however, does not mean preserving exactly the same competitive structures that suited the interests of the game twenty-five or fifty years ago. Unless some means is found to offer a minimum of prosperity for the clubs and their owners, the entire system is in danger of collapse.

One way or the other, these two sports have been the national pastimes in their respective countries for over a century. They have been created out of literally millions of individual acts of devotion in different times and places. This is not the kind of evolution that demands constant change and restructuring. Both games are simple to play and simple to understand. The essential feature that they share is the capacity for an individual match to produce a level of excitement and suspense rare in most other forms of entertainment. Though they wax and wane in popularity, they have shown that their cultural centrality is stronger than the often errant policies of those who might currently be in charge. Soccer and baseball are, after all, our national pastimes.

Notes

Preface

1. To be sure, the evolution of baseball and soccer has been compared before, notably by Allen Guttman (see, for example, *Games and Empires* (Columbia University Press, 1994), but such works have not looked at the detailed economic structure of sport. More recently, there has been some interest in making international economic comparisons (see, for example, Carlos Barros, Muradali Ibrahim, and Stefan Szymanski, eds., *Transatlantic Sport* [Cheltenham, U.K.: Edward Elgar, 2002]; or Rodney Fort and John Fizel, eds., *International Sports Economics Comparisons* [Westport, Conn.: Praeger, 2004]; or Robert Sandy, Peter Sloane, and Mark Rosentraub, *The Economics of Sport* [Basingstoke, U.K.: Palgrave Macmillan, 2004]), but these have tended to compare sports in general.

2. John Maynard Keynes, *The General Theory of Employment, Interest and Money* (Harcourt, Brace & World, 1964), p. 383.

Chapter One

1. A. Bartlett Giamatti, *Take Time for Paradise: Americans and Their Games* (New York: Simon and Schuster, 1991), p. 13.

2. Throughout this book we use the word soccer to denote "Association Football," to give the game its full title. While "football" is the more common term used in the United Kingdom and elsewhere, we avoid this, so as not to confuse it with American football. It is sometimes thought that the word "soccer" is an American invention for precisely this reason, but this is not so. According to the Oxford English Dictionary, the first recorded use of the word "soccer" was in 1889 by an English writer (although using a variant spelling, "socca"). The word has been commonplace in England and elsewhere ever since. It is thought to be an abbreviation of "association," used originally to distinguish it from the game of "rugby football," also popular in England.

3. Franklin Foer, *How Soccer Explains the World: An (Unlikely) Theory of Globalization* (New York: HarperCollins, 2004), p. 245.

4. To be sure, leagues often impose some minimum standards in relation to facilities for promoted teams, but sporting rather than commercial merit is paramount.

5. There were, however, two joint Major League Baseball/National Football League facilities constructed: the Minneapolis Metrodome in 1982 and Joe Robbie Stadium in Dade County, Florida, in 1987.

6. These figures on stadium costs, private and public, come from Judith Grant Long, "Full Count: The Real Cost of Public Funding for Major League Sports Facilities and Why Some Cities Pay More to Play" (Ph.D. dissertation, Urban Planning, Harvard University, April 2002).

7. Much of this evidence is reviewed in John Siegfried and Andrew Zimbalist, "The Economics of Sports Facilities and Their Communities," *Journal of Economic Perspectives* 14, no. 3 (2000): 95–114.

8. For a low estimate of the externality, consumer surplus, and public-good value of sports teams, see Bruce Johnson, Peter Groothuis, and John Whitehead, "The Value of Public Goods Generated by a Major League Sports Team: The CVM Approach," *Journal of Sports Economics* 2, no. 1 (2002): 6–21. For a somewhat more optimistic assessment, derived from an estimated increase in property rents, see G. Carlino and N. Coulson, "Compensating Differentials and the Social Benefits of the NFL," *Journal of Urban Economics* 56, no. 1 (2004): 25–50. For another sanguine assessment of the consumer surplus generated by a baseball team, based on fans' inelastic demand curve, see Roger Noll, "The Economics of Baseball Contraction," *Journal of Sports Economics* 4, no. 4 (2003): 367–88. For a critical discussion of the Carlino and Coulson study, see Dennis Coates, Brad Humphreys and Andrew Zimbalist, "Compensating Differentials and the Social Benefits of the NFL—A Critique," *Journal of Urban Economics*, forthcoming.

9. Sadly, there was nothing new about these disasters. In 1946, thirty-three people were killed when a wall collapsed at a stadium in Bolton, England; and the Ibrox stadium, home of the famous Scottish team, Rangers, suffered two major disasters, one in 1902 when twenty-five people died and one in 1971 when sixty-six perished.

10. See Stefan Szymanski and Tim Kuypers, *Winners and Losers: The Business Strategy of Football* (London: Penguin Books, 1999), chap. 2, for more details.

11. Deloitte & Touche, *Annual Review of Football Finance* (Manchester, U.K.: July 2003), p. 49.

12. The exceptions are baseball in Japan and basketball in China and Europe.

13. The Bosman judgment issued by the European Court of Justice in 1995 is a landmark in European sport that effectively guaranteed free agency to players. It is discussed in more detail in chapter 4.

14. The economic and legal analysis of sports league monopolies in the United States has been written about extensively. Some of the seminal works include: Roger Noll, ed., *Government and the Sports Business* (Brookings, 1974); Stephen Ross, "Monopoly Sports Leagues," *Minnesota Law Review* 71, no. 3 (1989): 643–761; Rodney Fort and James Quirk, "Cross-Subsidization, Incentives, and Outcomes in Professional Team Sports Leagues," *Journal of Economic Literature* 33, no. 3 (1995): 1265–99; Simon Rottenberg, "The Baseball Players' Labor Market," *Journal of Political Economy* 64, no. 3 (1956): 242–58; and Walter Neale, "The Peculiar Economics of Professional Sport," *Quarterly Journal of Economics* 78, no. 1 (1964): 1–14. An early important work on the economics of open soccer leagues is Peter J. Sloane, "The Economics of Professional Football: The Football Club as a Utility Maximiser," *Scottish Journal of Political Economy* 18, no. 2 (1971): 121–46.

15. Some might add Taiwan and South Korea to this list.

Chapter Two

1. This contemporary doggerel testifies to the unpopularity of the monarchy in Britain in the mid-eighteenth century.

2. He was hit on the head by a cricket ball and died a few weeks later. However, there is some controversy among historians as to whether the cricket ball was the cause of death.

3. In a letter dated November 14, 1748, one Lady Hervey wrote, "The Prince's family is an example of innocent and cheerful amusements. All this summer they played abroad; and now, in the winter, in a large room, they divert themselves at base-ball, a play all who are, or have been, schoolboys, are well acquainted with." Cited by Robert Henderson in *Ball, Bat and Bishop: The Origin of Ball Games* (New York: Rockport, 1947), p. 134.

4. Who knows, perhaps baseball, with royal support, might have become England's national pastime, while cricket might have been adopted, in protest, by the Yankee rebels.

5. See, for example, *Cricket Scores and Biographies of Celebrated Cricketers, 1744–1826*, vol. 1 (London: Lillywhite, 1862).

6. Like baseball, cricket is played with a bat and ball, there are pitchers (called bowlers), batters (batsmen), and fielders. There are innings and runs, and a ball caught on the fly is an out. In fact, any American who loves baseball will quickly learn to appreciate the subtleties of the game (in the experience of the authors it takes about two hours at a game, with proper instruction). One of the key differences between cricket and baseball is that in the former the batsman is under almost no pressure to swing at any ball: there are no strikeouts in cricket. Thus the batsman has the luxury of waiting to hit only those balls that he finds convenient. It is therefore not surprising that a batsman can remain at bat for more than ten hours, over a period of more than one day, making the typical game of cricket a very lengthy affair.

7. See Joseph Strutt, *Sports and Pastimes of the People of England*, book 2 (1801), chap. 3.

8. For the full extent of aristocratic patronage in the eighteenth century, see David Underdown, *Start of Play: Cricket and Culture in Eighteenth-Century England* (London: Penguin, 2000).

9. The parallel development of horseracing in England was primarily motivated by the same demand.

10. Eric Parker, *The History of Cricket* (London: Lonsdale Library, 1950), chap. 9. Parker lists no fewer than fifteen games played for this sum in 1792 alone.

11. The field is named after Thomas Lord, a well-connected entrepreneur.

12. Wicket has several meanings. First, the wicket designates the five sticks that roughly delineate a strike zone. Second, by extension, the wicket describes the area between the wickets at either end of the field. Third, wicket is used to denote the number of outs per team.

13. "Public" here in fact means what we today call "private," but at the time there was no such thing as a free education provided by state-run schools, and the only options were to engage a private tutor for your children, send them to one of the fee-charging schools open to any of the public who could pay, or not educate your children at all.

14. The modern Harry Potter is in many ways a fictional reincarnation of Tom Brown.

15. This phrase was coined by a reviewer of Charles Kingsley's novel *Two Years Ago*, also published in 1857. Kingsley and Hughes were friends and espoused a similar ideology. They feared that effeminacy was weakening the church and the nation and argued that an emphasis on rugged manly virtues would maintain the empire. Their views were hugely influential with British educationalists in the nineteenth century and also spread to the United States through movements such as the YMCA. In addition to supporting imperialism, advocates argued that the working class would be less likely to lapse into alcoholism and debauchery if they were properly occupied with sports.

16. The book also contained "A Dark Chapter in the History of Cricket," explaining the harm done to the game by gambling, and the well-known phrase "it's not cricket" was used to describe a game in which each side bet against itself.

17. Small details made for big differences. A gentleman could have the title "Esquire" after his name. On the scorecard, a gentleman's first initial would precede his surname (J. Smith), while a mere player's initial would follow after (Smith, J.).

18. *Spirit of the Times*, October 1, 1859.

19. The Doubleday myth was comprehensively refuted by Robert Henderson, former Reading Room chief of the New York Public Library, in his book *Bat, Ball and Bishop*. He writes that the first historical mention of baseball was in England in 1700, and that the game is described in a book published in England in 1744. This same book was listed for sale in the *Pennsylvania Gazette* in 1750, and thereafter several pirated editions were published in America. John Adams, the second president of the United States, wrote in his diary about playing "bat and ball" as a child. Adams was born in 1735. A Revolutionary soldier at Valley Forge referred to playing "at base" in 1788, and recently a reference was found to the banning of baseball within eighty yards of a newly built church in 1791 in Pittsfield, Massachusetts. These and other references date the origin of baseball to well before Spalding had Abner Doubleday inventing the game in 1839 in Cooperstown, New York. Still, it was Cartwright who provided the codification upon which the game as we know it evolved.

20. The first recorded admission fee to a baseball game was the all-star contest between the best players from New York against the best from Brooklyn on July 20, 1858. Some 4,000 spectators paid 50 cents apiece to watch the New York all-stars defeat those from Brooklyn, 22 to 18. Ron McCullough, *How Baseball Began* (Warwick, 1995), p. 37.

21. Robert Burk, *Never Just a Game: Players, Owners and American Baseball to 1920* (University of North Carolina Press, 1994), p. 6.

22. Harold Seymour, *Baseball: The Early Years* (Oxford University Press, 1960), p. 17.

23. Ted Vincent, *Mudville's Revenge: The Rise and Fall of American Sport* (New York: Seaview Books, 1981), p. 88.

24. Quoted in Seymour, *Baseball*, p. 16.

25. George Kirsch, *The Creation of American Team Sports: Baseball and Cricket 1838–72* (University of Illinois Press, 1989), p. 180.

26. Burk, *Never Just a Game*, p. 9.

27. Seymour, *Baseball*, p. 35.

28. *Spirit of the Times*, April 3, 1858.

29. A good account of this period is provided by John Allen Kraut in "The Rise of the National Game," *Annals of American Sport* (Yale University Press, 1929).

30. Kirsch, *The Creation of American Team Sports*, p. 93.

31. Seymour, *Baseball*, pp. 45–46.

32. Nevertheless, one of the older member clubs resigned in disgust because the Knickerbocker club had "desecrated its time honored principles of playing Base Ball for health and recreation merely" (ibid., p. 49).

33. Ibid., p. 50.

34. See David Voigt, *American Baseball,* vol. 1 (Pennsylvania State University Press, 1983), pp. 19–20.

35. Kirsch, *The Creation of American Team Sports,* pp. 235–36.

36. This and other betting scandals are ably described in Daniel Ginsburg, *The Fix Is In: A History of Baseball Gambling and Game Fixing Scandals* (Jefferson, N.C.: McFarland, 1995).

37. Of course, baseball was not the only threat to the church at the time. During the period 1870–90, professional theater was beginning to take hold as an entertainment form. The number of actors in the United States increased from 5,000 to 15,000 over this twenty-year period. According to Vincent (*Mudville's Revenge,* p. 159): "Baseball promoters and theater owners and managers were often the same people, and many a ball player was engaged with an acting troupe during the winter."

38. There is, alas, some disagreement on whether the team played fifty-seven or fifty-eight games. One of the games ended in a tie because the opposing team walked off the field to save a bet of one of its sponsors. By most standards, this would have constituted a forfeited game and hence a victory for the Red Stockings.

39. Vincent, *Mudville's Revenge,* p. 127.

40. Ibid., p. 130.

41. Kirsch, *The Creation of American Team Sports,* p. 251.

42. Ibid., p. 252.

43. Lee Allen, *100 Years of Baseball* (New York: Bartholomew House, 1950), pp. 24, 28.

44. Quoted in Ginsburg, *The Fix Is In,* p. 19; Ginsburg also provides a detailed description of betting on particular games.

45. Quoted in ibid., p. 17.

46. See, for example, Joe Durso's *Baseball and the American Dream* (St. Louis: Sporting News, 1986), pp. 16–18; and Vincent's *Mudville's Revenge,* p. 102.

47. Vincent, *Mudville's Revenge,* p. 107.

48. Allen, *100 Years of Baseball,* p. 27.

49. In Spalding's version, somewhat improbably, the idea was his own (see Albert G. Spalding, *America's National Game* [University of Nebraska Press, 1992], p. 175).

50. Ibid., pp. 176–77.

51. Details of how the tour was organized, and the correspondence between Wright and Alcock, are preserved in the Spalding Collection of the New York Public Library (the Harry Wright Materials). Microfilm copies are also held in the Baseball Hall of Fame Archive, Cooperstown, New York.

52. This observation remains valid to the present day.

53. Spalding, *America's National Game,* p. 5.

54. Ginsburg, *The Fix Is In,* p. 35.

55. A nice discussion of Hulbert's actions in 1875 is provided by John Rosenburg, *They Gave Us Baseball: The 12 Extraordinary Men Who Shaped the Game* (Harrisburg, Penn.: Stackpole Books, 1989).

56. It should give some solace to those who see no compelling reason for Pete Rose to be excluded from the Hall of Fame to know that William Hulbert is also not in the

Hall. Not Hulbert, but Morgan Bulkley, who served for only nine months as the NL's first president and accomplished nothing in that period, has been inducted at Cooperstown. Hulbert succeeded Bulkley as NL president, a position he retained until his death at age 50 in 1882. Bulkley was simply Hulbert's vehicle to buy acceptance of his plan for the NL from the eastern club backers.

57. William Akin, "William A. Hulbert," in *Nineteenth Century Star*, edited by Robert Tiemann and Mark Rucker (Kansas City, Mo.: Society for American Baseball Research, 1989); Robert Barney and Frank Dallier, "William A. Hulbert, Civic Pride and the Birth of the National League," *Nine: A Journal of Baseball History and Social Policy Perspectives* 2, no. 1 (1973).

58. Quoted in Barney and Dallier, "William Hulbert," p. 42.

59. Quoted in Peter Levine, *A. G. Spalding and the Rise of Baseball* (Oxford University Press, 1985), p. 22.

60. Because the launch of the NL was preceded by an article in the *Chicago Tribune* in October 1875 criticizing the NAPBBP and citing the need for a new league with certain characteristics, some have claimed that Hulbert got his ideas from the article's author, Lewis Meacham. More recent scholarship, however, has followed the interpretation of Harold Seymour (*Baseball*, pp. 76–78) that Meacham's article most likely came from Hulbert's head.

61. Ibid., pp. 24, 134.

62. Alas, although Hulbert's intransigent disciplining of these players sent a strong message and improved the game's image, it failed to root out player and umpire corruption. After a brief hiatus, scandals reappeared. For details, see Ginsburg, *The Fix Is In*.

63. Cited in Seymour, *Baseball*, p. 90. Translated into early twenty-first-century parlance, this maxim becomes, "What is good for Milwaukee is good for Major League Baseball."

64. Ibid., p. 94.

65. Interestingly, this article does not appear in the 1876, 1878, or 1879 constitutions. It appears to be a one-time opening in order to lure certain teams into the NL or deter other teams from competing with the NL. We are grateful to Tim Wiles of the Baseball Hall of Fame in Cooperstown for pointing this out to us.

66. Strutt, *Sports and Pastimes*, p. 168.

67. Ironically, the RFU also ended up banning the practice of hacking some years later. What really distinguished the rugby code (and later American football) from the soccer code was the practice of running with the ball in hand, long associated with the Rugby School.

68. These details are taken from a recent biography of Alcock by Keith Booth entitled, somewhat grandly, *The Father of Modern Sport* (Manchester, U.K.: Parrs Wood, 2002).

69. The annual Eton vs. Harrow cricket match at Lord's was an important date in London's social calendar from 1805, when it was organized by Lord Byron, until the 1960s.

70. Soccer was commonly referred to as the "Association game" in the nineteenth century—that is, the game authorized by the Football Association.

71. "Fixture" is commonly used in England to denote a scheduled match or game.

72. The notorious "Bodyline" Series of 1932–33, in which the English bowlers appeared to deliberately bowl at the Australian batsmen rather than the wicket, almost

led to the termination of diplomatic relations between the two countries and is a source of resentment to this day.

73. Nicknamed "Pa" Jackson, he earned this sobriquet in 1881 while returning on a train with the rest of the Cambridge University team after a match against the Blackburn Rovers. One of the players started singing and Jackson told him to be quiet. "Oh, pa, don't be so cross!" came the sarcastic reply. Recounted in the official *History of the Football Association* (London: Naldrett, 1953), pp. 157–58. On tours he demanded that his players always attend the postmatch dinner. On one occasion, when one of the team's best players turned up for the following day's match having failed to attend the dinner, Jackson immediately sent him home, *pour encourager les autres*. N. Lane Jackson, *Sporting Days and Sporting Ways* (London: Hurst & Blackett, 1932), p. 141.

74. Their name also passed into the (British) English language as a synonym for gentlemanly amateurism.

75. In fact, this was the culmination of a sequence of battles. First, there was an uproar with the introduction of the penalty kick in 1892. This offended the amateur gentlemen, since it implied a punishment for a deliberate foul, to which, of course, no gentleman would ever admit. Next, the FA banned "scratch" teams, on the grounds that these ad hoc matches were undermining proper competitions. Obliging gentlemen to socialize with professionals was the last straw. The history of this struggle is explained in the official *History of the Football Association,* pp. 203–28.

76. In later life, he was the founder of numerous golf clubs and an influential figure in English tennis (most of his autobiography, *Sporting Days and Sporting Ways*, published in 1932, is taken up with golf and tennis). Many years earlier, back in 1889, he was responsible for coordinating the first international tennis competition to be held in the United States between American and British players.

77. *The Sporting Chronicle*, March 23, 1888, p. 4.

78. *The Athletic News*, June 21, 1887, p. 6.

79. William McGregor, "The Origin and Future of the Football League," in *Association Football and the Men Who Made It*, edited by Alfred Gibson and William Pickford, vol. 3 (London: Caxton, 1906), p. 2.

80. Ibid., p. 3.

81. J. A. H. Catton, *The Real Football* (London: Sands, 1900), p. 70.

82. Gibson and Pickford, *Association Football and the Men Who Made It*, vol. 1, pp. 99–100.

83. Until 1997 the soccer club played in the original stadium used for the baseball league, which was known as the Baseball Ground.

84. The league had some early success, and in his 1899 *Baseball Guide,* Spalding wrote confidently of a glowing future for baseball in Britain. Sadly this never materialized, and by 1914 interest had almost completely evaporated.

85. Newton Crane, *Baseball* (London: George Bell & Sons, 1891), p. 104. The book explains the game as it is played in the United States, including a discussion of player contracts, and provides some match statistics for games between Preston North End and Aston Villa.

86. N.L. Jackson. *Association Football* (London: George Newnes, 1899), p. 211.

87. Ibid., p. 67.

88. Ibid., pp. 216–21.

89. Catton, *The Real Football*, p. 186.

90. Ibid., pp. 182–84.

91. *History of the Football Association,* pp. 151–53.

92. This rule was established even though only twelve teams in total entered the league in the first season.

Chapter Three

1. FIFA's official centennial history, written by some of the leading historians of soccer, provides a good overview of the institution. See Pierre Lanfranchi, Christiane Eisenberg, Tony Mason, and Alfred Wahl, *100 Years of Football* (London: Weidenfeld and Nicolson, 2004).

2. That match was played on April 11, 2001. The referee lost count during the game, and there remains some dispute over whether the score was 31 or 32 to 0.

3. Switzerland played a prominent part in the spread of soccer to the rest of Europe. In the late nineteenth century, it was a favored destination for sporting English gentlemen, and it housed a large number of finishing schools for the children of wealthy Europeans.

4. As might be expected, there are disputes and differences of opinion in relation to all of these historical claims. Most of these examples are taken from Bill Murray's *Football: A History of the World's Game* (Aldershot, U.K.: Ashgate, 1994), with some additional accounts from Willy Meisl, *Soccer Revolution* (London: Phoenix Sports Books, 1955); Eduardo Archetti, *Masculinities* (New York: Berg, 1999); Tony Mason, *Passion of the People? Football in South America* (London: Verso, 1995); Steven Main, *The History of Russian Football* (1991) (www.quark.lu.se/~oxana/archie/rfhist.html); Phile Ball, *Morbo; The Story of Spanish Football* (London: WSC Books, 2001); Pierre Lanfranchi and Matthew Taylor, *Moving with the Ball: The Migration of Professional Footballers* (New York: Berg, 2001); and Dave Litterer, "An Overview of American Soccer History" (www.sover.net/~spectrum/overview.html).

5. That is unless, of course, as in Australia, it was an opportunity to show oneself to be more English than the English, or, as in India and the Caribbean, it was an opportunity for a subject people to teach their supposed masters a lesson.

6. Lanfranchi and Taylor, *Moving with the Ball*, p. 25.

7. *History of the Football Association* (London: Naldrett, 1953), p. 198.

8. Meisl, *Soccer Revolution,* pp. 57–58.

9. Héctor Chaponick, ed., *Historia del Fútbol Argentino* (Buenos Aires: Editorial Eiffel, 1955), p. 121.

10. Angus Maddison, *The World Economy: A Millennial Perspective* (Paris: OECD, 2001), pp. 89–123.

11. Michael Edelstein, "Foreign Investment and Accumulation, 1860–1914," in *The Economic History of Britain Since 1700*, vol. 2, edited by R. Floud and D. McCloskey (Cambridge University Press, 1994), p. 175. James Foreman-Peck, *A History of the World Economy* (London: Harvester Wheatsheaf, 1995), p. 121.

12. B. O. Corbett, *Annals of the Corinthian Football Club* (London: Longmans, 1906), pp. vi–vii.

13. Robert Burk, *Never Just a Game: Players, Owners and American Baseball to 1920* (University of North Carolina Press, 1994), p. 93.

14. Ward is the only player in baseball history to record both 100 wins as a pitcher (Babe Ruth had 94) and 2,000 hits as a batter. Robert Berry, William Gould, and Paul Staudohar, *Labor Relations in Professional Sports* (Dover, Mass.: Auburn House, 1986), p. 52. He was also more than a ballplayer, eventually earning degrees in political science and law from Columbia University.

15. In 1884, with salaries rising from competition from the AA, the NL allowed pitchers to throw overhand and batting averages dropped 14 points. In 1886 the number of balls for a walk was increased to seven. In 1888 the number of balls for a walk was reduced to 4.

16. The buyout was for a total of $131,000 plus 10 percent of all 1892 gate receipts in the now twelve-team National League. But Von der Ahe's fortunes turned bleak. A stadium fire, two divorces, unpaid debt, and legal problems led him first to lose his baseball team and finally to a job tending bar at a small saloon until his death from cirrhosis of the liver in 1913.

17. The only catch was that Lajoie would be banned from playing any games in Pennsylvania. This ban was lifted when the major league agreement was signed in 1903.

18. Andrew Zimbalist, *Baseball and Billions: A Probing Look inside the Big Business of Our National Pastime*, paperback ed. (New York: Basic Books, 1994), p. 9.

19. David Voigt, *American Baseball* (Pennsylvania State University Press, 1983), p. 117.

20. Lee Lowenfish and Tony Lupien, *The Imperfect Diamond: The Story of Baseball's Reserve System and the Men Who Fought to Change It* (New York: Stein and Day, 1980), p. 90.

21. For an excellent, though perhaps overly sympathetic, biography of Judge Landis, see David Pietrusza, *Judge and Jury: The Life and Times of Judge Kenesaw Mountain Landis* (South Bend, Ind.: Diamond Communications, 1998).

22. Albert G. Spalding, *America's National Game* (University of Nebraska Press, 1992), pp. 256–57.

23. Mark Dyreson, *Making the National Team: Sport, Culture and the Olympic Experience* (University of Illinois Press, 1998), p. 64.

24. Sometimes known as the "Tribal Games," the St. Louis Olympics assembled and trained to play sports more than two thousand representatives of indigenous peoples—Native Americans, African pygmies, Tehuelche Indians from Patagonia, and Filipino tribes—as part of a "scientific" experiment to discover which races were most athletic, led by Professor W. J. McGee, an anthropologist who headed the American Bureau of Ethnology. As Baron de Coubertin observed, "In no place but America would one have dared to place such events on a program, but to Americans everything is permissible, their youthful exuberance calling certainly for the indulgence of the Ancient Greek ancestors, if, by chance, they found themselves among the amused spectators" (ibid., pp. 84–85).

25. Ironically, other than the 1994 strike-interrupted season, 1904 was the only time that the World Series was not played since 1903.

26. Eleven teams played in 1912, fourteen in 1920, and twenty-two in 1924.

27. www.quickstart.clari.net/qs_se/webnews/wed/cn/Qrugbyu-wc2003-oly-rogge. RBK7_DNK.html.

28. Lipton was a self-made Scot who had made his way to the United States in his early years and then returned to the United Kingdom, where he set up one of the world's first department stores. Later in life he entered the tea business, in which he soon became a global player. A sports lover, he encouraged all kinds, including soccer. He established the Lipton Cup in 1905, a trophy to be played for in matches between Uruguay and Argentina, where he also owned plantations. He had a great affection for all things American and treated the baseball tourists as long-lost cousins. Lipton was also a famous competitor in the America's Cup, noted for his failure to win the event despite making five attempts and for his good grace in accepting defeat.

29. Thorpe was ranked as the third greatest athlete of the twentieth century by a panel of American sports journalists for *USA Today* (behind Babe Ruth and Michael Jordan). Only one soccer player, Pele, made the list (www.usatoday.com/sports/ssat2.htm).

30. The most complete and authoritative history of Cuban baseball is Roberto González Echevarría's *The Pride of Havana: A History of Cuban Baseball* (Oxford University Press, 1999). An excellent treatment of the development of baseball in the Dominican Republic is Rob Ruck's *The Tropic of Baseball: Baseball in the Dominican Republic* (Westport, Conn.: Meckler, 1991).

31. Donald Roden, "Baseball and the Quest for National Dignity in Meiji Japan," in *Baseball History from outside the Lines*, edited by John Dreifort (University of Nebraska Press, 2001), p. 286.

32. When the gentlemen's London Association formed the breakaway Amateur Football Association in 1907, it is striking how many foreign associations wrote in support of the established FA; see *History of the Football Association*, pp. 219–20.

33. The Irish Republic won its independence in 1922, and with it its own Football Association, but Britain retained the six counties of Ulster. The United Kingdom continued to enjoy the privilege of four national associations through the creation of Northern Ireland.

34. Most notable among them was Norbert Elias. See N. Elias and E. Dunning, *Quest for Excitement: Sport and Leisure in the Civilizing Process* (Oxford, U.K.: Blackwell, 1986).

35. Malcolm Brown and Shirley Seaton, *Christmas Truce* (London: Pan Macmillan, 1994).

36. Shocked by the implications of this truce, the British and German High Commands prohibited any further fraternization, and these events were not repeated. Nevertheless, there is a wider connection between truce in wartime and sport going back to the ancient Olympic games, which required the endlessly warring city-states of Greece to observe a truce during the sporting festival. In modern times it is hard to imagine any sport other than soccer that could be played between warring parties.

37. George Will, *Daily Hampshire Gazette*, September 6, 2004, p. A6.

38. "The pools" is a form of gambling on soccer results that is popular in many countries. Participants pick the outcome of matches for the coming week for a small fee, and those who pick correctly can win very large jackpots.

39. Paul Preston, *Franco: A Biography* (New York: Basic Books, 1994), p. 700.

40. Allen Guttmann's classic *Games and Empires* (Columbia University Press, 1994) contains a chapter on the story of Jahn and the *Turnen* movement.

41. Norway has a remarkable soccer history, and for a nation of only 4.5 million it has achieved many outstanding results, beating most of the major nations in recent history. Indeed, it has played Brazil three times—winning twice and drawing once, probably the

best record of any team in the world against that country. But most Norwegians are still proudest of the victory against Nazi Germany.

42. Stanley Rous, *Football World* (London: Faber and Faber, 1978), p. 64.

43. Ibid.

44. In a recent book, *Scoring for Britain: International Football and International Politics 1900–1939* (London: Cass, 1999), Peter Beck suggests that the conventional view is wrong. He argues that it was not a propaganda boost for the Nazis (who lost), but for the English, who won, giving the British confidence again in their abilities. Whatever the interpretation, the political dimension of the match cannot be denied.

45. Victoria de Grazia, *The Culture of Consent* (Cambridge University Press, 1981), p. 175.

46. See Angela Teja, "Italian Sport and International Relations under Fascism," in *Sports and International Politics*, edited by P. Arnaud and J. Riordan (London: E & FN Spon, 1998), p. 156.

47. A. Ghirelli, *Storia del Calcio in Italia* (Turin: Einaudi, 1990), chaps. 1 and 3.

48. Ibid., chaps. 8–10.

49. de Grazia, *The Culture of Consent*, pp. 178–79.

50. Arpinati was murdered by Italian partisans in 1945.

51. Ghirelli, *Storia del Calcio in Italia*, p. 135.

52. Murray, *Football*, p. 69.

53. Ghirelli, *Storia del Calcio in Italia*, p. 100.

54. Murray, *Football*, p. 69.

55. Sindelar, the star of the Austrian team, was brutally marked out of the game. Openly opposed to the Nazis, and labeled by the Gestapo as "pro-Jewish and a social democrat" he "committed suicide" in 1939, a victim of the fascists on and off the pitch.

56. Ghirelli, *Storia del Calcio in Italia*, p. 133. See also Simon Martin, *Football and Fascism: The National Game under Mussolini* (New York: Berg, 2004).

57. Mason, *Passion of the People?* pp. 63–64.

58. Janet Lever, *Soccer Madness* (University of Chicago Press, 1983), p. 68.

59. Juan José Sebreli, *La Era del Fútbol* (Buenos Aires: Editorial Sudamericana, 1998), p. 187.

60. Quoted in J. Arbena, "Generals and Goles: Assessing the Connection between the Military and Soccer in Argentina," *International Journal of the History of Sport* 7, no. 1 (1990): 123.

61. Sebreli, *La Era del Fútbol*, p. 203.

62. Russ Williams, *Football Babylon* (London: Virgin Books, 1996), p. 104.

63. Shepherd's Bush was the site of the Olympic stadium.

64. The events of the 1908 Olympics are described in *The Olympic Story: Pursuit of Excellence* (Danbury, Conn.: Grolier, 1979), pp. 59–64; and in Alexander M. Weyand, *The Olympic Pageant* (New York: Macmillan, 1952), pp. 79–85.

65. Dyreson, *Making the National Team*, p. 164.

66. *The Times* (London), August 18, 1913.

67. Quoted in Arnd Kruger, "'Buying Victories Is Positively Degrading' European Origins of Government Pursuit of National Prestige through Sport," in *Tribal Identities: Nationalism, Europe, Sport*, edited by J. A. Mangan (London: Cass, 1996), p. 192.

68. George Orwell, "The Sporting Spirit," first published in the *Tribune* (London), December 1945; reprinted in Orwell, *Shooting an Elephant and Other Essays* (New York: Harcourt, Brace, 1950).

69. Wray Vamplew, *Pay Up and Play the Game: Professional Sport in Britain, 1875–1914* (Cambridge University Press, 1988), p. 269.

70. Ibid., p. 268.

71. Indirectly, the cause of the catastrophes was hooliganism, since the crowd was entirely fenced in to prevent a pitch invasion. The disaster occurred because fans had to enter the enclosure through a tunnel; the stewards were unable to see that the enclosure was full and so continued to allow fans to enter. By the time the message had reached the stewards, it was too late.

72. Hubert Dwertmann and Bero Rigauer, "Football Hooliganism in Germany," in *Fighting Fans*, edited by Eric Dunning and others (University College Dublin Press, 2002), pp. 75–87.

73. P. Marsh, K. Fox, G. Carnibella, J. McCann, and J. Marsh, *Football Violence and Hooliganism in Europe* (Oxford, U.K.: Social Issues Research Centre, 1996).

74. Ibid., p. 64.

75. www.biz.inter.nl.net/jimpex/english/interviews/papers/wes81121.html.

76. www.supertifo.it/storia_tifo/INGLESE/storia_del_tifo.htm.

77. *Clarín*, May 28, 1998.

78. Sebreli, *La Era del Fútbol*, p. 82. The murderer, a known fan of Boca Juniors called Pepito, was never brought to trial.

79. Juan Pablo Iribarne, *Barras Bravas* (www.people.bu.edu/palegi/jiribarn.html).

80. Other ugly incidents from history include forty-four deaths in Kayseri, Turkey, in 1967 following a riot at a soccer match; forty dead when fighting began during a preseason "friendly" between the Kaizer Chiefs and Orlando Pirates in Orkney, South Africa, in 1991; thirty killed in Tripoli, Libya, during an international match against Malta when a fan appeared wielding a knife and a stand collapsed in the panic; and twenty killed in Cali, Colombia, again when a stand collapsed as rival fans urinated on their opponents from above.

81. Among the first nations outside of Great Britain to stage an "international" match were Austria and Hungary in 1902, at a time when both formed part of Emperor Franz-Josef's Habsburg domain. Many years after Otto von Habsburg, great-nephew of Franz-Josef, pretender to the imperial throne and member of the European Parliament, on being told that a soccer match was played involving Austria and Hungary, is reputed to have said, "Oh yes, against whom?"

82. See, for instance, Kevin Young, "A Walk on the Wild Side: Exposing North American Sports Crowd Disorder," in *Fighting Fans*, edited by Dunning and others. The last well-known incidence of fan disturbance at a baseball game, however, goes back over twenty-five years to Disco Demolition Night at Comiskey Park in Chicago on July 12, 1979. Fans became unruly during a disco destruction ritual on the field after the first game of a doubleheader. Only six people were injured, but because part of the field was torn up, the second game was forfeited by the home team.

83. And to be sure, the consumption of alcohol inside sports facilities in the United Kingdom is illegal.

84. Unavoidably, occasional violence does erupt at games between opposing players and, in 2004, between players and fans at both baseball and basketball games. In the latter, the reaction of the league was swift and severe in an effort to control the outbreak and make it clear that violence wouldn't be tolerated in the future.

Chapter Four

1. Beckham's image was tarnished somewhat, though, by tabloid revelations about his private life that surfaced in the summer of 2004.

2. To be sure, in baseball some players are under contracts that permit them to negotiate improvements when they are traded.

3. To be precise, it is also possible that a player's productivity increases after he signs his contract. This too could lead to underpayment.

4. This figure is consistent with his market value depreciating at a rate of 25 percent per year.

5. Robert Burk, *Never Just a Game: Players, Owners and American Baseball to 1920* (University of North Carolina Press, 1994), p. 122.

6. They also engendered conflict between the low- and high-revenue major league clubs.

7. League classifications were defined in the National Agreement according to the average population of the host cities in each league. Each club then had to pay a "membership and protection" fee, according to the classification of its league. In the 1896 National Agreement, reservation rights were recognized for clubs in league classifications C through F. In that agreement, each club in Class A paid an annual membership and protection fee of $75. This fee diminished to $50 for Class B clubs, $40 for Class C, $30 for Class D, $20 for Class E, and $10 for Class F.

8. Several team owners (Brush of Cincinnati, Soden of Boston, and Spalding of Chicago) took partial ownership shares of the New York Giants. Their principal motive was to bail out Giants owner John Day, who was in desperate financial straits. The owners felt that a strong team in New York was essential. The widespread presence of cross ownership during the 1890s earned the decade the sobriquet of "syndicate ball." See, for one, Harold Seymour, *Baseball: The Early Years* (Oxford University Press, 1960), chap. 24.

9. See, for instance, Joe Cashman, "Babe Sold to Hose in Panic of 1914," *Boston Herald Record*, January 19, 1943.

10. It was not uncommon for baseball's top players to earn between $10,000 and $20,000 during the 1910s. In 1910 Christy Mathewson earned $10,000 and Nap Lajoie $12,000. Player-manager Honus Wagner was paid $18,000 that same year. Ty Cobb earned $20,000 as early as 1915. Babe Ruth, however, did not earn his first $20,000 contract until 1920 with the Yankees.

11. Eliot Asinof, *Eight Men Out: The Black Sox and the 1919 World Series* (Evanston, Ill.: Holtzman, 1963).

12. For a good discussion of Rickey's methods and his struggles with Landis, see, for one, Andrew O'Toole, *Branch Rickey in Pittsburgh: Baseball's Trailblazing General Manager for the Pirates, 1950–1955* (Jefferson, N.C.: McFarland, 2000).

13. Major league clubs also cut back their ownership of minor league teams, from 207 in 1951 to only 38 in 1957. Excellent sources on minor league baseball history include: *Organized Baseball*, Hearings before the Subcommittee on Monopolies and Commercial Law of the House Committee on the Judiciary, 82 Cong. 1 sess. (Government Printing Office, 1952); James Miller, *The Baseball Business: Pursuing Pennants and Profits in Baltimore* (University of North Carolina Press, 1990); Jerome Ellig, "Law, Economics and Organized Baseball: Analysis of a Cooperative Venture"(Ph.D. dissertation, Department of

Economics, George Mason University, 1987); Neil Sullivan, *The Minors: The Struggles and the Triumph of Baseball's Poor Relation from 1876 to the Present* (New York: St. Martin's, 1990); Seymour, *Baseball*; Burk, *Never Just a Game*; and Henry Fetter, *Taking on the Yankees: Winning and Losing in the Baseball Business, 1903–2003* (New York: Norton, 2003).

14. For a fuller discussion of the meaning and interpretation of baseball's presumed antitrust exemption, see Andrew Zimbalist, *May the Best Team Win: Baseball Economics and Public Policy* (Brookings, 2003).

15. In 1998 Congress passed the "Curt Flood Act," removing baseball's presumed antitrust exemption as it applied to the sport's labor relations. For a fuller discussion of the Flood Act and related issues, see Zimbalist, *May the Best Team Win*.

16. The story of Miller's role in building the union is well told in three books: Marvin Miller, *A Whole Different Ballgame: The Sport and Business of Baseball* (New York: Birch Lane, 1991); Charles Korr, *The End of Baseball as We Knew It: The Players Union, 1960–1981* (University of Illinois Press, 2002); Robert F. Burk, *Much More Than a Game: Players, Owners, and American Baseball since 1921* (University of North Carolina Press, 2001).

17. For details on the initial system of free agency and its subsequent evolution, see Andrew Zimbalist, *Baseball and Billions: A Probing Look inside the Big Business of Our National Pastime* (New York: Basic Books, 1992), chap. 1.

18. The median salary in 2003 was $652,088, having fallen from $750,000 in 2002.

19. These average salaries are based on figures from the Major League Baseball Players Association, which uses a slightly different methodology to compute salaries than the Player Relations Committee of the commissioner's office. According to the Players Association's figures, average salaries were also essentially flat between 1986 and 1987, but this appears to be due to a minor methodological change. Without this change, salaries would have increased by a small amount in 1987.

20. The MLB revenue-sharing system taxes a club 34 percent of its net local revenue. Thus if a player is judged to contribute $10 million to local revenue, without the revenue-sharing tax the owner would be willing to pay the player up to $10 million. With the tax, the owner would be willing to pay 34 percent less, or $6.6 million. Actually, because of the distribution system, the effective tax rate is around 47 percent for the low-revenue teams and 39 percent for the high-revenue teams. This lowers the wage offer even more.

21. Interestingly, although the provisions for unrestricted free agency are weaker in these sports than in baseball, the players' salary share in league revenues is higher in each of these sports than in baseball. If minor league costs are included, however, the baseball player share exceeds that in football and basketball. The much lower revenue base in the NHL makes it difficult to compare hockey with the other sports.

22. The share of major leaguers of Hispanic origin rose from approximately 2 percent during 1946–50 to approximately 10 percent during 1956–60, and to approximately 14 percent during 1966–70. See Burk, *Much More Than a Game*, p. 310.

23. Also, the breakup of the Soviet empire in 1989 led to an economic crisis in Cuba, which in turn led to increased defections of baseball players from that country.

24. An excellent discussion about Japanese baseball and its player transfer history with MLB can be found in Robert Whiting's *The Meaning of Ichiro* (New York: Warner Books, 2004).

25. He was nicknamed "Dixie" because of the dark tint of his skin and his black wiry hair; to the English of that era this nickname signified the notion that Dean was of Negro origin. The nickname stuck, although Dean himself always denied any African ancestry and was offended by any such insinuation.

26. In the decade 1994–2004, no one in the English Premier League scored more than thirty-four league goals in one season.

27. Yankees data from *Organized Baseball*, Hearings. Everton data from Stefan Szymanski and Tim Kuypers, *Winners and Losers* (London: Viking, 1999). Although precise accounting definitions may vary, both figures refer principally to revenue from selling tickets, refreshments, and trading of players.

28. In the jargon of economics, the marginal revenue product of a star player will tend to be lower the weaker the standard of competition.

29. Of course, this also reflected the fact that throughout most of the twentieth century Americans were far richer and therefore willing to pay more for their sports. Again in economic jargon, the income elasticity of demand for sport is positive and high.

30. Marshall Smelser, *The Life That Ruth Built* (University of Nebraska Press, 1993), p. 484.

31. A. Fabian and G. Green, eds., *Association Football*, vol. 3 (London: Caxton, 1960), p. 279.

32. S. Inglis, *League Football and the Men Who Made It* (London: Willow Books, 1988), pp. 21–22.

33. Ibid., pp. 24–25.

34. Tony Mason, *Association Football and English Society, 1863–1915* (Sussex, U.K.: Harvester, 1980), p. 104.

35. Inglis, *League Football*, pp. 38–39.

36. Fabian and Green, *Association Football*, vol. 3, p. 280.

37. Mason, *Association Football and English Society*, p. 97.

38. See the official *History of the Football Association* (London: Naldrett, 1953), pp. 404–5, 407.

39. This was a period of significant social unrest in England, and there was even talk of revolution, so the plan would have shocked businessmen and patriarchs alike. In the event, the soccer union did not join the national union.

40. According to the judge, "When a man exercises an undoubted right, the question of motive is not a sufficient cause of action." Quoted in J. Harding, *For the Good of the Game* (London: Robson Books, 1991), p. 100.

41. A. Ghirelli, *Storia del Calcio in Italia* (Turin: Einaudi, 1990), p. 90.

42. Ruth's salary peaked in 1930 and 1931 at $80,000, but as baseball's first marketing giant, Ruth earned as much as $250,000 a year in promotional and endorsement work.

43. Exceptionally, in Spain the "reserve teams" of the large clubs are permitted to play in lower divisions. However, reserve teams are not permitted to play in the same division as the senior team. Hence, in 1989, Real Sociedad reserves were denied promotion to the first division, while Atlético Madrid reserves were automatically demoted from the Spanish second division to the third when their first team was relegated from the first division in 2000. In 2004 the relegation of Celta Vigo's senior team to the second division denied the reserve team the promotion it had won from the third division. In both Spain and

Germany, however, reserve teams are allowed to play in cup competitions and to play against the senior team if drawn against each other.

44. Fans of the Women's National Basketball Association (WNBA) will find an eerie similarity to the NBA's motives for starting the women's league.

45. These details are from Steve Holroyd, "The First Professional Soccer League in the United States: The American League of Professional Football (1894)" (www.sover.net/~spectrum/alpf.html).Various articles in *The Sporting News* of 1894 also follow the league's rise and demise. See, for instance, "American Professionals: Another Football League Has Sprung into Existence," September 1, 1894; "Football: Cold Weather Sport," October 6, 1894; and "No More Football," October 22, 1894.

46. Several matches are recorded approvingly in the Reverend Pycroft's 1851 history of the game. Women were also responsible for introducing the distinctive form of over-arm bowling, which was then adopted by the men.

47. *History of the Football Association*, p. 533.

48. Ironically, the team folded just as the FA ban was being withdrawn, but this probably had more to do with industrial decline in the north of England than anything else. For a history of the team, see Gail J. Newsham, *In a League of Their Own! The Story of the Dick, Kerr Ladies Football Team* (London: Scarlett, 1997).

49. Ibid., chap. 5.

50. Harding, *For the Good of the Game*, p. 164.

51. See Ariel Scher and Hector Palomino, *Fútbol: Pasión de Multitudes y de Elites* (Buenos Aires: CISEA, 1988), pp. 85–87; and Tony Mason, *Passion of the People? Football in South America* (London: Verso, 1995), pp. 59–60.

52. Of course, in Australia "football" means Australian Rules, which is a venerable version of the football established in the 1850s and a close relative of Gaelic football, a game played in Ireland.

53. Juventus (Italy) paid River Plate (Argentina) 180 million lire for Omar Sivori in 1957.

54. Juventus (Italy) paid Varese (Italy) 370 million lire for Pietro Anastasi in 1968.

55. Although the Scots and the Irish had always played in England, technically they were either U.K. citizens or held the right to live and work in the United Kingdom, and hence were not considered foreign.

56. This, of course, is not to gainsay the significance of political connections in U.S. sports leagues. Indeed, George W. Bush's career received a jumpstart while his father was U.S. president. The new owning partnership of the Texas Rangers enlisted George W. to join their group with the expectation that his family's political connections would oil the way to a publicly funded new stadium for the team. Their expectations were realized. George W. became the managing partner of the Rangers and from there, governor of Texas. The subsequent step in his career is well known.

57. When Spain joined the EU in 1986, the five major soccer nations of Europe (Italy, England, Germany, France, and Spain) were all members.

58. www.images.fifa.com/fifa/handbook/regulatons/player_transfer/2003.

59. Szymanski and Kuypers, *Winners and Losers*, p. 98.

60. Figures reported in club accounts refer to total club employment, not just the players, but few doubt that the players account for the overwhelming majority of this expenditure.

Chapter Five

1. Jack Ewing, with Laura Cohn, Maureen Kline, and Rachel Tiplady, "Can Football Be Saved?" *Business Week*, July 19, 2004, cover story.

2. James Michener, *Sports in America* (Greenwich, Conn.: Fawcett, 1976), p. 441.

3. It is possible that this figure should be adjusted for the superstation payments that the Cubs make to MLB, which are probably on the order of $15 million annually. It is also possible, however, that the *Broadcasting & Cable* figure is conservative.

4. See Andrew Zimbalist, *May the Best Team Win: Baseball Economics and Public Policy* (Brookings, 2003), chap. 5.

5. The reason the net tax was just under 20 cents was that the team gets back roughly one-thirtieth of every dollar it contributed.

6. Bill Shaikin, "Fox Reaches Dodger Goals," *Los Angeles Times*, December 13, 2001, p. Sports-8.

7. Reality, alas, is likely to be a bit more complex than this, because at some later point Trump may be liable to pay a capital gains recapture tax. There are, however, ways to avoid this tax. Even if he does pay it, the capital gains tax rate is much lower than the income tax rate he faces, and he would benefit from the time value of money. In late 2004, the U.S. Congress was considering legislation that would allow sports teams to amortize all their intangible assets over a fifteen-year period. Although complicated, this legislation, if passed, would ultimately further extend the ownership tax shelter and increase franchise values.

8. That said, the rate of return experienced by George W. Bush from his partial ownership of the Texas Rangers was abnormally large. Bush invested some $600,000 as a minority owner in the early 1990s and received a reported $14 million when the team was sold to Tom Hicks in 1998.

9. Rodney Fort, *Sports Economics* (Upper Saddle River, N.J.: Prentice-Hall, 2003), p. 389.

10. John Moag, *Two Strikes and You're Out*, industry analysis by Moag & Co. (Spring 2002), p. 2. Using data through the early 1990s, Gerald Scully, *The Market Structure of Sports* (University of Chicago Press, 1995), pp. 118–25, finds even higher annual rates of return on sports franchise ownership.

11. Strictly speaking, a team can also meet the debt rule requirements if it has debt below $25 million. But no more than a handful of teams might be in this felicitous situation. The financial debt of an average MLB team at the beginning of 2004 was reportedly in excess of $100 million. For more information and an analysis of MLB's new, collectively bargained, debt rule, see A. Zimbalist, "MLB's Debt Rule Reveals More Smoke and Mirrors," *Sports Business Journal*, May 3–9, 2004.

12. An economist would say that the slope of the relationship between success and revenues is steeper (and, perhaps, more discontinuous) in promotion/relegation leagues.

13. Once again, the explanation for this phenomenon is that if a large city is undersupplied with teams in an open league, it is always possible for an entrepreneur to start a new team in the city and build its way up to the top tier of competition. Or, viewed differently, the open promotion/relegation leagues in Europe do not grant territorial monopolies to their teams. Territorial occupation is determined by competitive market forces.

14. Fay Vincent, *The Last Commissioner* (New York: Simon & Schuster, 2002), pp. 281–86.

15. Among other things, Ueberroth got the owners to agree to (a) increase his fining authority from $5,000 to $250,000; (b) bring the AL and NL offices under his umbrella; and (c) change the reappointment process for the commissioner from requiring a super majority to a simple majority. See, for one, John Helyar, *Lords of the Realm: The Real History of Baseball* (New York: Villard Books, 1994).

16. For a discussion of these collusion cases, see Andrew Zimbalist, *Baseball and Billions: A Probing Look inside the Big Business of Our National Pastime*, paperback ed. (New York: Basic Books, 1994), pp. 24–26.

17. For more details on these matters, see Zimbalist, *May the Best Team Win*.

18. For more information on the organization of these Shareholder Trusts and their team-by-team operation, see www.supporters-direct.org/englandwales/links.htm. Some might also observe that greater fan involvement, particularly when individual fans hold small amounts of shares, may lead the team to put too much emphasis on winning and eventually lead to financial distress. Of course, intelligent leadership of the Shareholder Trusts would argue for the long-term interests of the club, which ought to curtail financially imprudent behavior.

19. *The Deloitte Football Rich List*, March 2004, p. 12.

20. On July 17, 2004, the *London Guardian* reported that Libyan dictator Muammar Gaddafi wanted to buy a Premier League team and had his sights set on the newly promoted team Crystal Palace. Gaddafi bought a 5.3 percent stake in the Italian club Juventus in 2002 and reportedly is interested in investing in British soccer in order to improve political relations between Libya and the United Kingdom.

21. In England, Rupert Murdoch's Sky Broadcasting was prohibited by the U.K. competition authority from taking a controlling stake in Manchester United (primarily on the grounds that it would stifle the development of competition in broadcasting). We return to this issue in the next chapter.

22. This relationship is analyzed in great detail for the English market by Stefan Szymanski and Tim Kuypers, *Winners and Losers* (London: Viking, 1999).

23. Before 1994 this relationship in baseball was even weaker. For a fuller statistical treatment of this relationship in soccer and baseball, see Stephen Hall, Stefan Szymanski, and Andrew Zimbalist, "Testing Causality between Team Performance and Payroll," *Journal of Sports Economics* 3, no. 2 (2002): 149–68.

24. See Charles E. Sutcliffe and F. W. Hargreaves, *The History of the Lancashire Football Association* (1928; repr., Harefield, Middlesex, U.K.: Yore, 1992), pp. 223–24.

25. Football Intelligence and Research, *English League Football Clubs—Financial Status and Performance* (London, 1982).

26. Income in the Premier League is highly skewed, and some clubs, such as Manchester United and Arsenal, are capable of generating large surpluses. Generally, well-run PL teams are able to at least break even. The few examples of teams in financial crisis in the Premier League, such as Leeds United in 2003–04, had more to do with poor club management.

27. Premier League clubs tend to be net spenders in the transfer market (they pay out more in transfer fees than they receive). Transfers are not included in the wage and salary share. Of course, in return for transfer fees the clubs augment their assets (in the form of players).

28. The former Division II is now called FL League One, and the former Division III

is now FL League Two. The reader will recall that in 1992 the then Division I was renamed the Premier League, and what had been Division II in 1991 became Division I in 1992. Thanks to this Byzantine nomenclature, teams in the third tier of the English league system can now pretend they are on top of the pile.

29. Of course, another difference is that in baseball the salaries of affiliated minor league players are paid by the major league team.

30. In England and Scotland, the major creditors are usually banks that have a long-standing relationship with the club. Given the bad publicity involved with pressing for the liquidation of a local football club, many banks have played an important role in keeping insolvent clubs afloat.

31. *Leeds United Annual Report and Accounts*, May 2001. Book value reflects what the club had paid to acquire the talent in the first place.

32. According to press reports, in addition to Ferdinand, Jonathan Woodgate was sold for £9 million, Robbie Keane for £7 million, Harry Kewell for £5 million, Olivier Dacourt for £3.5 million, and Lee Bowyer for £100,000. Several players were transferred for a negligible fee or loaned to other teams. Given that at least 10 percent of these reported fees would have been paid to the player and that the club continued to contribute to paying part of the salaries of some players after they had been sold, the income realized by the club would have been even lower than this figure.

33. The "Salva Calcio" law was passed in December 2002 and adopted in February 2003.

34. Player trading, of course, along with providing revenue to the selling club, creates an offsetting cost to the buying clubs. Hence it does not alter profitability in the aggregate (though it might affect some leagues differently than others, depending on whether the league is a net exporter or net importer of players).

35. Florentia was easily promoted from this division and in the following season was allowed to jump up one more division, to play at the second level. In 2004 it won promotion back to Serie A.

36. Napoli was relegated from Serie A to Serie B in 2001.

37. For instance, the Salva Calcio law mentioned above was investigated by the European Commission for evidence of illegal state aid. In the end, the investigation was dropped, but the EC made clear that explicit subsidies to national soccer leagues would be challenged.

38. In 2003 the annual revenues of Manchester United were $304.1 million, while those of Real Madrid were $242.1 million. However, the growth rate of Real Madrid's revenues is considerably higher. Real Madrid's president, Florentino Perez, stated in mid-July 2004 that the club anticipated $171.5 million in merchandise sales alone in 2004 and that the club would "outstrip Manchester United as the most valuable brand label in world sport." Quoted in the *Sports Business Daily*, July 20, 2004, p. 6.

39. In the same year, Olympique de Marseilles was also investigated for inadequate financial guarantees but was allowed to remain in the top division.

40. Of course, since U.S. sports leagues are closed monopolies, the discipline of the market is less immediate and more cushioned than for normal competitive industries.

Chapter Six

1. Harold Seymour, *Baseball: The Golden Age* (New York: Oxford University Press, 1971), p. 345.

2. Baseball's early years of broadcasting created conflict on another front. Many minor league teams felt that the broadcasting of games was sharply lowering their attendance and requested that major league games be blacked out in their area. MLB obliged until the Justice Department, seeing this as a restraint of trade, forced a change in policy in 1949. Thereafter, MLB continued to follow a blackout policy for major league cities.

3. For an excellent discussion of the legal issues involved in the Sports Broadcasting Act, see Stephen Ross, "An Antitrust Analysis of Sport League Contracts with Cable Networks," *Emory Law Journal* 39, no. 2 (1990): 463–98.

4. Albert Powers, *The Business of Baseball* (Jefferson, N.C.: McFarland, 2003), p. 265.

5. The Yankees' owners in the 1950s were Del Webb and Dan Topping. Webb was in construction and had business relations with Arnold Johnson. Webb arranged for Johnson to buy the Philadelphia A's and move them to Kansas City at the end of the 1954 season. In the ensuing ten years, the Kansas City A's functioned as a virtual farm team for the Yankees, trading over forty players between the two major league teams, including Roger Maris.

6. These figures are before revenue sharing. Revenue sharing is discussed in detail in the next chapter.

7. Andrew Zimbalist, *Baseball and Billions: A Probing Look inside the Big Business of Our National Pastime*, paperback ed. (New York: Basic Books, 1994), p. 49; *Broadcasting and Cable*, July 29, 2002.

8. Again, actual revenue growth was likely considerably higher than this.

9. These issues are discussed in greater detail in Andrew Zimbalist, *May the Best Team Win* (Brookings, 2003), chaps. 1, 2, and 7. As we write in August 2004, a new dispute between Cablevision and Time Warner brought a halt to the transmission of New York Mets games to some 3 million local subscribers.

10. Baseball also receives central revenues from licensing and sponsorships. Licensing income is approximately $3 million per team. Corporate sponsorship data are incomplete, but sponsorship revenue appears to exceed licensing payouts comfortably. According to one source, MLB signed 30 percent more corporate sponsorship deals during 2003–04 than ever before. One deal was signed with Reebok that provides for $500 million over five years. Another was signed with Taco Bell, a three-year deal worth $25 million annually. Rick Horrow, "MLB at the Break: Three Major Growth Challenges," CBSSportsline.com, July 9, 2004. Nevertheless, baseball's central revenues are below $35 million per team in 2004; by contrast, in the NFL they are over $90 million per team.

11. Asa Briggs, *The History of Broadcasting in the United Kingdom*, vol. 1: *The Birth of Broadcasting* (Oxford University Press, 1961), pp. 107, 100.

12. *The History of the Football Association* (London: Naldrett, 1953), pp. 508–9.

13. Each team of the first two divisions traditionally held one vote each. When the two lower divisions were created in the 1920s, they were given a mere eight votes between them. However, since league decisions had to be carried by a three-quarters majority, small clubs still found it relatively easy to assemble a blocking coalition.

14. Nicholas Fishwick, *English Football and Society, 1910–1950* (Manchester University Press, 1989), p. 109.

15. ITV was a consortium of regional broadcasters who produced programming both jointly and independently.

16. Simon Inglis, *English League Football and the Men Who Made It* (London: Willow Books, 1988), p. 228.

17. Bob Lord, *My Fight for Football* (London: Stanley Paul, 1963), p. 134.

18. For more details, see Stefan Szymanski and Tim Kuypers, *Winners and Losers* (London: Viking, 1999), pp. 55–67.

19. Briggs, *History of Broadcasting in the United Kingdom*, vol. 5: *Competition*, p. 593.

20. Allen Guttman, *Sports Spectators* (Columbia University Press, 1986), p. 135.

21. Paul Gardner, *The Simplest Game* (New York: Macmillan, 1996), p. 96.

22. A. Ghirelli, *Storia del Calcio in Italia* (Turin: Einaudi, 1990), p. 316.

23. See, for example, Manuel Vázquez Montalban, *El libro gris de televisión española* (Madrid: Ediciones 99, 1973).

24. Duncan Shaw, "The Political Instrumentalization of Professional Football in Francoist Spain, 1939–1975" (Ph.D. dissertation, University of London, 1988), pp. 156, 157.

25. Unlike in the United States, cable TV was not an important platform in Europe, largely because the original motivation for laying cable, namely the difficulty of accessing remote communities using over-the-air signals, did not apply. However, deregulation of telecommunications in the late 1980s also led to the laying of large optical fiber cable networks for telephony, and in many countries this helped to develop a cable TV market as well.

26. Students of U.S. college sports will recognize an interesting parallel here to the breakaway of Division IA and its conferences from the NCAA football television contract in the early 1980s. See Andrew Zimbalist, *Unpaid Professionals: Commercialism and Conflict in Big-Time College Sports* (Princeton University Press, 2000).

27. Alfred Wahl and Pierre Lanfranchi, *Les Footballeurs Professionels* (Paris: Hachette, 1995), p. 220.

28. Deloitte & Touche, *Annual Review of Football Finance* (Manchester, U.K., 2003), p. 12.

29. Wahl and Lanfranchi, *Les Footballeurs Professionels*.

30. Geoff Hare, *Football in France: A Cultural History* (Oxford: Berg, 2003), p. 147.

31. Enders Analysis, *Canal+: The Showdown* (www.endersanalysis.com/enders/documents/Canal+%20The%20Showdown%20(Ref%202002-52).pdf [November 2002]).

32. Umberto Lago, Alessandro Baroncelli, and Stefan Szymanski, *Il Business del Calcio* (Milan: Egea, 2004), p. 79.

33. Deloitte &Touche, *Annual Review of Football Finance*, appendices, p. 16.

34. Ulrich Hesse-Lichtenberger, *Tor! The Story of German Football* (London: WSC Books, 2002), p. 274.

35. European Commission, "The European Model of Sport," consultation paper of DGX, Brussels, 1998.

36. See, for example, "G-14 Considering Superleague," *The Guardian*, February 4, 2003.

37. In the United States, the FCC had considered anti-siphoning rules in the 1950s, and rules were introduced to prevent the exclusive sale of rights to events such as the NCAA men's basketball championship to pay TV operators. These specific rules, however, were vacated by the appeals court in *Home Box Office, Inc. v. FC*, 567 F.2d 9 (D.C. Cir. 1977). See Philip Cox, "Flag on the Play? The Siphoning Effect on Sports Television," *Federal Communications Law Journal* 47, no. 3 (www.law.indiana.edu/fcli/pubs/v47/no3/cox.html).

38. See Guido Ascari and Philippe Gagnepain, "The Financial Crisis in Spanish Football," Working Paper (Universidad Carlos III de Madrid, Economics Department).

39. *OECD Round Table on Competition Issue Related to Sport*, OCDE/GD(97)128 (Paris: OECD, 1997), pp. 61–63.

40. See Philip Deacon, "Public Accountability and Private Interests: Regulation and the Flexible Media Regime in Spain"; and Liz Crolley, "Football and Fandom in Spain," both in *Contemporary Spanish Cultural Studies*, edited by Barry Jordan and Rikki Morgan-Tamosunas (London: Hodder Headline, 2000).

41. Susanne Parlasca and Stefan Szymanski, "The Negative Effects of Central Marketing of Football Television Rights on Fans, Media Concentration and Small Clubs," *Zeitschrift für Betriebswirtschaft* 4 (2002): 83–104.

42. S. Szymanski, "Collective Selling of Broadcast Rights to Sporting Events," *International Sports Law Review* 2, no. 1 (2002): 1–6.

43. www.europa.eu.int/eur-lex/pri/en/oj/dat/2003/l_291/l_29120031108en00250055.pdf.

44. www.europa.eu.int/eur-lex/pri/en/oj/dat/2004/c_115/c_11520040430en00030006.pdf.

45. If rights are sold in smaller bundles, the argument would go, then smaller broadcast companies would be able to obtain a share of rights. If a single broadcaster tried to acquire all the packages, this would then be treated as an antitrust violation.

46. See, for example, David Forrest, Rob Simmons, and Stefan Szymanski, "Broadcasting, Attendance and the Inefficiency of Cartels," *Review of Industrial Organization* 24 (2004): 243–65. However, it is true that broadcasting more live games of teams in the Premier League would undermine attendance at games in lower divisions if they were played at the same time.

47. Wladimir Andreff and Jean-Francois Bourg, "Broadcasting Rights and Competition in European Football," draft paper presented at the annual conference of the International Association of Sports Economics, Neuchatel, Switzerland, June 2003.

Chapter Seven

1. In most sports, of course, there is some value in watching the highlights soon after the game has ended, but within a few days the value of the television rights has almost vanished.

2. See, for instance, Mathew Baker and others, "The Old Ball Game: Organization of 19th Century Professional Baseball Clubs," *Journal of Sports Economics* 5, no. 3 (2004): 277–91.

3. Coincidentally, the first season of the English Football League in 1888–89 was also rather unbalanced, with Preston North End winning the championship without losing a single game. It won 82 percent of its games and tied the remainder.

4. Some economists also worry about the imbalance of individual matches. But this seems like a pretty academic concern. This is because most fans go to see the home team win, and the bigger their victory, the happier they are likely to be. The competitive balance problem is principally about the outcome of championships, not individual games.

5. Recently, a measure of competitive balance has been proposed by the economist Brad Humphreys of the University of Illinois, which he calls the competitive balance ratio (CBR). This is the ratio of the between-season to the within-season measure. According to Humphreys's ratio, competitive balance fell by nearly one-third in the American League in the second half of the 1990s, and by 14 percent in the National

League, thus denoting an increase in imbalance in both leagues. See Humphreys, "Alternative Measures of Competitive Balance in Sports Leagues," *Journal of Sports Economics* 3, no. 2 (2002): 133–48.

6. The "idealized standard deviation" is the standard deviation adjusted for the number of games played by each team. The greater the number of games, the less random the final outcome at the end of the season and, hence, the smaller the expected standard deviation. The "range" is the distance between the top- and bottom-performing teams. The "decile ratio" is the ratio of the win percentage of the team at the 90th percentile to the team at the 10th percentile.

7. To be sure, no league will want perfect balance (complete equality of playing talent) among its teams. The way to maximize league-wide revenues is for the teams in larger markets (and with more win-sensitive fans) to win more frequently than those in smaller markets. Of course, given control over league policy by individual clubs that act in their own best interests, what is objectively in the league's best collective interest may not be attainable. This is especially so when voting rules in the league require supermajority support for certain policy changes.

8. This literature is summarized in Stefan Szymanski, "The Economic Design of Sporting Contests," *Journal of Economic Literature* 41 (December 2003): 1137–87. Also see the special symposium issue on competitive balance in the *Journal of Sports Economics* (May 2002), edited by Andrew Zimbalist; and Martin Schmidt and David Berri, "Competitive Balance and Attendance: The Case of Major League Baseball," *Journal of Sports Economics* 2, no. 2 (2001): 145–67.

9. James's index, which is similar in spirit to Humphreys's competitive balance ratio, is equal to the average standard deviation of win percentages each year plus the standard deviation of team win percentages over the entire decade, divided by the idealized standard deviation of these percentages (if teams were of equal competitive strength). This number is then divided into 100 and expressed as a percentage. Bill James, *The New Bill James Historical Baseball Abstract* (New York: Free Press, 2003); see page 19 for an explanation of the construction of and rationale behind this index, which is intended to reflect league balance in particular years as well as team performance mobility over time.

10. Statement reprinted in S. A. Sullivan, ed., *Early Innings: A Documentary History of Baseball, 1825–1908* (University of Nebraska Press, 1995), p. 113. Also see E. W. Eckard, "The Origin of the Reserve Clause," *Journal of Sports Economics* 2, no. 2 (2001): 113–30.

11. Cited in Roger I. Abrams, *Legal Bases: Baseball and the Law* (Temple University Press, 1998).

12. *Organized Baseball*, Hearings before the Subcommittee on Monopolies and Commercial Law of the House Committee on the Judiciary, 82 Cong. 1 sess. (Government Printing Office, 1952), p. 30. Frick testified on July 31, 1951. Frick served as commissioner from 1951 until 1965.

13. Ibid.

14. Simon Rottenberg, "The Baseball Players' Labor Market," *Journal of Political Economy* 44, no. 3 (1956): 242–58.

15. Szymanski, "Economic Design of Sporting Contests," pp. 1159–61, reviews the evidence.

16. As we shall see, capturing competitive balance is not a simple matter, especially in a single measure. In James's index, for instance, both the 1940s and 1950s score 34 percent, implying the same level of balance for the two decades. Yet no teams really dominated baseball in the 1940s, while the Yankees and Dodgers did so in the 1950s.

17. "Net" refers to the deduction of stadium expenses (operations and debt service). Because of this deduction, a team like the Yankees, which faces a revenue-sharing marginal tax rate of almost 40 percent, receives an indirect subsidy from MLB's other teams if it builds a new stadium. In late July 2004 it became known that the Yankees were proposing to build a new stadium (next to the existing one) and to contribute some $700 million toward its construction (and seeking around $300 million in public infrastructure investment). If the Yanks contributed $700 million, under the 2002 CBA they would reduce their revenue-sharing obligations by approximately $280 million over time. Alternatively, if the Yankees paid $70 million in debt service annually, they would reduce their revenue-sharing taxes by $28 million per year.

18. Other factors may alter this outcome. For instance, if revenue sharing makes the finances of a low-revenue team less precarious, the team owner may be more willing to take risks in signing a free agent.

19. Selig quoted in the *Sports Business Daily*, July 14, 2004, and October 28, 2003.

20. If teams increased their player development budgets instead of increasing their major league payroll, team performance could still improve. However, (1) this effect would take time, (2) there is little evidence to suggest that there has been a significant increase in the player development budgets of teams receiving revenue-sharing transfers, and (3) the correlation between player development budgets (lagged and present) and team win percentage is weak.

21. *Basic Agreement between the 30 Major League Clubs and Major League Baseball Players Association*, effective September 30, 2002, p. 106.

22. Confronted with this evidence, the Brewers have claimed that they would be putting additional funds into player development. The evidence does not support this contention. According to a prospectus provided by the Brewers to prospective investors in July 2003, the team budget for payroll and player development would stay flat between 2004 and 2006, despite estimated increases in net revenue-sharing receipts of over $3 million during this period. For a more detailed discussion, see Andrew Zimbalist, *May the Best Team Win: Baseball Economics and Public Policy*, rev. ed. (Brookings, 2004), Postscript.

23. It is important to be clear here. Even if payroll distribution were made more equal, there would be no guarantee that competitive balance would be improved. Higher payrolls simply increase the probability of better team performance; they do not guarantee it. So, if the revenue-sharing system were working properly, it would lead to a more equal distribution of payroll, which would increase the probability of greater balance.

24. www.rsssf.com/tablesp/portchamp.html#liga.

25. www.imperial.ac.uk/business/dynamic/other/RiminiGroup/report120304/Reports/Financial%20Crisis%20in%20the%20Portuguese%20Footbal%20(final)%20(3).pdf.

26. www.rsssf.com/tablesn/noochamp.html.

27. www.rsssf.com/tableso/oekrchamp.html.

28. www.rsssf.com/tablesg/grkchamp.html.

29. The other six championships were all won by a single team, Trabzonspor. www.rsssf.com/tablest/turkchamp.html.

30. www.rsssf.com/tablesi/italchamp.html.

31. www.rsssf.com/tabless/spanchamp.html.

32. www.rsssf.com/tablese/engchamp.html#c1993.

33. Several, though, have introduced postseason playoffs for promotion in recent years.

34. Luigi Buzzachi, Tommaso Valletti, and Stefan Szymanski have developed one method for comparing between-season balance in open and closed leagues; see "Equality of Opportunity and Equality of Outcome: Open Leagues, Closed Leagues and Competitive Balance," *Journal of Industry, Competition and Trade* 3, no. 3 (2003): 167–86.

35. See Szymanski, "Economic Design of Sporting Contests," table 1, p. 1154.

36. But Spain did win the European Championship (once).

37. Uruguay might also be considered an over-performing nation, but its World Cup victories came in 1930 and 1950, when the competition involved relatively few teams and was not taken as seriously as it is now.

38. In fact, Greece had to play the hosts twice, being drawn against them in the opening match of the group stage, a match that Greece also won against the odds.

39. See B. Taylor and J. Trogdon, "Losing to Win: Tournament Incentives in the National Basketball Association," *Journal of Labor Economics* 20, no. 1 (2002): 23–41. The NBA has altered its rules in an effort to remove any direct incentive for teams to perform poorly.

40. See Andrew Zimbalist, "Sports as Business," *Oxford Review of Economic Policy* 19, no. 4 (2003): 503–11.

41. Some tentative steps are now being taken. In 2002 the G-14, the lobby group of Europe's biggest clubs, agreed in principle to introduce a limit of 70 percent on wages as a percentage of revenue, effective from 2005–06. While this will be independently audited, the sanctions for noncompliance are not clear. In England, the Football League, which controls the second-, third-, and fourth-tier divisions, has created a "salary cost management protocol," limiting wage spending to 75 percent of revenues; the protocol was applied to the fourth tier in 2003–04 and to the second tier in 2004–05. If these limits are actually observed, it is likely that they would be challenged as antitrust violations by the players. In this case, however, the leagues may be protected by the Bosman ruling, which specifically acknowledges the importance of maintaining competitive balance.

42. See Joe McGinniss, *The Miracle of Castel di Sangro* (New York: Time Warner Paperbacks, 2000), for an entertaining account.

43. The qualification rule has been changing almost yearly, however. In 2003–04, the fifth team qualified plus two additional teams, chosen on the basis of their performance in supplementary tournaments.

44. Since the matches in each round are determined by a random draw, in each round a fraction of games is between teams that play in the same division.

45. See S. Szymanski, "Income Inequality, Competitive Balance and the Attractiveness of Team Sports: Some Evidence and a Natural Experiment from English Soccer," *Economic Journal* 111 (2001): F69–F84.

Chapter Eight

1. Some might argue that the issue of performance-enhancing drugs constitutes a crisis in baseball. We discuss this matter below.

2. Although South Americans have been a significant adornment to the European game, most soccer players in Europe are themselves Europeans.

3. In 2001, when the European Union was negotiating the amendment to the Treaty of Rome that would permit the expansion of the European Union from fifteen to

twenty-five members, several sports governing bodies lobbied to include an exemption in the treaty but met with firm rejection.

4. For an earlier treatment of this idea, see Tom Hoehn and Stefan Szymanski, "The Americanization of European Football," *Economic Policy* 28 (1999): 205–40.

5. A famous example of this came after World War II, when FIFA was more or less bankrupt. The British governing bodies agreed, in 1946, to host a friendly match between teams representing Great Britain and "the rest of Europe," attended by 135,000 at Hampden in Scotland, with the proceeds being donated to FIFA.

6. Some might argue that baseball is also reaching this status in Taiwan.

7. See, for one, Amy Yee, "Sports Marketing: Efforts to Stoke Global Interest in U.S. Baseball Have Paid Off in Japan," *Financial Times*, November 12, 2004, p. 12.

8. See Amy Chozick, "Global Pitch," *Wall Street Journal*, October 18, 2004, p. R6.

9. U.S television ratings are based on the average number of households watching a show, where one rating point is equal to 1 percent of the total number of television households in the country. In 2004 there were approximately 110 million television households in the United States.

10. The percentage of whites on major league rosters fell from 76 percent in 1992 to 60 percent in 2003. Mike Fish, "Major League Problem: What Happened to Black Baseball Players?" *SI.Com*, May 16, 2003.

11. In 2001 blacks accounted for 43.2 percent of Division I college football players, 57.1 percent of basketball players, and only 6.7 percent of baseball players.

12. Mark Newman, "MLB Announces Initiative for Kids," *MLB.com*, August 9, 2004.

13. Jim Salisbury, "Robinson's Legacy Dims on the Diamond," *Black Athletes Sports Network*, July 15, 2004.

14. MLB's youth problem is also not helped by decreasing the number of reduced-ticket-price family days, not opening the ballparks until after the home team has taken batting practice, and not allowing fans to go on the playing field after the game.

15. Lee Jenkins, "Another Chance for Baseball to Settle Its Score with Drugs," *New York Times*, December 12, 2004, section 8, p. 1.

16. During the 2004 season, another slugger, Gary Sheffield, admitted to previously using a cream steroid but, similar to Bonds, claimed that he did not know it was a steroid when he used it.

17. See, for instance, Andrew Zimbalist, "No Easy Answers to MLB's Steroid Scandal," *Sports Business Journal*, December 13–19, 2004.

18. In the soccer world there has been a consensus that the abuse of performance-enhancing drugs is less of a problem than in sports that rely on pure power. After all, performance-enhancing drugs cannot account for the balletic skills of a Pele or Maradona (who has long suffered from a recreational drug–abuse problem). Some national governing bodies take the problem more seriously than others, and several have long had substantial testing programs. The English FA, for example, currently conducts over 1,000 tests per year. Nonetheless, there are grounds to believe that doping is becoming a serious problem. In November 2004 a Turin judge convicted the Juventus doctor of administering performance-enhancing drugs, including EPO (which enhances endurance), to stars such as Zinedine Zidane and Alessandro del Piero over the period 1994–98. Neither the club chairman nor the players were accused of any wrong-doing.

19. The formal office of the commissioner, of course, was not established until January 1921. Its predecessor, the National Commission, was even weaker.

20. Owners have frequently characterized each other in even more negative terms. One early stinging indictment of owners came from Albert Spalding himself when he was an owner of the Chicago NL club and on the verge of being elected league president. Spalding wrote: "The trouble now was not with gamblers or with players, but with club officials, generally termed magnates, and it will be readily understood how difficult a matter it was to deal with them . . . [their] personal cussedness and disregard for the future welfare of the game. . . . With these men it was simply a mercenary question of dollars and cents. Everything must yield to the one consideration of inordinate greed." Albert G. Spalding, *America's National Game* (University of Nebraska Press, 1992), pp. 301–2.

Index

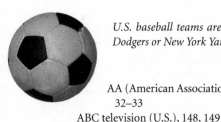

U.S. baseball teams are listed by city or state (for example, Los Angeles Dodgers or New York Yankees).